THE CAREER COUNSELOR

**CONTEMPORARY CHRISTIAN
COUNSELING**

THE CAREER COUNSELOR

LESLIE L. PARROTT, ED.D.
AND
LES PARROTT III, PH.D.

CONTEMPORARY CHRISTIAN
COUNSELING

General Editor
GARY R. COLLINS, PH.D.

The Career Counselor
Contemporary Christian Counseling
Copyright © 1995 by Word, Incorporated

Library of Congress Cataloging-in-Publication Data:

Parrott, Leslie, 1964–
    The career counselor: guidance for planning careers and managing career crises/Leslie Parrott & Les Parrott III.
        p.   cm.—(Contemporary Christian counseling: 11)
        Includes bibliographical references and index.
        ISBN 0–8499–1074–9   (hard cover)
        ISBN 0–8499–3677–2   (trade paper)
        1. Vocation.   2. Pastoral counseling.   3. Vocational guidance.   I. Parrott, Les.   II. Title.   III. Series.
    BV4740.P37   1995
    253.5—dc20   95–3274
                                                                             CIP

5 6 7 8 9 0 LBM 7 6 5 4 3 2 1

Printed in the United States of America

We dedicate this book to Leslie's mom,
Kay Spruce Young,
with love and affection
—to a woman who was unexpectedly forced
back into the workplace,
and whose depth of character has astounded us
as she has faced her greatest challenge.

Contents

Preface

This book has been written primarily for Christian counselors and pastors working with individuals at every stage of the career-life journey. In this volume we have summarized much of what we know about vocational counseling methods that are consistent with Christian understanding. Part One provides a conceptual overview of a Christian perspective on vocational counseling. Part Two deals with specific developmental and situational challenges. Part Three addresses special skills and resources that are essential to the vocational counselor.

The case illustrations in this book come from our counseling experiences. However, all case material has been disguised and names have been changed to protect those whose stories are discussed.

We are grateful to several people who helped with the preparation of this manuscript. This book would never have been written without the leadership, vision, and kindness of Gary Collins. From the beginning of this project it has been clear that Gary is committed to a high quality process as well as an excellent product. For his wisdom and expertise we are deeply grateful.

The publishing team at Word, including Terri Gibbs, Editor of Academic and Reference Works, and Lois Stück, our copyeditor, have given us heart-felt support and thoughtful input. They have contributed greatly to the quality and integrity of this work.

Jeff Trautman, director of the Christian career placement agency, Intercristo, has contributed greatly to our thinking. His pioneering efforts to apply biblical insights to the career journey have been invaluable to us.

Our colleagues at Seattle Pacific University, especially those in the Office of Student Life and the Career Development Center, have offered professional support, prayers, and encouragement as we prepared this manuscript. The students who have participated in our counseling and vocational counseling courses have also offered helpful feedback on the content of this book.

Finally, we want to thank all of those individuals who have trusted us at some point in their personal quest to find meaning and mission in the world of work. The lessons we have learned through your lives are deeply valued. This book was inspired by you.

Leslie Parrott
Les Parrott

PART I

The Big Picture

Chapter One

The World of Work

THE NATIONAL ATTITUDE TOWARD WORK has gone through an unsettling shake-up in recent decades—like the rearrangment of the skyline after an earthquake. Every working member of every family and all prospective workers and their dependents are touched by the shifting views of what work is and by the new meanings attached to it. No worker is left unshaken by the jolt of this work-quake and the aftershocks that continue to keep us unnerved. To better understand the tremors in today's job market, consider some of the factors that have contributed to these shifting conditions:

The jobs revolution can be attributed, in great part, to the introduction of high technology into the workplace. How people work today and where they work is different from what it used to be. Computers, faxes, copy machines, voice mail, E-mail, communications centers, Picturephones, teleconferencing, 800 telephone numbers, and inter-net have impacted workers at all levels everywhere. Some career people who hold responsible jobs now work at home. Others take their office on the road with mobile equipment that matches the full-service operation back at headquarters. Some people work shorter weeks and longer days than they used to. Some work by project on a contract basis that pays them in lump sums.

We have a nephew just out of Penn State with a degree in chemical engineering. There was a time when he would have been a direct employee of the national company who recruited him. Instead, he serves as a vendor paid by the branches who need his skills. He gets several checks a week as he flies coast-to-coast training their people. A decade ago, college graduates would have rejected this kind of job, considering it risky. But he loves it.

Massive data banks and instant communications have scrambled jobs in middle management, eliminating many. Even libraries, which are prosaic by nature, have turned to high-tech with vigor. At least in the workplace, we are moving closer to James Mischner's observation: "Those who do not learn to use the computer will abdicate their right to make decisions to those of us who do."

The Changing Role of Women in the Workplace. Gone is the day when father brought home the bacon and mother cooked it. Before World War II, mother's place was in the home and homemaking was her job. Her daughters were never encouraged to enter the professions, for doctoring and lawyering were the province of men. During the war, great numbers of women streamed through the factory gates to take jobs vacated by men away in uniform. After the war, Rosie-the-Riveter types lost their reluctance for work outside the home and invaded the job market in ever increasing numbers. More than 45 percent of the labor force today is female. Women are hired to fill two-thirds of all new jobs created. Women are in about 40 percent of the 14 million executive, administrative, and managerial jobs, nearly double from twenty years ago.[1] Working women have been a major force in the work-quake.

Minorities Are Becoming a Larger Element in the Population. Most members of minority groups have been treated as second-class citizens, some more than others, but they have made their mark on the American culture whether they were native-born or immigrant. African Americans constitute about 11 percent of the United States population, although Hispanics will soon become the largest minority group in America. In terms of percentage, Asian Americans are the fastest growing group. Many African Americans and Hispanic people lack the skills needed for the new jobs of the present and future. Asians, lacking social acceptance, have turned to computer science and other high-tech areas where their expertise has been widely recognized. A major challenge confronts American society in trying to help minority groups who are growing at a faster rate than the American population as a whole.

A Maturing Society Keeps Growing Older. Despite modern advertising's emphasis on a youth culture, the United States is experiencing a change in which middle-aged and older people will dominate the society by their sheer numbers. The proportion of older citizens is greater now than during any previous period in American history. As the year 2000 approaches, the baby boom generation (those born between 1946 and 1964) will be middle-aged and approaching elder status. The maturing of America profoundly affects the social and economic values and trends of the future. Less attention is likely to be paid to youth as market makers focus more intently on the needs of middle-aged and older people. Long-term health care will become more important. Workers aged sixty and over who are in good health may want to delay retirement, believing their occupations give their lives meaning, purpose, and an identity they find nowhere else. Of course, people over sixty who stay in the work force keep job opportunities from younger workers. With unsolved issues still in doubt, what to do with older workers still looms large on the work horizon.

The Disquieting Factor of Downsizing. National and international companies have waged nerve-racking employment cutbacks on a major scale. Even more important is the fact that downsizing is here to stay. Thanks to the wizardry of the computer industry, as well as a new concern in many places for quality over profit, qualified people are being laid off in shocking numbers.

The Rising Demand for Better-Trained Workers. As the Ford Motor Company says, "The quality goes in before the name goes on." That means high-skilled but fewer employees. Mindless jobs on the assembly line are being taken over by sophisticated robots. Those who program the computers that activate these robots have skills accruing from years of education and training. The people who guard the gates to union membership are looking for qualified people more than ever before.

The Dominating Influence of Small Businesses. Although the major corporations are getting large—mostly by acquisitions and further internationalization—the wave of the future is focused on small businesses. A hospitable climate has been created for new businesses by favorable laws, changing consumer preferences, the frustration and resistance of customers to computer voices, and the emergence of the friendly neighborhood franchiser. These factors, among others, have encouraged the development and growth of small businesses, which tend to be user-friendly, focused on quality, and in control of costs. Over-the-counter trading for equities in small stocks has become a significant factor in the portfolios of serious traders and investors. Boutiques have come back into the marketplace through the malls and even the department stores in both Europe and America. Cottage industries, which died with the assembly line, are gaining new favor with buyers looking for quality, uniqueness, and personal service.

Minimum-Wage Jobs Are in Full Supply. While politicians fought to raise the minimum wage, the increased pay level is both a blessing and a curse. It is a boon to teenagers who want extra money but a bane to breadwinners who need full-time jobs to make their living. These minimum-wage jobs are the new "assembly line" jobs without the benefit of union wages and benefits.

The Population Is Moving South and West and Into the Suburbs. The U. S. population is shifting to the south and west, with Texas and Florida leading the way. Smaller states like Arizona, Nevada, and Alaska showed population increases near the 40 percent range during the 1980s. With this migration of people, economic and political influence has shifted southward and westward as well. Almost as dramatic as this population shift is the movement from cities to the suburbs and even into the nonmetropolitan areas beyond the suburbs. The population shift is certainly being felt in the job market, especially in construction, road building, and consumer-goods industries.

A Shift Toward Multiple or Successive Careers. Consider this scenario:

> *Andrew, a husband and father in his midthirties, was restless. He enjoyed a fair level of success as a salesman for a local manufacturer. His supervisor was happy with him and offered to increase his regional responsibilities. However, something about the move just did not feel right. In college Andrew majored in fine arts and had enjoyed drama. Sales was certainly nothing like the career Andrew had envisioned for himself. The more Andrew thought about it, the more he began to feel like he was giving up his dream and opportunity was running through his fingers like sand. Andrew decided it was now or never. He wanted to try something new. So in spite of great promise in his present position, Andrew cut ties with his company to pursue a career in the arts.*

Multiple and successive careers like Andrew's are accepted as an alternate to the old idea that a person was to land a job in his or her youth and then let it lead where it would until retirement.

The Cataclysmic Impact of the Information Age. The last, but by no means the least, reason for the jobs revolution is the birth of the information age. In the days of the Continental Congress, it took a week or more for information to reach Boston from Philadelphia. Modern citizens watch congressional debates live on C-Span. Interactive television, instant two-way communications, lightning-fast printing presses, supersonic travel, and the Super Information Highway have inundated the world with news, views, and data of all kinds for strategizing the future or just planning a day's work. For instance, traders in the commodity pits in Chicago stop dead every day at 12:20 P.M. sharp when the highly respected weather report is given by Tom Skillings on the WGN superstation. The advantages of expanded information are obvious, but some say the result will be information pollution and we will drown in the flood of data. Regardless of its impact, the information age has changed the way we work forever. The majority of today's jobs now involve gathering, processing, and using information in one form or another.

There is a bottom line to this brief overview of the changing dynamics in the workplace. It is this: *Vocational counseling is more important now than ever before.* To expand on this idea, we will examine (1) the meaning of work, (2) the purpose of work, and (3) the role of vocational counseling.

THE MEANING OF WORK

Philosophers, psychologists, theologians, and plain everyday people have grappled since ancient times with the meaning of work. Plato is quoted most often: "Do thine own work, and know thyself, each of these two parts generally cover the whole duty of man, and each includes the other. He who will do his own work well, discovers that his first lesson is to know himself, and what is his duty." Thomas Carlisle was more poetic when he wrote, "Blessed is he who has found his work; let him ask no other blessedness, he has a work, a life-purpose, he has found it and will follow it."[2]

John Gardner, leader of the Washington-based think tank Common Cause said, "What can be more satisfying than to be engaged in work in which every capacity or talent one may have is needed, every lesson one may have learned is used, every value one cares about is furthered?" Gardner is indeed right. Work has the power to satisfy deep needs in human experience.

However, for the young adult who is searching for a career or for the person who lost his or her job in a company's downsizing, philosophizing gives way to pathos: "What am I to do?"

Everyone has his or her own view on the meaning of work. Understanding this personal view or philosophy within each counselee is the cornerstone of vocational counseling. Following are six views adapted from *Modern Work and Human Meaning*.[3] During our years in counseling and consulting, these views have constituted the kaleidoscope of approaches people use to invest their work with meaning.

1. *To some, work Is a blessing.* For early Protestant immigrants, labor and wealth were signs of one's election. Hard work and

personal salvation were indelibly linked. This theological perspective resulted in a moral intolerance for laziness and an insufferable ambition that still dominates the view of work for many Americans. If work is a human blessing and success the greatest blessing of all, then more work is better than some work, and much work is the best of all.

The Puritan legacy manifests itself most often in Americans today as compulsive workaholics. The focus for the workaholic is on results and achievement. In the world of the workaholic, service is a by-product of personal achievement, not its primary goal.

2. *Others see their work as a calling.* For the early Pietists, work was an expression of their faith. They pointed to the words of Paul: "Nevertheless, each one should retain the place in life that the Lord assigned to him and to which God has called him. This is the rule I lay down in all the churches. . . . Each man, as responsible to God, should remain in the situation God called him to" (1 Cor. 7:17, 24). While Paul was referring to faith in Christ, Martin Luther, and other commentators who followed him, identified work as both a call and a virtue. For Pietists, ambition and achievement were not religious; in fact, personal ambition was sinful. The Pietists feared that secular work for its own sake could detract from serving God.

3. *To some, work is a curse.* Slaves in the ancient world and later in America saw work as a curse. They sang about its heavy burden and the relief they sought in heaven. Flowing from the early American Black tradition, a work ethic emerged in which labor was neither a blessing nor a calling. Work in the old South was a heavy burden identified with suffering. Work was toil and sweat. Who could look forward to another day—dawn to dark in the cotton fields with all the bending, stooping, and sweating their work called for?

Even today, many people see work as a strong negative in their life. Vacations, days off, sick leave, and holidays relate to the personal feelings of those who declare with relief, "Thank God It's Friday." The most important days of the week and a prayer for good weather is focused on Saturday and Sunday. In this perspective of work, the weekend is more important than the week.

4. *With some people, labor is a commodity to be bought and sold.* With the advent of the Industrial Revolution, laborers moved in droves from fields to factories, from agriculture to manufacturing. The slave block was replaced with an arena where the muscle power of workers was bought and sold. Time and skill were bartered for the good life in the cities. This view allows the market to define the worth of each laborer. For a majority of people in the modern work force, work as a commodity is evaluated in pay, perks, and benefits that reflect the worker's responsibility and authority. One of us once asked an older gentleman who frequently passed our house in carpenter's apparel what he was making. Expecting to hear about some creative project, it was surprising when he gave the terse answer, "Twenty-two dollars an hour." He may not have understood the intended question, but it was clear that his work was a commodity for sale by the hour.

5. *Some view work as a basic human right.* Unionists and humanists have historically been associated with the message that work is a basic human right. Unions always cry "unfair" when their perceived rights have been abridged. More recently, many within the religious and political community have joined in this concept of work as a basic right. The sign on the wall inside the campaign headquarters in Little Rock that starkly said, "Jobs stupid!" clearly declared President Clinton's stance. Many analysts believe he won the election on jobs as a basic human right. "The most urgent priority for U. S. domestic economic policy is the creation of new jobs with adequate pay and decent working conditions," a recent pastoral letter from the Catholic Bishop said. "The prime goal must be to make it possible for everyone who is seeking a job to find employment which befits human dignity."[4] According to a statement from the body of the Presbyterian Church, "As our economy continues to evolve, we will have to advocate not just more jobs, but better jobs, jobs that are exciting and fulfilling. Moreover, we will have to rethink the meaning of work."[5] These sentiments are also voiced by politicians of all varieties. According to President Clinton, jobs is a top item on the national agenda.

6. *Some view work and vocation as synonyms.* The most dominant view of labor within the church community is the idea of

work as vocation. Work with a continuing purpose is vocation. Work is what I do each day, while vocation is what I do with my life of work. There are four commonly held elements in the view of work as vocation:

- One person's work contributes to everyone's good. All work is seen as an avenue for service to God or to one's neighbor. In everyone's job, there is an element of the public good.
- Work is meaningful in itself. No task is too sordid or too base to be considered meaningful as a worthy vocation. A hotel maid may make beds to the glory of God if she sees her work as vocation. If not, her job may be an unbearable burden.
- Vocation is universal, not the privilege of the few. This is a bold affirmation that all human beings of whatever station in life can participate in implementing the purposes of God through their labor, and it is true.
- Vocation is individualistic and purposeful. Each individual must answer the questions, "What is the task to which I am called?" "For what purpose was I created?" "What would God have me to do?"

The expression of vocation is a personal decision. However, the common purpose of the community is not to be lost in the search for personal achievement. The call to community comes before career development and corporate profit. Personal job choice is not predominantly determined according to "what I want and need" but according to "what is wanted and needed in the community." This view is not only right, it's smart.

THE PURPOSE OF WORK

In addition to a personal view of work, one's psychological need for work is also vital to understanding the meaning of work. Psychologist Abraham Maslow developed the concept of the role of work in helping people meet their important personal needs.[6] Maslow looked at the needs of the human heart in ascending order, as motivational steps in a ladder. Thus, the need above could not be satisfied until the need below was fully met. After the most basic need for *survival* is satisfied, the working person is motivated to move up to *security,* which is the second rung of the ladder. Then comes *love, achievement,* and finally, *self-fulfillment.* Each need is fulfilled as a person moves upward, toward heightened levels of human dignity and personal maturity.

The most fortunate worker is the one who feels most fulfilled. Persons seeking vocational counseling are frequently propelled by the power of unmet needs and the hope of a positive resolution. Consider these five needs identified by Maslow as they relate to the vocational journey—survival, security, appreciation, achievement, and self-actualization.

A JOB PROVIDES SURVIVAL

The primitive need for physical survival lies at the base of the motivational ladder in work. Because these psychic needs are basic and self-centered, they are potent—our lives depend on them. Until the questions of survival are settled, they preoccupy and immobilize vocational advancement. All vocational counselors encounter some clients at this level of need; however, some vocational counselors develop an entire practice for persons struggling at this lowest level of the need hierarchy. Their unemployed clients need a job for survival.

Matthew, who is a vocational counselor for an inner-city job placement center knows a lot about jobs for survival. He is located in an urban church. Advertising for his work is by word of mouth. He has an overwhelming client load. His people are typically homeless. Some are residents in temporary shelters, while others live on the street. The problems these people face in securing jobs are herculean. Without a personal telephone number, legitimate address, professional wardrobe, personal identification, social security card, or steady employment history, they are stuck until Matthew can pry a job loose for their survival. These job seekers desperately need vocational advocacy. The counselor who can help them get a survival job is their angel in street clothes.

With experience, Matthew has learned to pick up on signals that distinguish a highly motivated client from one with a casual interest. Without a personal drive, the dispossessed person finds it impossible to get employment even with professional advocacy. The focus of Matthew's vocational counseling process is to find work that will supply the most basic physiological needs of his client. Most of the placements are in manual labor positions. The counselor helps the client draft a basic resume and provides a dozen copies for distribution to potential employers. The counseling center serves as a telephone answering service and, after a comprehensive screening process, further serves as a source of personal reference for the client.

There is a whole family of issues related to the problems of physical, emotional, spiritual, and financial survival. Obtaining a job is by no means the complete answer. But without a job, the other issues are not likely to be faced. Of the placements made with direct assistance by Matthew, half of the workers eventually bail out of their positions—some after they receive their first paycheck. There are others, however, who do become grounded in their work and begin to rebuild their broken lives, demonstrating dramatically that a vocational counselor can play a significant role in the process of restoring human dignity.

Work as Security

The second step in the hierarchy of needs is safety and security. When a swimmer has been rescued from the surf, the next step after survival is a move to higher ground. Survival is always followed by a desire for security. Workers at this need level are striving for a stable future. Clients who face a forced career transition (graduation, layoff, firing, business failure) or a crisis in their personal lives (relocation, death, divorce) grapple with issues surrounding safety and security in varying degrees of intensity.

> *Diane, a committed wife and mother, had invested her time and talents in ministry at the church where her husband served as senior pastor. After thirty-five years of*

marriage, Diane was abandoned by her unfaithful spouse. Her social and professional life, as well as her financial security—all of which had centered around her husband and the church—were demolished. Although she was a well-respected and gifted person, Diane was faced with the daunting challenge of finding a job with enough financial reward to support herself at fifty-four years of age. Trained as an educator, her credentials had lapsed and could not be renewed without additional coursework. Her previous employment history included several years in office administration, which had ended a decade ago. Emotionally devastated, physically vulnerable from a lifelong struggle with severe juvenile diabetes, and alone, Diane sought the support of a vocational counselor to negotiate this unchosen career transition.

Dealing with clients at this level is always difficult for vocational counselors. In recent years, centers consulting with adults on career changes have experienced a 25 percent annual boost in consultations.[7] George Barna estimates that by the year 2000, the average adult will make four to six career changes during his or her lifetime.[8] Gary Collins and Timothy Clinton address the realities facing adults in the contemporary work force: "Unlike their grandparents and parents, few workers today are able to stay with the same unchanging job throughout life. *Flexible* is the password for the future. Whether or not they like the idea, workers in the future will have to keep their skills fresh or risk being relegated to menial, low-paying jobs. In an era of swift technological changes, experience often counts far less than up-to-date skills and a willingness for workers to keep learning."[9]

Involuntary career transition is a great leveler of persons. In the film *Lost in America,* two midlevel professionals suffering from midlife crisis decide to resign from their positions, cash in their nest egg, and travel across the country. Passing through Las Vegas, one spouse looses the couple's entire savings in a gambling frenzy. Faced with this loss, the couple embark on a job search—they need money to get back home. Comedy ensues when the wife, a highly educated former personnel officer, is interviewed by the teenage manager of a fast-food restaurant, who has to "sleep on it" before he can make a hiring decision. The camera shifts to the unemployment office, where the husband is attempting to find leads for a job—any job. When asked about his previous salary level, he rattles off a six-figure income. With a sarcastic grin, the unemployment counselor asks her colleague to "bring over the stack of six-figure executive openings" for him. After an agonizing interview, the jobless man finally lands work as a school crossing guard. Although this story is intended to be funny, most vocational counselors are all too familiar with the scenario. Forced transitions are difficult at every level of professional skill. People need job security.

WORK AS A SOURCE OF APPRECIATION

The third level of personal need on the job is for belong–ingness, acceptance, or appreciation. Work allows us to associate with a group of colleagues who are united toward a common purpose. As we participate in the organizational community, contribute to group goals, and function as members of a team, we can feel deep satisfaction. Alienation from the group or feelings of rejection in work lead to disillusionment and often propel individuals to negotiate a career transition.

> *Greg was in his late twenties. After college he had completed a degree in architecture and practiced his profession in two reputable Seattle firms. He was a well-paid employee but deeply dissatisfied. His complaints were not about the tasks involved in design but rather about being a member of the staff. He had severe headaches and was mildly depressed. Unhappy, his private escape was a fantasy that entailed resigning from the firm and running off to Canada to run a sidewalk espresso cart. Over time, Greg described his colleagues as offbeat artistic types who maintained erratic, flamboyant lifestyles. They put in long, hard hours of work followed by evenings at the latest chic night spots. In short, Greg did not belong. He was a conservative Christian with a serious, businesslike presence. Each day was an experience in alienation. The barren socialscape was so draining that he was unable to focus on his tasks.*

Following an extensive evaluation of personality, values, and interests, Greg took an experimental course in the M.B.A. program and completed an internship in a corporate setting. Through both, he found the level of collegiality that he had longed for in the past. He soon quit his architectural job and pursued an M.B.A. with an emphasis in nonprofit organizations. His needs for belonging were finally met.

WORK AS SELF-ACHIEVEMENT

As need for belongingness is satisfied, the longing to achieve self-esteem emerges as the fourth level of need. Achieving a sense of competency in work acts as a catalyst for the fulfillment of this achievement need, although the character of personal competency changes as individuals progress developmentally through their career journeys.

Jason served as an assistant manager at a supermarket. After nearly a decade of work he was an established professional, and his manager had recognized him for his savvy in negotiating with outside venders who marketed their goods through the store, including independent bakeries, produce farmers, and the gourmet specialty lines. Jason had carved out a niche in the company as a specialist. Then the supermarket's general manager appointed him to a broader managerial post. As part of his new responsibilities, Jason was to train and offer professional development experiences to his colleagues. Taking a step back from his direct operational responsibilities to manage others created a high level of anxiety within Jason. He found the new role awkward. He had little time for the past activities that had been fulfilling. He had once felt like a competent professional, but now he felt like a novice. Overwhelmed with a lack of personal achievement, Jason sought vocational guidance.

Each level of career expansion and adjustment brings with it new developmental tasks and corresponding psychological issues to be resolved and mastered. The struggle for competency, while not continual, is punctuated by quantum leaps of anxiety as new horizons emerge on the vocational journey. Edgar Schein, a specialist in organizational career development, identified seven roles that the worker transitions through on the way to competency. Each of the stages has central developmental tasks to be resolved and psychological issues to be dealt with. (See figure 1.1.) Because many people are not able to adjust to new levels of responsibility, there is a truism among corporate

Seven Roles on the Way to Competency

Role	Psychological Crisis	Vocational Competency Tasks
Student	• acceptance of personal responsibility for his or her choices	• developing and discovering values, interests, and abilities • making wise educational decisions • finding out about occupational possibilities
Applicant	• the capacity to tolerate ambiguity and uncertainty • the ability to present himself or herself assertively	• learning how to look for a job, apply for a job, and negotiate a job interview • learning how to assess information about an organization or employment setting • making a realistic and valid job choice
Apprentice/ Trainee	• the capacity to depend on others • the ability to deal with reality—what the organization is really like • overcoming insecurity	• learning the ropes of an organization • helping others • following direction • achieving acceptance
Colleague	• independence • accepting responsibility for success and failures • establishing a balanced lifestyle	• becoming an independent contributor • finding a personal niche in the organization as a specialist • reassessing original career goals in light of new self-knowledge and growth potential in the organization

Role	Psychological Crisis	Vocational Competency Tasks
Mentor	• assuming responsibility for others • deriving satisfaction from the successes of others • accepting the role of established professional • finding opportunities for continued lateral growth	• training and mentoring others • interfacing with other divisions in the organization • managing team projects
Sponsor	• disengaging from primary concern about self to become more concerned about the welfare of the organization • managing personal emotional reactions to high stress levels • balancing work and family • planning for retirement	• analyzing complex problems • shaping the direction of an organization • handling organizational secrets • dealing with organizational politics • developing new ideas • sponsoring the creative projects of others • managing power and responsibility
Retiree	• finding satisfaction in his or her past career accomplishments • being open to new avenues of personal growth	• adjusting to changes in standard of living and lifestyle • finding new ways of expressing his or her talents and interests

Fig. 1.1

Source. Adapted from E. H. Schein, *Career Dynamics: Matching Individual and Organizational Needs* (Reading, Mass.: Addison-Wellesley, 1978), 36–48. Used by permission.

workers about people who are promoted one level above their competency: People tend to be promoted until they reach their level of incompetence.[10]

WORK AS SELF-ACTUALIZATION

Finally, as self-esteem begins to blossom, workers are motivated to ascend to the highest level of personal need:

self-actualization. The qualities of a self-actualized person reflect integrity, creativity, wisdom, competence, generosity, and a strong drive to make a significant and often sacrificial contribution to others. Although Abraham Lincoln has often been cited as one who was fully actualized, there are many ordinary people who reach this inward level.

> *Anne was a vivacious woman who, after raising her children, returned to school. Succeeding in college as an adult learner, she continued her education with a Master of Arts in English Literature and finally a Ph.D. In her late forties she entered the classroom at a small Christian college and embarked on a twenty-year career. She became a much-loved professor. She instilled a love for poetry and fine literature into the hearts of students through her creativity and personal passion for the great writers. Finally, in her midsixties, Anne retired to care for her husband, who had been diagnosed with terminal cancer. After he died, she sought the help of a career counselor in creating a plan for her retirement that would incorporate her love of literature, advanced teaching skills, and creativity. She wanted to be a volunteer in social-service organizations and churches. Anne was a self-actualized woman seeking new avenues for investment of herself. Her grief and loss became the catalyst for a new kind of sacrificial giving. She gave herself—and loved the process.*

THE ROLE OF VOCATIONAL COUNSELING

It is one thing to acknowledge the centrality of meaningful work in our lives and another to navigate the career journey. Psychologists, sociologists, and counselors invest enormous amounts of time, energy, and expertise in dispelling the mystery of career decision making and assisting people in career discovery. Their work in the art and science of vocational counseling has contributed both a theoretical foundation for vocational decision making and practical skills for the vocational counseling process.

Career counseling as a behavioral science and profession was born early in the twentieth century. With the Industrial Revolution, sweeping changes came to the world of work. Large factories replaced homes and small workshops as manufacturing centers. Educational and political privileges, which had once belonged largely to the upper class, spread to the growing middle class. Machines displaced some jobs, but other workers found new job opportunities with machinery. Both workers and employers had to adjust to a new, cold and impersonal relationship. In addition, many people lived and worked under harsh conditions in the expanding industrial cities.

But the rise of industrialization in the late 1800s also sparked a spirit of reform to compensate for the new impersonal systems of urban life. In this spirit, Frank Parsons, a young American engineer deeply committed to social change, introduced the world to the field of vocational guidance in 1908.[11] Parsons' book, *Choosing a Vocation*, published in 1909, was followed by the First National Conference on Vocational Guidance in 1910.[12] Several speakers, including the president of Harvard University, called on science to take this new field seriously. It did. The incorporation of the National Vocational Guidance Association (NVGA) came three years later in 1913.[13] By 1921, the NVGA had defined vocational guidance as: "The process of assisting the individual to choose an occupation, prepare for it, enter upon, and progress in it. [Vocational counseling] is concerned primarily with helping individuals make decisions and choices involved in planning a future and building a career—decisions and choices necessary in effecting satisfactory vocational adjustment."[14] Since that time, the work of career development theorists has concentrated on the theoretical development of occupational choice.

Although gaps exist between theory and practice, the effective vocational counselor has a grasp on career development theory as a framework for the examination and understanding of the clients' situation and behavior.

Theories of occupational choice place an emphasis on assessing the interests and abilities of the worker. Frank Parsons' original work blossomed into a theory of occupational choice known as the "trait and factor theory." This theory incorporates the three facets of "personal analysis, job analysis, and matching through scientific advising for occupational choice making."[15] Vocational psychologists associated with the University of Minnesota furthered this model and propelled it into the mainstream through the development of aptitude tests and personality inventories.[16] Now trait and factor theory is the foundational model of career development work in a majority of college and university career centers as well as in larger, more established programs such as the Veterans Administration, the YMCA, and the Jewish Vocational Services.[17]

Career Psychologist John Holland's theory of occupational choice emerged in the 1950s and is still used extensively in contemporary vocational counseling. Holland's theory of occupational choice is based on personality as expressed through interests and career fit. At the heart of his theory are the following assumptions:

1. Most people can be categorized as one of six personality types.

2. There are six kinds of work environments.

3. People search for environments that will allow them to express their skills, abilities, and values.

4. Our behavior is determined by an interaction between our personality and the character of our work environment.

The six basic personality types that Holland used to categorize people and environments are:

1. realistic—involving physical activity that requires strength, skill, and coordination (i.e., farming, surveyor, mechanic, forestry);

2. investigative—involving critical thinking, creative observation, investigation, and organization of physical, biological, and cultural phenomena rather than socially oriented activities (i.e., mathematician, chemist, and physicist);

3. artistic—involving creative self-expression and unsystematic, unordered, emotional interaction with physical, verbal, or human materials to produce art forms or products (i.e., writer, actor, musician, artist);

4. social—involving interpersonal activities focused on curing, enlightening, training, and developing people (i.e., social worker, vocational counselor, teacher);

5. enterprising—involving persuasive and influential verbal activities focused on obtaining power and status (i.e., salesperson, politician, entrepreneur);

6. conventional—involving ordered and systematic activities to obtain organizational goals (i.e., accountant, office clerk, payroll technician).[18]

Since people and work environments are rarely one pure type, Holland's typology uses a cluster code of three types, dominant and secondary, for each person.[19] This enables an individual to make occupational choices that result in congruence between personality and working environment. Holland postulates that increased levels of congruence lead to increased levels of stability, achievement, and fulfillment in vocational life. To that end, he has developed the *Self-Directed Search* and the companion resource, *The Occupations Finder*, which matches the personality codes with 456 occupations classified by the same three type codes.[20] His theory of career personality has also been incorporated into a widely used career assessment tool, *Strong Interest Inventory*, which will be described in detail in chapter 12, "Assessing Personality, Interests, Aptitudes, and Abilities."

Unlike the theory of occupational choice, which points to an already established personality, career development theories emphasize the *process* of personal and personality development as the determining factor in vocational choice. It was also in the 1950s that interest in occupational choice from a developmental perspective emerged. Donald E. Super is perhaps the preeminent figure of the 1990s in developmental career theory, and he promotes a "loosely unified set of theories dealing with specific aspects of career development, taken from developmental, differential, social, personality, and phenomenological psychology and held together by self-concept and learning theory."[21] Super's theory, rather than being limited only to occupation, encompasses six major life roles: homemaker, worker, citizen, leisurite, student, and child. Each of these roles plays a part of varying importance over the developmental life span of an individual and is a significant factor in the development of career maturity. Super's construct of career maturity involves a constellation of physical, psychological, and social characteristics. Career maturity incorporates the elements of planning, exploration, information, decision making, and reality orientation as an individual moves through the passages of childhood, adolescence, and adulthood.[22]

CONCLUSION

In this chapter, we have tried to explain the major factors in the work-quake that has changed the job skyline in America. We then proceeded to explain the meaning of work, the purposes of work, and vocational counseling as the product of problems generated by the twentieth-century jobs phenomenon. The role of the vocational counselor is needed for the public good. In the next chapter, we will consider the work of the vocational counselor within the specific framework of the Christian faith and calling.

NOTES

1. J. Naisbitt and P. Aburdene, *Megatrends 2000: Ten New Directions for the 1990s* (New York: Morrow, 1990).

2. Thomas Carlisle, *Past and Present* (1843), quoted in George Seldes, *The Great Thoughts* (New York: Ballantine Books, 1985).

3. J. C. Rains and D. C. Day-Lower, *Modern Work and Human Meaning* (Philadelphia: Westminster Press, 1986), 96.

4. Catholic Social Teaching on the U. S. Economy, First Draft of the U. S. Bishops' Pastoral Letter, *Origins* 40, no. 22/23 (15 November 1984): para. 158.

5. "Toward a Just, Caring, and Dynamic Political Economy," Presbyterian Church (adopted 1985).

6. A. H. Maslow, *Motivation and Personality*, 2d ed. (New York: Harper, 1970).

7. S. Garland, "Those Aging Baby Boomers," *Business Week*, 20 May 1991, 109, quoted in G. R. Collins and T. E. Clinton, *Baby Boomer Blues: Understanding and Counseling Baby Boomers and Their Families* (Dallas: Word, 1992).

8. G. Barna, *The Frog in the Kettle: What Cristians Need to Know about Life in the Year 2000* (Ventura, Calif.: Regal Books, 1990).

9. Collins and Clinton, *Baby Boomer Blues*, 21.

10. L. J. Peter, *The Peter Principle* (New York: Morrow, 1969).

11. C. McDaniels and N. C. Gysbers, *Counseling for Career Development: Theories, Resources, and Practice* (San Francisco: Jossey-Bass, 1992).

12. F. Parsons, *Choosing a Vocation* (Boston: Houghton-Mifflin, 1909).

13. V. G. Zunker, *Career Counseling: Applied Concepts of Life Planning*, 3d ed. (Pacific Grove, Calif.: Brooks/Cole, 1990).

14. G. E. Myers, *Principles and Techniques of Vocational Guidance* (New York: McGraw-Hill, 1941), 3.

15. D. Brown, et al., *Career Choice and Development* (San Francisco: Jossey-Bass, 1984), 8.

16. V. G. Zunker, *Career Counseling: Applied Concepts of Life Planning*, 4th ed. (Pacific Grove, Calif.: Brooks/Cole, 1994).

17. D. E. Super, "Vocational Development Theory: Persons, Positions, and Processes," in *Perspectives on Vocational Development*, ed. J. M. Whiteley and A. Resnikoff (Washington, D.C.: American Personnel and Guidance Association, 1972).

18. J. L. Holland, *Making Vocational Choices: A Theory of Personalities and Work Environments*, 2d ed. (Englewood Cliffs, N.J.: Prentice Hall, 1985).

19. R. S. Sharf, *Applying Career Development Theory to Counseling* (Pacific Grove, Calif.: Brooks/Cole, 1992).

20. J. L. Holland, *The Self-Directed Search Professional Manual* (Odessa, Fla.: Psychological Assessment Resources, 1987); and J. L. Holland, *The Occupations Finder* (Odessa, Fla.: Psychological Assessment Resources, 1987).

21. D. E. Super, "A Life-Span, Life-Space Approach to Career Development," in Brown, et al., *Career Choice*, 199.

22. McDaniels and Gysbers, *Counseling for Career Development*.

Chapter Two

God's Will, Calling, and the Career Journey

SCOTT, LIKE MANY YOUNG PEOPLE who grew up in Christian homes, never assumed a personal faith. After high school, he attended a competitive secular university where he plunged into a double major in communications and computer science. He was outstanding in his class. His creativity, aptitude with computer programming, marketing, and high energy level caught the attention of his peers and professors. By his senior year, Scott had completed an internship with a national corporation and was named on their patent for a new electronic device he had helped to develop and market. Because the city where Scott lived was a Mecca for people in technical careers, he was aggressively recruited out of college and joined a growing company. Scott was on his way. He knew it, and so did everybody else.

Through the prayers of Scott's family, outreach of a caring pastor, and the encouragement of a special friend, Scott reluctantly joined a Bible study group. To his surprise, the authenticity of the members' faith and the power of the Scriptures propelled him toward a positive crisis in his personal faith. Scott committed his life to the Lord.

Faced with a newfound desire to live his life to honor Christ, Scott began questioning the purpose of his career. "How can a technical specialist do the work of the Lord in a secular company?" "Do I need to give up my career and dedicate my life to full-time Christian ministry?" These were among the many questions that gave him pause for thought.

Scott was confused. He had conflicting advice. Even the Bible failed him on making a specific career choice. Scott was frustrated. His supervisor at work had noticed the growing ambivalence in Scott and offered him a significant promotion, intending to provide Scott with a new challenge that would recapture his professional motivation. Three months later Scott took two weeks off from work and sought professional guidance.

Scott faced the risk of what theologian Garry Friesen identifies as "a costly delay because of uncertainty about God's individual will."[1] Time was of the essence. His vocational engine was in neutral when Scott should have been in gear with the rest of his life. If a work change was right, he needed to get on with it. In the meantime, his reputation for integrity among his work colleagues was weakening.

PITFALLS IN SEEKING GOD'S WILL

According to Garry Friesen, there are four debilitating traps that ensnare Christians who are naive about finding God's will for their lives. They include:

1. Justifying unwise decisions on the grounds that "God told me to do it."

2. Fostering costly delays because of uncertainty about God's will for the individual.

3. Rejecting personal preferences when faced with apparently equal options.

4. The practice of "putting out a fleece"—allowing circumstances to dictate the decision.[2]

These common traps are explained below in the context of how people make decisions. They take on deeper meaning for the career counselor when they are linked with a decision-making model such as the one developed by Clarke Carney and Cindy Wells, authors of *Discovering the Career Within You*. By linking Friesen's traps with the Carney and Wells model, the road to better decisions becomes smoother.

Carney and Wells conceptualize decision making in a two-by-two model. The result is four distinct decision-making styles that point to "planful decisions" as most effective. On one axis of their model is self-knowledge. The other axis concerns information about the client's environment (see figure 2.1).[3]

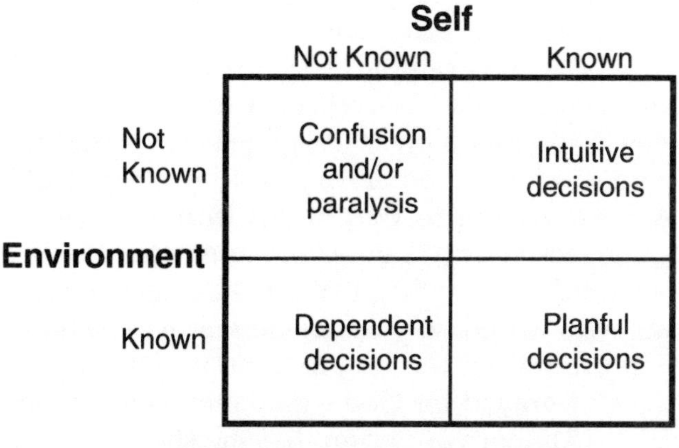

Self

	Not Known	Known
Not Known	Confusion and/or paralysis	Intuitive decisions
Known	Dependent decisions	Planful decisions

Environment

Fig. 2.1 **Learning decision strategies**

In the following pages, Friesen's four pitfalls are integrated with Carney and Wells' decision-making model for determining God's will.

1. THE DEPENDENT DECISION STRATEGY AND GOD'S WILL

The dependent decision strategy in Friesen's first quadrant is practiced by the person with low self-knowledge but high environment knowledge. Dependent decisions are made by people with little insight about themselves but great confidence in information supplied by others. This strategy is simple. Defer the career choice to God or to a trusted authority figure.

When faced with a complex vocational decision, dependent people simply defer. They let someone else decide.

Friesen's trap of "putting out a fleece" is a form of dependent decision making. Many sincere but misguided Christians are looking for a special sign. In their anxiety about making a decision that conforms to God's will, they seek a supernatural confirmation signal. They allow circumstances invested with spiritual meaning to dictate their decision.

In *The Myth of Certainty: The Reflective Christian and the Risk of Commitment*, Daniel Taylor addresses the naive desire for a neat formula that clarifies God's specific will. Taylor says, "It can be a powerful temptation for the Christian to disguise his or her covert discomfort with the ambiguity and risk involved in vocational decision making with an overt desire to comply to the supernaturally revealed will of God."[4]

Chris affords a good example of a sincere Christian tempted to let circumstances make her decision. Chris felt a deep desire to be an ethical and moral presence in the heart of the business world. To do so, she needed an M.B.A. from a reputable university. After applying to two highly competitive M.B.A. programs, she received one polite but impersonal rejection letter, and one letter announcing that she had been accepted as an alternate who would only be able to matriculate if another student withdrew from the program before fall quarter. Because Chris had prayed for God's guidance, she wondered if the almost closed door was a sign that she should not pursue this path. Heartbroken and confused, she received a telephone call from a friend who was looking for an administrative assistant. Was God sending her a message that her M.B.A. vision was too lofty? Not necessarily.

Friesen says , "Circumstances define the context of the decision and must be weighed by wisdom . . . not read as road signs to God's individual will." He also warns against viewing open doors as specific guidance from God requiring one to enter. Actually, open doors are *opportunities* for service but not necessarily God-given messages to be obeyed as a loyal army recruit. Sometimes obedience to God's will includes the option of saying "no" to opportunity. Likewise, it is an equal danger for individuals to view closed doors as signs of God's will.

Opportunities—opened or closed—are just one spoke in the wheel that will collapse if no other spokes are in place.

Abraham Lincoln encountered a closed door fourteen times on his road to the presidency. But he faced closed doors for what they were: just closed doors, not the end of the world. Ultimately, he was elected president, freed the slaves, and preserved the Union.

Rejecting personal preferences also leads to dependent decision making. The tendency of sincere but immature Christians to reject personal preferences as a matter of sacrifice is nonproductive in decision making. It is another form of dependent decision making. The results are negative.

Judy, a woman in our church, fell into this trap. She was flamboyant and animated. Everyone recognized her gifts in music, and no one doubted her devotion to Christ. Her dramatic skills were tapped each Sunday evening for a role in the skit based on the morning sermon. These skits often communicated at a new level to people who only heard the sermon superficially in the morning. During the week this high-energy woman worked in a community center and studied evenings to become a nurse.

Finally depleted of energy and frustrated by low grades, Judy sought help. Almost immediately, it became clear that Judy was overwhelmed with anxiety over the clinical phase of her degree—working with patients. She had to face her discomfort at the sight of blood honestly, along with her trepidation of pain-inducing procedures, and her distaste for the staunch professionalism and hierarchical nature of the medical environment.

The story that Judy told included an earlier promise to God that she would become a missionary nurse. This promise was both a sign and proof of her sacrificial love. As we discussed her situation, Judy discovered that a vocational decision based on sacrifice rather than desire is not a responsible decision. God always desires our *love* more than our sacrifices.

Frederick Buechner writes about confusing sacrificial behavior with God's will in his book *Wishful Thinking: A Theological ABC.*

There are all different kinds of voices calling you to do all different kinds of work, and the problem is to find out which is the voice of God, rather than that of society, say, or the superego, or self-interest. By and large, a good rule for finding this out is the following: The kind of work God usually calls you to is the kind of work (a) that you need most to do, and (b) that the world needs most to have done. If you really get a kick out of your work, you've presumably met requirement (a), but if your work is writing deodorant commercials, the chances are, you've missed requirement (b). On the other hand, if your work is being a doctor in a leper colony, you've probably met requirement (b), but if most of the time you're bored and depressed by your work, the chances are that you've not only bypassed (a), but probably aren't helping your patients much either. *Neither the hair shirt nor the soft berth will do.* The place God calls you to is the place where your deep gladness and the world's deep hunger meet.[5]

Ultimately, every pilgrimage calls for sacrifice. While in a Berlin prison for his involvement with the German underground's efforts to overthrow Hitler, Dietrich Bonhoeffer confided in a letter to his dear friend Eberhard Bethge:

It's painful to me, to be sure, that the improbable has happened, and that I shall not be able to celebrate the day with you; but I've quite reconciled myself to it. I believe that nothing that happens to me is meaningless, and that it is good for us all that it should be so, even if it runs counter to our own wishes. As I see it, I'm here for some purpose, and I only hope I may fulfill it. In the light of the great purpose all our privations and disappointments are trivial.[6]

From a contemporary vantage point, we can easily see how Bonhoeffer's sacrifice served significantly in the fulfillment of God's larger vision.

In a booklet entitled *How to Find Your Mission In Life,* Richard Bolles, author of several best-selling career exploration books, contradicts the validity of sacrifice as a determining factor in career decision making. He says, "When we exercise our best talent, our greatest gift, *that which brings us the most delight to use* in the place(s) or setting(s) which God has caused to appeal to us the most, and for those purposes which God most needs to have done in the world, we are surrendering to God's will."[7]

A dependent decision can produce unhappy results if it is used out of fear of making an independent choice or avoiding the responsibility of exploring the options. People do not find God's will by throwing darts at a vocational board on the wall, and deferring a choice out of indecision does not avoid the problem. The dependent decision is out of the hands of the decision maker. The decision may turn out well, but it could just as well turn sour.

2. CONFUSED AND PARALYZED IN SEEKING GOD'S WILL

The third quadrant helps explain the dilemma of individuals caught in a decision-making situation without knowledge of themselves or the environment. Confused and paralyzed, these persons are unable to decide anything.

Aaron was a person without knowledge of himself or his own world. He was a skilled carpenter who built and remodeled houses. He worked with his father and brother as successful subcontractors. His own home was witness to his talents.

In his late thirties, however, Aaron began to experience pain in his wrist and lower arm. The eventual diagnosis identified an irreversible problem that threatened his livelihood. Construction was the only work he knew.

Faced with the prospects of a total career change, Aaron had become depressed, confused, and paralyzed. His friends and family worked hard to allow him the space he needed to grieve and regroup. But Aaron determined that his paralysis was caused by his inability to know God's will. The deteriorating results of his disease made it urgent for Aaron to move in a new direction while he had the strength. Why couldn't he discern God's will?

Aaron had fallen victim to the trap of delaying a decision because of uncertainty about God's will. Yet with little knowledge of himself outside of his carpentry skills and limited knowledge of the world of work, Aaron was seeking God's guidance in a virtual vacuum.

While Aaron and others are faced with personal choices and vocational options that are almost limitless, the Bible does not speak directly to the matter of specific vocational choice. During biblical times, vocational decisions were predetermined by family and environment. Jesus, a carpenter's son, became a carpenter. Asking a young Israelite if he had discovered God's will for his life's work would have elicited a blank stare. Not so today. Vocational choices are personal, and the options are almost limitless.

Friesen believes that "the choice of a career or job falls into the area of freedom" for those not called to their work by direct revelation. Their decision is to be made on the basis of wisdom. One's choice of occupation is to be made on the same basis as every other decision within the moral will of God: wisdom. "Believers need to find God's guidance in relation to their aptitudes, abilities, gifts, desires, and opportunities. Which vocation offers the greatest potential for my service to the Lord and the most fulfillment for my life? The obvious prerequisite to a wise decision concerning one's vocation is a good understanding of one's aptitudes, abilities, gifts, and desires. Such self-knowledge takes time, a variety of life-experiences, and diligence."[8]

In their book, *Your Work Matters to God*, Sherman and Hendricks address the responsibility each person has to value God's will as it is revealed in his or her personal resources such as personality, talent, abilities, interests, and so forth.[9] The incorporation of these resources demands a planned decision-making strategy.

3. GOD'S WILL AND THE INTUITIVE DECISION STRATEGY

The second quadrant is the intuitive decision strategy, a stance that is low on environmental knowledge but high on self-knowledge. It is a decision-making process based on a gut-level reaction, which happens in the context of self-knowledge but without knowledge of the situational or relational expectations. The raw materials of intuitive decisions include more feeling than thought. Internal signals and feelings illumine the way, with little time taken for data gathering or conscious planning.

Falling into Friesen's trap of claiming divine guidance leaves a person in the pitfall of intuitive decision making. Although it is the responsibility of every believer to remain open to God's direction by any means, justifying unwise decisions on grounds that "God told me to do it" is dangerous. However, divine guidance is sometimes hard to distinguish from intuitive hunches, wishful thinking, or personal bias.

Jamie knew he was unhappy in his profession and wanted out. However, with two teenagers and a spouse who had just returned to college to complete her degree, he felt trapped. One Sunday during the open-altar prayer time at his church, he wept and prayed for direction. As the pastor delivered his sermon, Jamie was struck with the meaningfulness of the pastorate and the vibrancy of the church community. In his mind's eye he could picture himself delivering a sermon behind a pulpit before his own congregation. His dry spirit was infused with passion and energy, which his wishful thinking generated. Believing this vision was a divine call to the ministry, Jamie announced to his family that he would be resigning his work on Monday to follow God's will for his life: the pastoral ministry. This career change meant that his wife would defer her schooling again as he studied for the ministry. The children were separated from their peers at a crucial time in their adolescence. When the family tried to discuss the decision, he agreed that it would be difficult, but he affirmed that God had clearly called him through a vision. He said he could trust God to provide for all of their needs and his.

As I (Les) have said in another book:

> Feelings are like a compass. An emotional surge is more powerful for most than a rational deliberation. Sometimes hunches (intuition) or feelings are regarded as inward signs of God's leading. Some view intuition as the direct voice of the Holy spirit.

While God may certainly influence our feelings in order to tell us something, we must be cautious about putting too great an emphasis on intuition.

Nowhere does the Bible tell us that we should attempt to discern God's will merely through inner feelings. Intuition is helpful in providing insight into one's unconscious. It reveals some of our deepest desires and may tell us something about what God desires for us. However, we cannot conclude that every desire is directly from God. Desires are influenced by further information and experiences. Feelings are important in discovering God's will, but they are not the infallible voice of God.[10]

In Jamie's case it is easy to see that his deeply felt need for an escape could easily be confused with his sincere desire to hear God's voice and follow God's call.

Doug Sherman and William Hendricks of Career Impact Ministries have dedicated their lives to challenging people with a biblical view of work. They counsel, "I certainly would advise against basing a career decision on the notion that God has somehow committed Himself to giving a mystical, inner prompting one way or another. While inner impressions and feelings are valid and normal, it is impossible to define with certainty either their source or their meaning. Consequently, we must not invest these subjective impressions with divine authority."[11]

4. GOD'S WILL AND THE PLANFUL DECISION STRATEGY

A planful decision involves knowledge of both the self and the environment. This strategy demands rational consideration of alternatives, costs, and rewards. Therefore, the pace of this approach is slow. It takes time to gather information, explore options, and experiment with possible choices. This approach also places a high value on the consideration of personal feelings about the choices (intuition) and the opinions of experts and loved ones (dependence). A meaningful decision will marshal as much insight as possible about self, others, and the environment. One of the best examples of this approach is the young person who wants to be a professional athlete. Such a decision had better include a harsh assessment of personal abilities, a reality check on the competition, the counsel of coaches, and the Judgment-Day honesty of friends. Otherwise, the decision may be no more than wishful thinking.

Garry Friesen says a planful strategy for discerning divine guidance is provided by four foundational principles:

1. The revealed plans and principles of God (in Scripture) are to be obeyed.

2. In those areas where the Bible gives no command or principle, the believer is free and responsible to choose his or her own course of action in harmony with the tenor of the Scriptures. Any decision made within the moral will of God is acceptable to God.

3. In nonmoral decisions, the objective of the Christian is to make wise decisions.

4. In all decisions, the believer humbly submits to the outworking of God's sovereign will as it touches each decision.[12]

Dwight Carlson, author of *The Will of the Shepherd*, has developed a questionnaire that presents a series of steps leading to discerning God's will in decisions. The checklist is not to be tabulated or scored. It is simply a tool that clarifies the issues and delineates where an individual may be in the process of discovering God's guidance (see figure 2.2).

STAGES OF PLANFUL CAREER DECISION MAKING

Remember Scott, whose experience of changing vocations was told in the beginning of this chapter? He was confused in discerning God's will between advancement in his technical career or a pastoral ministry. Scott's decision-making process came about through what career specialists conceptualize in eight stages: awareness; self-assessment; exploration; integration; commitment; implementation; reevaluation; renewed

Checklist for Making a Major Decision

Below is a series of steps for knowing God's will in a particular matter. The steps are arranged in the form of a checklist. The checklist can help alert people to factors that might need to be dealt with before God's will is revealed to them.

The matter you want to know God's will in is: _____.

Step 1: Obedience to God's already-revealed will

A. Have you accepted Jesus Christ as your personal Savior?
   Yes   No
B. Is there any known sin in your life?   Yes   No
C. Are you being obedient to God's will to the extent to which it is now revealed?   Yes   No

Step 2: Openness to any means or results

A. Are you willing to follow God's will when he reveals it to you, regardless of what his will is or what it might cost you?
   Yes   No
B. Are you open to any means he might choose to lead you, whether supernatural/miraculous or some less dramatic means?   Yes   No

Step 3: God's Word

A. Do you have an adequate intake of God's Word?   Yes   No
B. Are you familiar with what the Scriptures really say about the issue for which you are seeking guidance?   Yes   No

Step 4: Prayer

A. Do you have a daily prayer time when you seek God's will and fellowship with him?   Yes   No
B. Have you specifically asked God's will regarding the matter for which you are seeking his guidance?   Yes   No
C. Are you too busy to adequately meditate and wait on him?
   Yes   No

Step 5: The Holy Spirit

A. Have you acknowledged the presence and function of the Holy Spirit in your life?   Yes   No
B. Does the Holy Spirit now fill your life?   Yes   No

Step 6: Counsel

A. Do you consistently fellowship with other Christians and hear God's Word proclaimed?   Yes   No
B. Is there any possibility of a medical problem for which you should obtain help?   Yes   No

C. Should you specifically seek the counsel of another, whether a minister, Christian friend, professional counselor, etc.?   Yes   No

Step 7: Providential circumstances
A. Have you adequately considered the providential circumstances that are available to you?   Yes   No

Step 8: Evaluation
A. Are you tired?   Yes   No
B. Have you specifically evaluated the reasons for and against the decision you are considering and your underlying motives (preferably on paper)?   Yes   No
C. Have you considered the needs of the world around you?   Yes   No
D. Have you considered your own abilities?   Yes   No
E. Have you considered your own desires and whether or not they are possible within God's will?   Yes   No
F. Will your decision harm your body or hurt others?   Yes   No
G. Will it hinder your spiritual growth, walk with Christ, or testimony?   Yes   No
H. Will it hinder the spiritual growth of others?   Yes   No
 I. Is it the choice that is most pleasing to God?   Yes   No
J. Is it the best and wisest choice using your enlightened judgment?   Yes   No
K. Have you prayerfully evaluated the matter alone, without unnecessary time pressure?   Yes   No

List any steps that should be done before you conclude what God's will is in the matter. Is there anything else he wants you to do or consider?

Step 9: The decision
A. Should you postpone the decision as to what God's will is in the matter?   Yes   No
B. Should you decide but wait for its fulfillment?   Yes   No
C. Do you already know God's will but not his timing?   Yes   No

Step 10: God's peace
A. Having determined God's will in the matter, do you have a deep, inward peace about the decision?   Yes   No
B. As time passes and you continue to reflect and pray about the decision, do you have an increasing assurance from him that the decision was the right one?   Yes   No

Figure 2.2

Source: Adapted from Dwight Carlson, M.D. *The Will of the Shepherd* (Eugene, Ore.: Harvest House, 1989). Used by permission.

awareness (see figure 2.3).[13] With help from a vocational counselor, Scott worked through the eight stages of planful decision
making. This then led Scott to continue in his current vocation, accepting the promotion offered by his supervisor and
moving ahead with his life.

The Decision Cycle

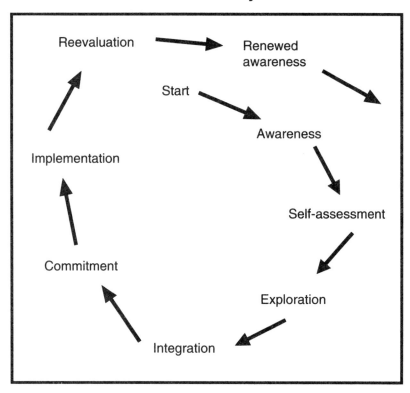

Figure 2.3

1. *Awareness.* The hallmark of the awareness stage is a feeling of increasing discomfort or pressure for change. This is
often a feeling of excitement mingled with doubts and fears
about the future. This stage may also be characterized by feelings of panic that cause someone to delay for fear of making
the wrong choice. Conversely, someone may act rashly, even
prematurely.

The task of this stage is to *clearly define the problem*. For Scott, the problem was not that he was unhappy in his career. The problem was that he had never intentionally approached his career from the standpoint of his newfound Christian values and beliefs. He had never attempted, directly or indirectly, to allow God to guide him in his work endeavors. He had never approached his career-life from the standpoint of ministry. When he finally did, his fears made it difficult to act.

2. *Self-assessment.* Self-assessment helps individuals decide how significant the decision is, what they want to accomplish by it, and what effort or sacrifice they are willing to make to achieve it. The decision maker must answer the question, "What do I most want the outcome of this decision to be?" This allows a person to check alternative solutions against beliefs, attitudes, and values. At this point, individuals determine what they want and what they are willing to give up to accomplish the desired outcome.

Scott began to build a list of possible settings within the church and parachurch to which his skills might be donated for direct evangelical endeavors. He decided he would give up two of his four monthly golf outings to work in a ministry outside his organization. This decision expanded Scott's vocational vision beyond the bounds of his job and created possibilities for a career in a Christian organization in the future.

3. *Exploration.* The goal of exploration is to *identify and examine possible courses of action*. The challenge is to gather enough information to generate quality alternative strategies. For Scott, the most exciting alternative generated was an opportunity to serve as one of the computer information systems coordinators needed for the Billy Graham Crusade scheduled in his city.

4. *Integration.* The purpose of this stage is to *assess the likelihood of turning the options and hopes into realities*. To accomplish this we must weigh the influence of other important factors, such as commitments to significant others, financial resources, and time constraints.

Now is the time to reevaluate beliefs and attitudes as we ready ourselves for commitment. The process of integration is often impacted by an inability to sort through feelings of guilt, fear, or dependency.

5. *Commitment.* This stage is defined by a willingness to *move forward on the basis of hopes and preparation.* Although there is no guarantee of success, there is a determination to move forward in the face of unresolved fears and unavoidable risks. While commitments are difficult to make, it is destructive to invest energy compulsively as an attempt to keep alternatives alive. The outcomes of a commitment pursued to the best of our abilities usually produce, at the very least, a harvest of growth and learning.

Based on his commitment to use his giftedness in service, Scott accepted the supervisory position and entered the managerial training course. He simultaneously applied to the Billy Graham Evangelistic Association to serve as a computer coordinator.

6. *Implementation.* The goal in this stage is *to act on a decision.* This requires the initiation of a new course of action. If assessment, exploration, and integration have been complete, difficulties encountered in implementing a goal will not be a complete surprise. However, implementation of a goal is often blocked or delayed. Hurdles and setbacks may appear bigger in reality than they did in imagination, even when following a clear course of action.

When Scott offered to serve on the Billy Graham campaign staff, he was not accepted. His skills were excellent, but the date of his conversion was so recent the supervisor felt Scott needed more time to mature. Disappointed, Scott respectfully deferred. However, Scott did commit himself to a servant style of leadership in his organization. After only nine months he was able to invite his first colleague to a relationship with Christ.

7. *Reevaluation.* The ongoing process of reevaluation involves regularly examining new information and experiences to see if they have brought about a change in perspective or possibilities. Regular exposure to the Word of God is also crucial for the ongoing reevaluation process of every individual seeking to discern the will of God in his or her vocational life. Robert Mulholland, author of *Shaped by the Word,* advises, "We build, maintain, and defend a complex structure of habits, attitudes, and perceptions, of dynamics of personal and corporate relationships, and of patterns of reaction and response to the world. This complex structure enables us to cope with life. But

this structure also becomes an ever-thickening crust of self that imprisons and limits us."[14]

8. *Renewed awareness.* This stage often leads to a new level of awareness (the feeling of increasing discomfort or pressure for change). It should lead a decision maker back into the cycle of planful career decision making. The process begins again at an advanced level. These eight steps need not be cumbersome. The goals in some stages may be achieved easily and quickly, but each step is important in making a planful career decision based soundly on wisdom in seeking God's will.

THE CALL TO MINISTRY

Every vocational counselor encounters people struggling to discern whether or not they are called to full-time Christian ministry. What signs can we look for in helping them answer God's call? Jesus personally called the disciples to follow him. Paul fell to the ground, blinded by a bright light, and later received a personal message from Ananias who told him, "You will be [God's] witness to all men of what you have seen and heard" (Acts 22:15) If God's call was always this dramatic, the help of a counselor would not be necessary. However, the Holy Spirit still calls men and women with the same definiteness of two thousand years ago.

CHRISTIAN BIOGRAPHIES AS A TOOL

Biographies of great Christian pastors, evangelists, and missionaries from past and present are one of the best tools vocational counselors have in helping people identify a call to ministry. Here are four brief examples followed by a summary of the four unique steps that each person encountered in his or her call.

1. *William Carey,* the combination schoolteacher preacher, had formerly been a shoe cobbler. As he read *Cook's Voyages "Round the World"* and taught his geography class from his own homemade leather globe, it flashed painfully upon him how small a portion of the human race yet possessed the merest knowledge of Jesus Christ and his salvation. He decided to investigate the subject thoroughly. From the Bible he concluded

that salvation was not for a limited few but for all who believe. The charge to bear this news into all the world seemed to lay an obligation of some sort on the entire Christian church in general and on himself in particular.

With the map of the world unrolled, and consulting books that described the various countries, Carey ascertained as nearly as he could the extent of Christianity in every country, its population, its government, and its social and religious conditions. Like a stunning blow, the fact hit his mind—more than 400,000,000 people lay in the blackest of spiritual darkness. Carey concluded that the gospel must be taken to these heathen. This truth so burned within him that he could scarcely talk or preach, and he could never pray without referring to the subject.

How far Carey was influenced by his geographical study, and how far he drew his impulse directly from the Bible, we can not tell. But once the Savior's will was clear to him, he felt the burden upon himself personally to do what he could for the salvation of the lost. In Carey's own mind, doubt now had no place. The principle of missionary evangelism had become as clear to him as anything in the Bible, and the duty as imperative as that of paying one's lawful debts.

2. *Mary Slessor* of Calabar, whose father was an alcoholic, had a praying missionary-minded mother who dreamed that her son, Mary's brother, would someday be a missionary to Africa. Mary Slessor, who was personally interested in Africa, never considered herself a likely missionary prospect. When the brother died before ever reaching Africa, Mary began to feel impressed that she must go to take his place. This impression never left, and in 1874 when the death of David Livingstone stirred the world and created a new enthusiasm for Africa, Mary Slessor concluded that she must answer the call. Thus by two deaths, Mary reached a decision and presented herself to the mission board in 1875. On August 6, 1876, she sailed to Africa on the *Ethiopia*.

3. *Dr. Oswald J. Smith* tells how God called him to preach:

"My desire to preach had grown stronger day by day. I felt as though I could not wait for the time to come. I would lie awake night after night making up sermons and preaching them over and over to myself. So desperate did I become that one time I planned to go to a place some ten miles away and ask the minister to let me preach in his church, arguing that if I failed, no one would know me and thus I would find out whether or not I could preach. . . . How to get into the ministry was the question. . . . I knew within myself that I could preach, I felt it in my very bones, and my whole soul cried out for an opportunity to put myself of trial."[15]

4. *Billy Graham* has less drama than many in his call to preach. As he entered Trinity College in Florida, things began pointing toward a call to preach. He started by giving his testimony in a street meeting. Then he began going into the swamp to practice on the birds and creeping things as he preached from a big cypress stump. His first real chance came when a nearby pastor asked him to fill in during his absence. When the pastor returned, a revival tide was on. Billy kept on preaching as the urgency became more real. He walked through the doors as they opened. This was his call.

FOUR STEPS TO ANSWERING GOD'S CALL

As we look at these calls of a pastor, an evangelist, and two missionaries, which date from the present back through many generations, you may note that each call had four unique steps. With some people these steps are drawn out over a period of years; with others they seem to come in rapid succession. There is rare exception to this progression. The four steps are:

1. *Recognition of the need.* Some zealous leaders have advocated that a recognition of the need, especially as concerns missions, is a call to full-time service. This is not true. Theoretically, all Christians see the need, but most of us must stay home to pray and give while others with special gifts and calls are sent into the pastorate or mission field. The biblical church at Antioch sent out Paul and

Barnabas while the laypersons stayed to pray, to give, and otherwise to strengthen the local church.

2. *A desire to fill the need.* The outstanding characteristic of William Carey's call was his earnest desire to fill the need. Many others have been prodded to action by the burning desire to win humanity to Christ. It was this desire—not training and methods—that made Peter a powerhouse in the revival following Pentecost.

3. *Ability to help fill that need.* At no place in the Scripture can you find God calling for men and women with talents and abilities. However, the Bible has much to say about the stewardship of the talents we do have. On the part of every called worker, there is the full consecration and development of these special abilities. Those with no enthusiasm and commitment to channeling their talents in other areas of life probably will not be a success in full-time service either.

4. *A growing impression that this is "my life's work."* Time is one of the best tests for a call to the ministry. If you feel that God might be calling you to special work, quietly thank him and hide the impression away in your heart. Keep walking in the light he gives. If the call is of God, there will be a persistent and deepening conviction of the need and of your desire to fill the need, and an increase in your consecrated abilities to help meet the need. Billy Graham is a good example of this truth. As he accepted the doors that opened, his spiritual insights into human needs and his passion to get Christ to the unsaved increased.

FIVE PHASES OF AN EMERGING CHRISTIAN LEADER

Dr. J. Robert Clinton, Professor of Leadership at Fuller Theological Seminary, proposes a developmental framework for people responding to a call to ordained ministry. Dr. Clinton identifies five phases based on rigorous examination of the lives of respected spiritual leaders such as A. W. Tozer, Watchman Nee, and Amy Carmichael: Phase 1—Sovereign Foundations; Phase 2—Inner-Life Growth; Phase 3—Ministry Maturing; Phase 4—Life Maturing; Phase 5—Convergence.[16]

Phases 1 and 2 are the initiation and confirmation of a call to ministry. In Sovereign Foundations, God weaves personality characteristics, positive and negative life experiences, and spiritual giftedness into a firmly developing character. This foundational period is usually marked by a "conversion or an experience of all-out surrender and commitment to a lifetime that counts for God."[17]

In Inner-Life Growth, the emerging leader usually receives some form of training—formal or informal—in connection with ministry. Through opportunities for modeling, mentoring, Bible school, or seminary, the individual experiences ministry. During this phase of training, the person's task is not primarily the ministry, but the inward preparation to be conformed to the character of Christ.

The formation of a call to ministry is affirmed and expanded as an individual learns three important inner-life lessons. Clinton calls these integrity checks, obedience checks, and word checks.[18]

Integrity Checks. An integrity check is a test that God uses to evaluate intentions in order to shape character. This check is a springboard to an expanded sphere of influence, and it involves behaving consistently with one's expressed convictions, resisting temptations, and withstanding persecution.

Obedience Checks. The obedience check is a process that teaches an individual to recognize, understand, and obey God's call. It is a personal response to revealed truth.

Word Checks. A word check tests the individual's ability to understand a word from God (e.g., an assignment to a special ministry) and then to allow God to work it out in his or her life.

Each of these three are sometimes combined with the others. For example, a revealed truth will test integrity and obedience.

Phases 3, 4, and 5 encompass the years of active ministry. In Ministry Maturing the emerging leader is focused on gaining ministry competence and evaluating productivity, activities, and fruitfulness in the ministry.

During Life Maturing, personal giftedness has been discovered and is channeled toward clear ministry priorities with discernment and fruitful results.

Finally, Convergence is marked by the spiritual leader's fulfillment of a role that matches gift-mix, experience, and temperament in such a way that enhances the best that the leader has to offer.

God's will is not a mystical unknown beyond the comprehension of common Christians. God gave us our minds and talents, which he expects us to use. He has given us our life experiences, which are the teachers of the soul. He has given us the Scriptures, which are our fundamental guide for service, attitudes, and relationships, as well as salvation. And in this era, God has given us professional Christian counselors who can guide people in making one of the greatest decisions of their lives.

NOTES

1. G. Friesen and J. R. Robinson, *Decision Making and the Will of God: A Biblical Alternative to the Traditional View* (Portland, Ore.: Multnomah, 1980), 126.

2. Ibid.

3. C. Carney and C. Wells, *Discover the Career Within You*, 3d. ed. (Pacific Grove, Calif., Brooks/Cole, 1991), 20–21.

4. D. Taylor, *The Myth of Certainty: The Reflective Christian and the Risk of Commitment* (Waco, Tex: Jarrell, 1986).

5. F. Beuchner, *Wishful Thinking: A Theological ABC* (New York: Harper and Row, 1973), 95. Italics added.

6. E. Welty and R. Sharp, *The Norton Book of Friendship* (New York: Norton, 1991), 475.

7. R. Bolles, *How to Find Your Mission in Life* (Berkeley: Ten Speed Press, 1991), 12–14. Italics added.

8. Friesen and Robinson, *Decision Making*, 335–55.

9. D. Sherman and W. Hendricks, *Your Work Matters to God* (Colorado Springs: NavPress, 1987), 142.

10. L. Parrott III, *Helping the Struggling Adolescent: A Guide to Thirty Common Problems for Parents, Counselors, and Youth Workers* (Grand Rapids: Zondervan, 1993), 129.

11. Sherman and Hendricks, *Your Work Matters*, 142.

12. Friesen and Robinson, *Decision Making*, 226.

13. Carney and Wells, *Career Within You*, 23.

14. M. R. Mulholland, *Shaped by the Word: The Power of Scripture in Spiritual Formation* (Nashville: The Upper Room, 1985), 110.

15. L. Parrott, *How to Choose Your Vocation* (Grand Rapids: Zondervan, 1952).

16. J. R. Clinton, *The Making of a Leader: Reconizing the Lessons and Stages of Leadership Development* (Colorado Springs: NavPress, 1988), 30–31.

17. Ibid.

18. Ibid.

Chapter Three

The Power of Family in Career Development

JULIE WAS AN INTELLIGENT, ENTHUSIASTIC woman in her mid-twenties. She invested much of her discretionary time procuring donations from area businesses to send shipments of toys to orphans in Romania. She had developed the contacts on her own and initiated the entire effort. When she talked about those children, her eyes lit up her entire face.

But here she was in my (Leslie's) office, shifting uncomfortably in her chair as she talked about her stalled efforts to make a career decision. A recent college graduate, she had spent time investigating opportunities to work as a travel agent, yet nothing was falling into place. Knowing her level of business savvy and professionalism, I was surprised to hear that she wasn't able to find an entry-level position in a local travel agency. After reviewing her resume and hearing a summary of her job search strategies, I had a growing hunch that an underlying barrier had preempted Julie's efforts.

As we talked, I began to ask exploratory questions. "Julie,

who among your circle of family and friends is invested in or anxious about the outcome of your career decisions?"

"It's funny you should ask that. My father called just last night to check on the status of my job search. It didn't go very well. He gave me a long lecture, said I wasn't really trying hard. I got so upset that I hung up."

"How anxious are you about making this career decision?"

"Do you really want to know? I'll show you."

Julie held out her hands that had been hidden in her lap. They were severely inflicted with a rash that left them red and raw with the top layer of skin almost completely peeled away. "This is how anxious I am about making this decision!"

In the remainder of our session Julie unfolded the story of parents who had encouraged her to apply to travel agencies. All she could understand was that they would enjoy the availability of the free travel benefits for the whole family. The combination of their pressure and her guilt had convinced her that she owed it to them after all they had done to help her complete her education. Once this was uncovered, Julie was able to see how her efforts to obtain a position in the travel industry were failing in great part due to her own unconscious self-sabotage. Her dream was to work in a not-for-profit agency focused on the needs of Romanian orphans and, eventually, to work directly in a Romanian orphanage.

In our work together, Julie came to develop strategies for clearer communication, increased empathy, and a confident determination to pursue the calling of her heart. Her dream was realized through exploring three areas: family rules, family roles, and family triangles. Let's take a look at each of these important areas.

FAMILY RULES

Each family has its own unique set of rules. These rules create an environment of consistency and predictability within the family structure. For example, one family may operate by the rule that everyone should get a graduate education. It is not discussed; it is simply expected. Another family, on the other hand, may live by the idea that real achievement is succeeding in the business without the intrusion of formal training.

While family rules may be explicit, they are more often unspoken, operating outside the conscious awareness of each family member. No one may say, "You have to get a Ph.D.," but the rule is unconsciously articulated and formed from picking up subtle and not so subtle attitudes. Hearing family stories about the glory and achievement of Dad's graduate training, for example, can be a way of saying, "You should do the same."

Family rules unconsciously guide individuals toward an almost predetermined career path. They describe what family members should do and how they should behave. But sometimes family rules fly in the face of a young person's real desires as Julie's family rules did.

Julie had to cultivate her own beliefs and values about work in order to transcend her family's rules for what she should be. She had to accept the fact that she was an active participant in the family system.[1] Once Julie raised her awareness of the unconscious rules she was operating by—the rules her family unknowingly perpetuated and instilled in her—she was more able to make conscious, intentional decisions about her career.

FAMILY ROLES

Jeff was an unknown when he appeared in my (Leslie's) office to discuss his career development. He was dressed casually, but his seriousness was notable. As he flipped open his daytimer to a list of questions he had prepared for our discussion, he said, "I'd like to nail it down today." While Jeff lacked even a cursory knowledge of his interests and abilities, he wanted to identify a career choice and map out a detailed plan of implementation during our first session. We talked for a while about some of his thoughts, and then I asked, "Jeff, what really prompted you to come to a me today? Why do you feel an urgency about making this decision now?"

It didn't take long for tears to well up in Jeff's eyes. He dropped his gaze, and we sat together silently for a few seconds. Then, with a deep sigh Jeff revealed that his older brother, who was on a fast track in a very successful career, had been killed recently in a car accident. Suddenly, the happy-go-lucky Jeff, who had been content with his retail job at an outdoor equipment supplier, felt the mantle of "oldest and only son" falling on his shoulders. Now that Jeff's role in the family had changed, everything about his future looked different.

Birth order and sibling dynamics are significant factors in shaping one's role in the family, and they are critical to the career decision-making process.[2] Psychologist Richard Bradley suggests that careers are shaped, in part, by our family constellations, by the career choices of our siblings. Siblings tend not to select the same careers but usually choose to go in different directions. The point is that roles played out within the family often develop into occupational or vocational pursuits.[3]

Jeff had crossed the professional career track off his list of options since his older brother had chosen a profession. Jeff's role as a fun-loving, carefree youngest child had comfortably developed into a vocational choice to work with outdoor, adventure-related equipment. The death of his brother, however, had redefined the boundaries of Jeff's role in the family and created a crisis of career identity. Understanding these basic tendencies between siblings helped him to understand his part in the system and aided him in making a less compulsive, more informed career decision.

FAMILY TRIANGLES

As Helen flopped herself into a chair in the counseling office, her body language screamed defeat. The way she sat was a white flag of surrender. This was such a change from the Helen of past career sessions that I (Leslie) was taken by surprise.

"Helen, what has happened? Did you get turned down for the position?"

"No! I was accepted right away."

"I thought that was exactly what you wanted, but you sure don't seem excited about it."

"I was excited—well that seems like forever ago now—when they first called to let me know. I could have turned cartwheels!

But I decided to call my parents and let them know about my good news. That's when everything exploded."

Helen had initiated career counseling several weeks earlier because of a growing awareness that she had no clues about her future career goals and dreams. She had worked hard in counseling to identify her interests, abilities, and values and to strategize a plan to implement them. Part of her plan was to apply to a competitive study-abroad program. The program included about ten weeks of academic travel with a faculty advisor. This would be a great boost to her major in English. Though her parents were aware that she had applied to the program, the family wheels didn't start turning until after she announced her acceptance. At this point her mother stepped in aggressively suggesting that Helen seemed depressed and despondent. Her mother then scheduled an appointment for Helen to see a psychiatrist. Her relatively uninvolved father suddenly encouraged Helen to consider dropping out of school since she seemed to have "lost all sense of direction." Helen had endured interviews with a puzzled psychiatrist and fought her parents' escalating efforts to move her back home. Finally, she gave in and passed up the opportunity to go abroad. As a result, things at home with the family were serene once again.

Ironically, just as Helen was discovering a career path she felt committed to and excited about—the very thing her family supported in theory—her parents moved in to resist it. Why?

The answer is found in a family triangle.[4] Triangulation happens anytime a third party becomes involved in an anxious or conflictual two-member relationship—even if they are all related. In some families, a person becomes so entrenched in a triangulated role that his or her identity cannot be separated from it. That was Helen's problem.

Through counseling, Helen was able to identify the role she had played over the years as mediator between her mother and father. Her presence in the family helped keep the peace. Because this was a particularly bad time in her parents' relationship, they were depending on her heavily, albeit unconsciously, to absorb the stress between them. Helen's plan to leave for ten weeks was so threatening to the family's delicate relational balance that a crisis ensued.

Eventually, Helen transcended what she called the "strangulation of triangulation." She realized that as long as she continued to carry such a substantial responsibility for her parents' relationship she would have little energy to invest in her own career development. Her role in the triangle sabotaged her attempts to develop a separate identity. Though she had missed her opportunity for study abroad, she took other steps that set healthier boundaries between herself and her parent's relationship.

Research has confirmed that families are a powerful force in the process of career development for a son, daughter, or sibling. For some individuals, family will be an extremely empowering presence in negotiating the career development process. For most, however, their families will present a mixed legacy with several vocational hurdles to overcome for true vocational development to occur. Rabbi and family therapist Edwin Friedman powerfully captures this reality:

> The position we occupy in our family of origin is the only thing we can never share or give to another while we are still alive. It is the source of our uniqueness, and hence, the basic parameter of our emotional potential as well as our difficulties. This unique position can dilute or nourish natural strengths; it can be a dragging weight that slows our progress throughout life, or an additive that enriches the mixture of our propelling fuel. The more we understand that position, therefore, and the more we can learn to occupy it with grace and "savvy," rather than fleeing from it or unwittingly allowing it to program our destiny, the more effectively we can function in any other area of our life.[5]

THE GENOGRAM: A TOOL FOR UNDERSTANDING CAREERS AND FAMILY

One of the most helpful tools for family exploration in career counseling is the family genogram.[6] It is a relational family tree that reveals recurring life patterns across three generations, and it can speed up the process of awareness and greatly facilitate career counseling. The genogram was developed from research on family systems by Murray Bowen and is widely used to help people unravel family mysteries.[7] The genogram records three basic pieces of information: family structure, family information (including stressors), and family relationships.

MAPPING THE FAMILY STRUCTURE

The backbone of the genogram is a graphic depiction of the family structure across three or four generations (see figure 3.1). Each male is represented by a square and each female is represented by a circle. A marriage is represented by a solid line connecting the two persons. Children are listed in birth order, beginning on the left with the oldest. Divorce is represented by a double slash through the marriage line. The genogram begins at the bottom of the page with the client's nuclear family and extends through the generations. The extended families represented by the mother and father are shown on different sides of the chart.

Genogram Format

A. Symbols to describe basic family membership and structure. Include on genogram significant others who lived with or cared for family members—place them on the right side of the genogram with a notation about who they are.

male ☐ female ○	birth date → 43–75 ☒ ← death date
Index Person (IP): ☐ ◎	Death = X
Marriage (give date) (Husband on left, wife on right)	Living together Relationship of liaison:
Marital Separation (give date)	Divorce (give date)
Children: List in birth order, beginning with oldest on left	Adopted or foster children

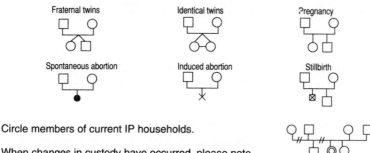

Circle members of current IP households.

When changes in custody have occurred, please note.

B. Family interaction patterns. The following symbols are optional. The clinician may prefer to note them on a seperate sheet. They are among the least precise information on the genogram, but may be key indicators of relationship patterns the clinician wants to remember:

Very close relationship

Conflictual relationship

Distant relationship

Estrangement or cutoff
(give dates if possible):

Fused and conflictual

C. Medical history. Since the genogram is meant to be an orienting map of the family, there is room to indicate only the most important factors. Thus, list only major or chronic illnesses and problems. Include dates in parentheses where feasible or applicable. Use DSM IV categories or recognized abbreviations where available (e.g., cancer, CA; stroke, CVA).

D. Other family information of special importance may also be noted on the genogram:

1. Ethnic background and migration date
2. Religion or religious change
3. Education
4. Occupation or unemployment
5. Military service
6. Retirement
7. Trouble with law
8. Physical abuse or incest
9. Obesity
10. Alcohol or drug abuse (symbol=   )
11. Smoking
12. Dates family members left home: LH '74
13. Current location of family members

It is useful to have a space at the bottom of the genogram for notes on other key information including critical events, changes in the family structures since the genogram was made, hypotheses, and other major family issues or changes. These notations should always be dated and should be kept to a minimum, since every extra piece of information on a genogram complicates it and therefore diminishes its readability.

Fig. 3.1

Source: B. Carter and M. McGoldrick, *The Changing Family Life Cycle: A Framework for Family Therapy*, 2d ed. (Needham Heights, Mass.: Allyn and Bacon, 1989). Used by permission.

RECORDING FAMILY INFORMATION

Once the family structure, or tree, of the genogram has been drawn, the next step is to add family information. There are three basic levels of information to record: demographic information, critical life cycle events, and functioning information. For a career-oriented genogram, the demographic information should include ages, dates of birth and death, geographic locations, educational experiences, current and previous occupations, and unemployment.

Critical life-cycle information should be focused on significant factors both within the family and in the external environment. Family therapists Betty Carter and Monica McGolderick have conceptualized the family system as flowing both vertically (as family patterns move through the generations) and horizontally (as families move through the life cycle).[8]

Vertical stressors are created when families adopt entrenched styles of relating. For example, the family rules and themes Julie identified and the triangulation that Helen experienced are both vertical stressors. They were styles of relating, deeply engrained and unconscious. Other vertical stressors include attitudes, expectations, labels, loaded issues, myths, and taboos that families collect and pass down through the generations.

Horizontal stressors are the result of either a developmental crisis within the family or a crisis precipitated by a force in the external environment. Developmental stressors are tied to predictable family life transitions such as marriage, birth of children, launching of children, retirement, and death. External horizontal stressors include war, debilitating illness, natural disasters, divorce, untimely death, and bankruptcy. Information related to both vertical and horizontal stressors should be recorded on the genogram.

The next step is to record information about each family member's medical, emotional, and behavioral functioning. Information about alcoholism, depression, and disabilities that have impacted the career journey of family members should be included. It is also important to include information about family members who reveal a high level of functioning—those who are considered successful, competent, and healthy. When looking at previous generations, the client may need to look for indirect clues such as, "Aunt Sarah never left the house," to discern functioning information.

MAPPING FAMILY RELATIONSHIPS

The final phase of constructing the genogram centers on family relationships. This is the most inferential part of the genogram and is based on the observation and intuition of family members. Which members of the family are distant, estranged, or cut off from each other? At the other extreme, which family members are close or overly close? Whose relationship would be characterized as conflictual? Are some people both distant and conflictual? Are others enmeshed and conflictual? What are the relational patterns in the transgenerational family? Many career paths have been impacted by the quality and tone of relationship patterns. As there are symbols representing people, there are symbols that enable the recording of relationship information on the genogram: three solid lines represent a very close relationship, a zigzag line represents a conflictual relationship, and a broken line represents a distant relationship. Estrangement or cutoff is indicated by two solid lines that are separated with a break and a slash (see figure 3.2).

PUTTING THE GENOGRAM TO WORK

A genogram can be created in the context of the counseling session or assigned to the client as homework. Either scenario will probably require that the client contact family members to gather information. It is important that you equip the client to set a comfortable tone for these conversations with relatives. We recommend that the client always tell the person in advance what he or she would like to accomplish. For example, the client might say to the relative, "I've been doing a lot of thinking about our family lately, and I'd like to learn more. Because you know more family history than I do, I'd like to ask you some questions." Emily Marlin, author of "If Your Family Tree Could Talk," suggests the following list of questions:[9]

Genogram of Family with Young Children: Freud Family, 1866

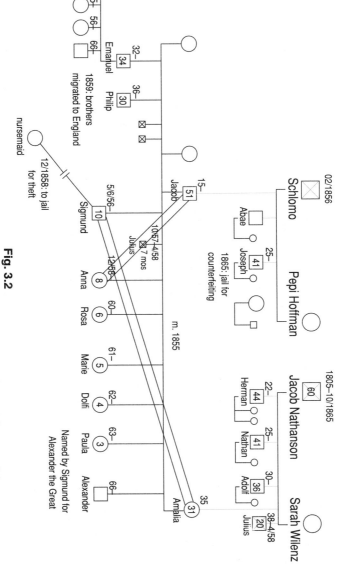

Fig. 3.2

Source: B. Carter and M. McGolderick, *The Changing Family Life Cycle: A Framework for Family Therapy,* 2d ed. (Needham Heights, Mass.: Allyn and Bacon, 1989). Used by permission.

- How did you like school, and what was your fondest school memory?
- What was your most terrible school memory?
- What kinds of relationships did you have with family members when you were growing up? What about now?
- How would you describe yourself at ages seven, fourteen, and twenty-one?
- What kinds of work have you done in your life?
- What was the most valuable thing your parents taught you?
- When were you married? What was the courtship like?
- What was the hardest thing you ever had to do?
- What was the happiest period in your life? The most difficult?

A primary purpose of this exercise is to uncover and identify any personal or environmental barriers that may impact movement toward the client's career goal.[10]

INTERPRETING THE IMPACT OF FAMILY THEMES ON CAREER DEVELOPMENT

Because the family plays such a key role in defining our destiny, it is important to synthesize the information from the genogram into a set of coherent statements. From the genogram and an autobiographical understanding of the client, you can gain insight into the value the family places on earning an undergraduate education, earning a graduate education, earning financial wealth, attaining personal achievement and prestige, developing individual talents, being self-giving, and being a success. You will also want to give consideration to the number of career transitions the father and mother went through as well as the importance of career to the self-definition of each of them. Each client, under the supervision of a vocational counselor, will interpret whatever events and relationships are important to the family story. No two are alike.

INFLUENTIAL FAMILY THEMES WORK SHEET

One approach to this task is to use a work sheet containing a list of unfinished sentence stems: Women are . . . Men are . . . Success is . . . Failure is . . . A career is . . . Being a woman and having a career is . . . Being a man and having a career is . . . Education is . . . Achievement is . . . Developing talents is . . . Being self-giving is . . ., and so on. As you guide the counselee through this work sheet, refer to the family genogram to inform your answers. This list should be representative of how the *family* might finish these sentence stems, rather than how the counselee believes personally. The goal is to uncover how the client's family of origin has shaped the client's career aspirations.

REWRITING FAMILY THEMES AS COMMANDMENTS

It may be useful to synthesize the genogram data even more into a list of family "commandments" for life.[11] Such a list would change the sentences above into a declarative form. For example, in one client's family, the family rule about earning an education can be stated in a declarative form: "Johnsons get their Ph.D.s." Almost every member of the extended family has chosen to fulfill this family value. In another client's family, that value might be stated, "Formal education is useless; what's practical is common sense." It is not hard to imagine how easily either of these family values could provoke inner turmoil for a client who does not share the inclination to pursue the family path.

IMPLEMENTING PLANS AGAINST FAMILY TRADITIONS

Career counseling's move for generating alternatives, obtaining occupational information, and making choices will take place against the backdrop of family information. The usual eight steps outlined in chapter 2 will be followed and the genogram will be a useful tool to this end.

It is important that you warn the client that if he or she chooses a career path divergent from family norms, it may be necessary to deal with broadly based family resistance. Understanding this probability can enable the client to withstand the resistance without engaging in a disruptive family discussion. Preparation is crucial when a client attempts to present a divergent point of view and work to resolve differences with the family.

Once the client understands what may lie ahead, he or she may be buoyed by knowledge of the twelve typical behavioral responses that people tend to rely on when a loved one has not lived up to an expectation.[12]

1. The family may resort to ordering, directing, or commanding. "I don't care what your counselor says. Do what I tell you to do because I know what's best for you."

2. The family may attempt to block the client by warning, threatening, or promising. "If you change your major, I'll stop paying your tuition."

3. Some family members will respond with moralizing or preaching. "You shouldn't change directions because other people will think you are immature and indecisive."

4. Some will offer other solutions or advice. "I'd suggest that you talk to your uncle about that. He's our accountant and knows more about the field than your adviser does."

5. Others will teach, lecture, or respond with logical arguments. "If you take responsibility and stick with your original plans, you'll be more marketable."

6. Some will resort to judging, criticizing, or blaming. "I couldn't be more disappointed in you."

7. They may praise or agree. "I've always been proud of you."

8. They might label or stereotype. "You're spoiled and inconsiderate of others."

9. They may analyze and diagnose. "You're not doing well because you're not trying hard enough."

10. They may reassure and sympathize. "Everyone goes through a phase like that. It will pass."

11. Some might probe and interrogate. "Why do you suppose you hate your job?"

12. They might withdraw or distract from the issue. "Why don't you quit and hide in the mountains?"

A team of career-development specialists have provided the following suggestions to help clients resolve the possible conflicts that may arise with the family because of a career decision:[13]

1. Know what you like to do, can do, and prize the most. This will raise your level of self-confidence.

2. Be sure the career information you use is the best available. Make a list of the resources you used in making your decision and offer to share the resources with those interested.

3. Select a favorable place to discuss your plan.

4. Be positive, clear, and precise in presenting your choice. You may want to role-play with an unbiased counselor to receive feedback on what is unclear or confusing.

5. Be open to learn from what others say. You can invite reactions without feeling obligated to change your decision.

6. Be willing to listen to others. Remember to put yourself in the shoes of the person receiving your news. This will increase your empathy to that person's response without demanding defensiveness on your part.

7. Be patient. Understand that it may take a while for the person to change his or her perspective.

8. Build on your commonalties and minimize your differences. If you are not in total disagreement about everything, remember to emphasize the areas of agreement.

9. Accept responsibility for your part of the conflict. Don't blame or placate—work it through.

10. Act assertively. If pressure to "live up to a family tradition or family rule" would make you feel resentful or angry, declare your feelings and request that the family not hold such fixed expectations of you. Let family members know of your hopes for their partnership with you in the transition process.

FAMILY IMPACT ON INDIVIDUAL CAREER DEVELOPMENT STYLES

Not every client is in need of career assistance in conjunction with family exploration. People seeking to negotiate career-development decisions or transitions will generally fall into one of the following categories: (1) free agent–decided; (2) free agent–undecided; (3) family agent–decided; or (4) family agent–undecided.[14]

FREE AGENT–DECIDED

These individuals have a healthy level of distinctiveness within their family. Family relationships are not characterized as overly close or enmeshed. These individuals are not struggling with a career decision but are solidly committed to a career goal. They are neither tangled in a morass of confusion about their career values and goals nor struggling to negotiate through the murky waters of overlapping or indistinct family boundaries.

For the Free Agent–Decided individual, the career-development process tends to be straightforward. The direct intervention of a vocational counselor is not usually necessary. Free Agent–Decided individuals will have a tendency to access resources and establish contacts on their own. Their decision-making style can be characterized as predominantly self-directed, virtually eliminating the necessity for an assessment and treatment strategy.

FREE AGENT–UNDECIDED

These individuals exhibit a high level of healthy distinctiveness or differentiation within their family but are faced with the task of making a career decision. These individuals are uncertain about their career goals and values, but they are not

troubled by the paralyzing pressures of diffuse family relational boundaries. For these individuals, career indecision is
more of a naturally unfolding developmental task than a
struggle.

Free Agent–Undecided individuals will also have a tendency to effectively utilize career-development assistance.
When they seek vocational counseling, they focus more on self-
assessment, skill building for the job search, or the provision
of information related to marketplace opportunities, options,
or relevant contacts. The decision-making style of the Free
Agent–Undecided individual is characterized by a tendency
to seek direct intervention. Traditional career assessment resources are generally appropriate for this population.

FAMILY AGENT–DECIDED

Individuals with this stance are low in distinctiveness or
self-differentiation within their family but are committed to a
clear career goal. They may seek wholeheartedly to live out
their family values to gain a personal identity as an extension
of the family system. Psychologists have called this condition
"identity foreclosure," a premature identity formed without
enough personal exploration and questioning to construct an
authentic personal identity.

Family Agent–Decided individuals may also be genuinely
congruent with the values of their family of origin and comfortable with a highly cohesive relational system. Especially
when dealing with clients from diverse cultural experiences,
this may be a factor of diversity in family and life norms.

Although Family Agent–Decided individuals tend to initiate direct intervention, they may have a tendency to exhibit a
subtle difference in demeanor: a quality of compulsive
drivenness in the career development process (different in tone
and intensity from the self-directedness of the two Free Agent
styles above). This drivenness may also be accompanied by a
lesser ability to fully utilize the available resources. Thus the
decision-making stance of the Free Agent–Undecided is one of
dependent drivenness. This is perhaps the most difficult stance
for the career counselor to discern and requires a more
thoughtful and thorough assessment process.

Effective assistance for these individuals will include an assessment of family. It is recommended that a tool such as the family genogram be constructed and interpreted for an exploration into family values, themes, goals, and relational dynamics. This will enable the Family Agent–Decided individual to resolve any deeper internal conflicts that may be unconsciously sabotaging the career development process.

FAMILY AGENT–UNDECIDED

These individuals suffer from low levels of self-distinctiveness or self-differentiation from their family of origin when facing the career decision-making process. Family Agent–Undecideds struggle with the double bind of unclear family relational boundaries and an inability to clarify their personal career values and goals. They are less likely to access career development resources unless they recognize them as a valid place to conduct career exploration, experience a quantum leap in anxiety related to developmental tasks, or receive pressure from other family members to make a career decision. The career decision-making stance of the Family Agent–Undecided is one of immobilization. Internally they experience a sense of being stuck and apprehensive with no developmental movement.

Effective career assistance to hurting people helps them identify the presence and intensity of their own anxiety and the anxiety of members of their family system. It will also provide a context for an assessment of the family system. Only after clarifying the impact of the family can true personal goals and values be identified and explored as well as the impact they may have on homeostasis, or balance, within the family system. The power of the family is no small matter.

NOTES

1. W. E. Bratcher, "The Influence of the Family on Career Development," *The Personnel and Guidance Journal* (1982): 87–91.

2. R. W. Bradley and G. A. Mims, "Using Family Systems and Birth Order Dynamics as the Basis for a College Career Decision-Making Course," *Journal of Counseling and Development* 70 (1992): 445–48.

3. R. W. Bradley, "Using Sibling Dyads to Understand Career Development," *The Personnel and Guidance Journal* 62 (1984): 397–400.

4. J. C. Zingaro, "A Family Systems Approach for the Career Counselor," *The Personnel and Guidance Journal* (1983); 24–27; M. Bowen, *Family Therapy in Clinical Practice* (New York: Jason Aronson, 1978).

5. E. H. Friedman, *Generation to Generation: Family Process in Church and Synagogue* (New York: Guilford Press, 1985), 34.

6. R. W. Okiishi, "The Genogram as a Tool in Career Counseling," *Journal of Counseling and Development* 66 (1987): 139–43.

7. M. McGoldrick and R. Gerson, "Genograms and the Family Life Cycle" in, *The Changing Family Life Cycle: A Framework for Family Therapy*, 2d ed., B. Carter and M. McGoldrick (Needham Heights, Mass.: Allyn and Bacon, 1989).

8. Carter and McGoldrick, *Changing Family Life Cycle.*

9. E. Marlin, "If Your Family Tree Could Talk," *Self,* January 1988, 88–91.

10. E. Yost and M. Corbishley, *Career Counseling: A Psychological Approach* (San Francisco: Jossey-Bass, 1987), 21.

11. R. R. Kurtz, "Using a Transactional Analysis Format in Vocational Group Counseling," *Journal of College Student Personnel* (1974): 447–51.

12. T. Gordon, *Teacher Effectiveness Training: Supplement to the Instructor's Outline* (Pasadena, Calif.: Effectiveness Training Associates), 1972.

13. C. Carney and A. Reynolds, "When Others Challenge Your Career Choice: Strategies for Conflict Resolution," in *Discover the Career Within You*, ed. B. Carter and M. McGoldrick (Pacific Grove, Calif.: Brooks/Cole, 1991), 272.

14. L. Parrott, "Career Decision-Making and Family Functioning" (Ph.D. diss., Seattle University, 1993).

Chapter Four

Applying Biblical Insights to Career Counseling

ALTHOUGH THE BIBLE IS RICH IN MATERIALS—parables, principles, and precepts—for living, it is challenging to find biblical insights that can be applied directly to career counseling. One biblical scholar who specializes in vocational counseling states, "There are no [biblical] how-to steps for busy North American evangelicals. The challenge we face is to understand our situation in light of biblical truths. That is what discipleship is all about: making choices in light of biblical truths we have discerned."[1]

Lee Hardy, Christian philosopher and author of *The Fabric of This World, Inquiries into Calling, Career Choice and the Design of Human Work,* reminds us that it should not come as a surprise that biblical guidelines for the responsible choice of an occupation "have not been thoroughly worked out by the Christian community at large."[2] The freedom to make an occupational choice has been studied by only a small minority of Christian thinkers and theologians.

One vocational counselor said, "Applying biblical insights to career counseling is like mingling poetry and prose. The poetry is God's grand vision for an individual, while the prose is found in the practice of translating that vision into specific, obtainable steps."

Dedicated vocational counselors working from a Christian perspective have attempted the practical application of principles and precepts related to work, while theologians focus their studies on a biblical view of a calling. Nonetheless, one gifted pioneer in vocational counseling, John Shea, uses the transformational qualities of biblical stories to inform the career journey.

This chapter will focus on intervention exercises and techniques based on (1) the application of biblical principles and precepts and (2) the application of biblical stories to careers.

APPLYING BIBLICAL PRINCIPLES AND PRECEPTS TO CAREER-LIFE PLANNING

The fertile soil of biblical principles offers a good harvest of directives in vocational planning. John Bernbaum, and Simon Steer have created a study guide titled *Why Work? Careers and Employment in Biblical Perspective* that does an excellent job of applying biblical insights to vocational issues. The authors approach the topic with an infectious joy.

> As we think about the subject of our jobs and future career aspirations, we need to pause a moment in order to thank God for his graciousness to us. God has not left us on our own to struggle in the darkness, groping to find direction for our lives where there are no discernible landmarks. All Scripture is "God-breathed" and is "useful," so each one of us may be "thoroughly equipped for every good work" (2 Tim. 3:16–17). That is an exciting truth. Despite the difficulties of the issues we face as we try to assess our own gifts and abilities and how we should use them in our work, we have a priceless resource available to us.[3]

In the workbook *Life Planning: A Christian Approach to Careers*,[4] Kirk Farnsworth and Wendell Lawhead have designed several helpful exercises that apply to one's values, abilities, gifts, and interests with an integration of biblical insights throughout. Farnsworth and Lawhead introduce Old Testament Scriptures that deal with God's laws of limited cropping, firstfruits, interest-free loans, and tithing (e.g., Lev. 25:1-7; Deut. 14:22–23, 27–29; 24:19; 26:10–11). Clients are invited to apply these laws to their present-day values and principles in the workplace. Then the New Testament is used as a groundwork of life values with Scriptures that apply to anxiety about the future, material possessions, honor and justice, and an eternal perspective on life (e.g., Matt. 6:25–34; Phil. 4:4–9; and Col. 3:1–17).[5]

Another series of exercises by Farnsworth and Lawhead are designed to help clients use the Scriptures to identify their gifts, talents, and abilities (e.g., Exod. 35:30–35; Rom. 12:3–8; 1 Cor. 12:4–11; 13:1–3, 8; 14:6, 26; Eph. 4:7–12; 1 Peter 4:9–11). Against this scriptural backdrop and in the context of group discussion, clients work to identify their own spiritual gifts, which the authors define as "abilities that are used for the edification of others rather than in self-service."[6]

APPLYING BIBLICAL STORIES TO THE CAREER JOURNEY

Narrative theologian John Shea has called us to view biblical stories as a means of "configuring ourselves correctly." He believes the power in these stories will teach us, change us, and make God's presence alive within us. [7]

Biblical stories share several common elements:

1. They begin with ordinary people in ordinary situations.

2. The actors are ordinary people, but God devised the plot.

3. They are not smooth stories but are interrupted by radical new possibilities that replace the ordinary hopelessness in life.

4. They turn on human decisions.

5. They leave us with new wisdom and understanding.

Through Bible stories God calls us to move from barrenness to fruitfulness, from sin to redemption, from hopelessness to faith, from the ordinary to the extraordinary, from depression to celebration, and from chaos to unity. [8]

One of the most in-depth and unique applications of the biblical model was developed by Jeff Trautman, director of Intercristo.[9] Based on the Old Testament narratives of Abraham, Jacob, Joseph, and Moses, Trautman's model focuses on the enduring vocational lessons extracted from these stories and applied to the individual lives of clients.

Trautman has organized the biblical stories around four key concepts:

- God's vocational vision
- beliefs essential to God's better future for us
- basic choices
- our role in God's agenda for reconciling the world

This model is designed as a ten-week process for use with groups or in individual counseling. The presentation materials and exercises for personal application and planning are presented in the workbook *How to Find Your Best Future: A Biblical Approach to Living Abundantly in a Turbulent World.*[10] The four stories are presented as a counseling resource. With the help of a good counselor, the experiences of a biblical character are applied to the vocational dilemmas at hand.

THE STORY OF ABRAHAM

The key elements of Abraham's story are:

1. *God's promises to make Abraham a great nation and to give him a long-desired son.* The application of this story helps clients to understand that God has a personal vision for their future. God has a plan and will fulfill it in spite of their uncertainty.

2. *Abraham's faith endured the uncertainty of traveling to a distant land, a barren wife, and a command to sacrifice his son.* The client may see that God's timing in life is always perfect even though it rarely feels soon enough.

3. *Abraham discovered a better future through God's plans and promises.* Clients may see that it is best to take obedient risks toward the fulfillment of their best future. The obedient risks God required of Abraham included:

- *The risk of choosing the unknown over the known.* Abraham had to leave the comfort and convenience of life in Haran and journey to a place he had never been.

- *The risk of saying "no" to an earned opportunity for personal gain.* Abraham's success in recovering the King of Sodom's people and resources resulted in the king offering him a financial windfall. But Abraham refused to claim it so he would not compromise his faith in God's promises for his future.

- *The risk of alienating significant others.* Abraham required his coworkers and family to undergo minor surgery and be circumcised as a symbol of their loyalty to God.

- *The risk of entrusting into God's care the resource in life you waited so long to acquire.* After enduring pain and disappointment while trying to have a son to inherit God's promise, and when Abraham's heart's desire was finally fulfilled, God asked him to give his son back to him. Abraham took this risk obediently and prepared Isaac for sacrifice.

4. *God's basic agenda for the world as revealed in the story of Abraham is to enlarge the family of faith.* The application of this in career counseling is to enable clients to see God's movement in their lives from the pursuit of a personal vision to involvement in God's global vision through his timing and their obedience.

APPLYING THE LESSONS OF ABRAHAM TODAY

The life of Abraham closely follows the vocation pattern researchers identify as the "transformer."[11] *Transformers* are those individuals who find their calling and vocation after a major career shift and remain faithful to that vision for the remainder of their lives. The lessons of Abraham are evident in the life of another transformer—Norman Vincent Peale.

The death of Norman Vincent Peale on Christmas Eve 1993 marked the end of an incredible life. An interview with Peale for a research project on longevity (Peale was already in his nineties), revealed some insights into his vocational journey.

As a young man, Peale wanted to be a journalist. As the associate editor of his college newspaper, he was drawn into the charged atmosphere of the newspaper business. After graduating from Ohio Wesleyan, Peale worked at the *Findley Ohio Morning Republican* and at the *Detroit Journal.* He loved his work and was diligent.

One day while covering a fire in Detroit, Peale saw a twelve-year-old girl trapped in a burning building. To save her, someone had pushed a plank between her building and one next door—about eight feet away. She was paralyzed with fear and couldn't cross it. Peale shouted up to her, "Honey, do you believe in God?" She nodded. "Do you believe he is right there with you?" She nodded again. "Well, he will guide you across that plank." With continued coaching by Peale, she made it safely across. After this incident a sergeant said to Peale, "Good job, boy. You ought to be a preacher." He responded, "I'm no preacher; I'm a reporter." But as time passed, Peale could not escape a haunting feeling that he was supposed to be "a messenger of the Good News instead of the daily news."

Still ambivalent about his career direction, Peale eventually left the newspaper business and returned to school to study theology. This move marked the risk of saying "no" to earned opportunity out of obedience to God. Then attendance at one of the first churches he pastored went from twenty to nine hundred in his first year of ministry. God blessed Peale and made him a blessing to others.

Nevertheless, Peale struggled hard to overcome shyness and, after working hard on his techniques, he put some of these into a manuscript for others. When he finished writing *The Power of Positive Thinking*, Peale took a risk and sent it to a publisher—who rejected it. Much later, his wife discovered the manuscript in the trash and submitted it to another publisher. It was accepted. Since 1952, *The Power of Positive Thinking* has sold millions of copies. Peale also started a magazine, *Guide-*

posts, and he and his wife, Ruth, founded a publishing company for inspirational publications.

As a pastor, Peale was a pioneer in integrating psychology and Christianity. After World War II Peale was trying to minister to people broken by job loss and depression. He consulted a psychiatrist and established a partnership with him in his church. This sparked a new era for ministering to the needs of people. However, Peale faced much criticism for this and other attempts to integrate practical psychology with Scripture. He paid the price in alienation. At one point Peale was so discouraged that he planned to resign his pastorate at the Marble Collegiate Church. A visit to his dying father encouraged him to remain, and it was there at the same church that he finished a long and flourishing career.[12]

A secular interviewer concluded, "This aspiring journalist ended up reaching millions of people in a way that he never expected. Seventy years after he made the decision to go into seminary, his influence is still spreading."[13] It is not difficult to see God's movement in the lives of Ruth and Norman Vincent Peale from the pursuit of a personal vision in journalism to involvement in God's global vision, through God's timing and the Peale's obedience. But as in the life of Abraham, so in the life of Norman Vincent Peale, God's timing, though perfect, rarely feels soon enough.

The Story of Jacob

The key elements of the story of Jacob are:

1. *Jacob's attempts to control and manipulate family members to attain the opportunities reserved for his brother, Esau, failed completely and alienated him from his family.* This truth applies in many situations involving family relationships. God advances the desires of the heart through uncontrolled opportunity, not through manipulation. Even if manipulation worked, the risks are too great. The results often tear families apart.

2. *Jacob learned to work with difficult people like Laban without compromising his commitment.* In career counseling, the clients learn not to bail out when the going gets tough. God uses imperfect people to advance the desires of the heart.

3. *Jacob discovered in a life-changing dream that God was on his*

side even when circumstances seemed out of control. Jacob's experience helps clients see that they have a basic choice to make: release control of your life and trust God with your heart's desire.

4. *God's basic agenda as revealed in Jacob's story is to use the heart's desires of his people to carry out his plans and promises.* This applies to clients who need to see that God uses the desires of the heart to advance both his plans and promises in the world and in their lives specifically.

APPLYING THE LESSONS OF JACOB TODAY

Jacob's vocational journey is similar to the pattern researchers have labeled the "homesteader." *Homesteaders* stay in the same field all their lives, committed and captivated by the work they have chosen. Many of the lessons in the Jacob story are also illustrated in the life of Mother Clara Hale who founded the Hale House center for child care in New York City, a nonprofit agency dedicated to the care of infants of addicted mothers.

The granddaughter of a slave, Clara's family history was extraordinary. Her father died when she was only two. To earn money, her mother cared for children, and Clara helped. When Clara was sixteen, her mother died. In spite of her high school diploma, Clara Hale could only find work as a domestic because she was black. Yet God worked to advance the desires of Clara's heart even through negative circumstances of limited employment options.

After her marriage to Thomas Hale, Clara moved her family to New York where she served as a building superintendent in return for a rent-free apartment. Tragedy struck again, however, when Thomas Hale died of cancer at the age of thirty-seven. To support her family, Clara took in children as her mother had before her. Rather than give up, Clara, simply kept going, releasing control over what she could not change, and trusting God with her heart's desires.

Years later, in 1969, Clara's daughter Lorraine saw a woman sleeping on a porch stoop with her baby. Concerned, she gave the woman her mother's address and telephone number. The next day the woman handed her baby over to Clara Hale, who helped the homeless mother get her life together so she could take proper care of her child. Word spread. Hale soon had a new vocation: taking care of children of women who were addicts. This uncontrollable circumstance turned into an opportunity for God's grace to reach through Mother Hale to hundreds of mothers, and children.

Eventually, Lorraine Hale completed her Ph.D. in early childhood development and began working with her mother. She also incorporated their center as a not-for-profit agency that could receive government funding. Since that time, Hale House has cared for more than eight hundred children.

It was said about Mother Hale, "She genuinely loved what she did in her life. She had a quality that children soaked up like sunshine, and the way she related to them was both brilliant and matter-of-fact."[14] God was able to use the desires of Hale's heart to advance his plans and promises to hundreds of children who desperately needed care. The unmitigated desires of Jacob and of Clara Hale and their ultimate fulfillment are an inspiration and beacon of hope for many clients in vocational counseling.

The Story of Joseph

The key elements of the story of Joseph are:

1. *God's vision for Joseph transcended his teenage dreams.* This was true even though Joseph's future was sometimes bleak. Joseph is a good example of someone limited by the authority within his own family. God's vision included Joseph's unlikely rise to power in an alien prosperous land, the reunion with his estranged brothers, and the spectacular development of the tribes of Israel. The story of Joseph enables clients to understand God's vision for their future. God guides them toward the highest and best use of their gifts and talents in spite of life's inevitable setbacks.

2. *God redeemed Joseph's setbacks.* God can use times of unseen progress to equip his people for greater service. Like Moses, who was being prepared for leadership during forty years in the wilderness, Joseph grew in the inner person during his prison experiences. When the time came for the fulfillment of his dream, Joseph was ready. This is why he

could say to his brothers at their tension-packed meeting, "You intended to harm me, but God intended it for good to accomplish what is now being done"(Gen. 50:20).

3. *Joseph's unjust setbacks were transformed into personal progress as he practiced perseverance.* Success did not come in one moment but in a succession of events. Joseph played a key role in Potiphar's household, in prison, among those who had lost hope, and finally as the government agent in Egypt's famine-relief program. This story can help clients to understand their need to persevere during times of great discouragement.

4. *God's agenda for the world as revealed in Joseph's story is to prepare his people to be salt and light in a world that is bland and dark.* This story helps career counselors lead their clients to see that God joins with his people in making them a part of the solution rather than a part of the problem. Paul caught this same vision in his first letter to the Christians in Thessalonica: "Make it your ambition to lead a quiet life, to mind your own business and to work with your hands, just as we told you" (1 Thess. 4:11).

APPLYING THE LESSONS OF JOSEPH TODAY

Joseph's vocational path is similar to one that researchers have labeled the "explorer." *Explorers* make periodic career changes throughout their lives. These changes may be motivated by unmet expectations, lack of job fit, internal need for growth, external factors, short-term opportunities, family considerations, or just circumstances. There is nothing wrong in judicious career changes that fit an overall goal.

The late Senator J. William Fulbright was an explorer whose life illustrates many of the lessons evident in the story of Joseph. As a result of his judicious career changes, Fulbright helped millions of people in their own work needs.

Born in Missouri in 1905, Fulbright grew up in Arkansas. Like Joseph, William Fulbright was a promising young man. He was a Rhodes scholar and studied three years at Oxford University. After returning from England, Fulbright worked a series of four jobs: first a businessman, then a lawyer, later a law professor, and then a university president. Even though circumstances turned against him on occasion, God used these hard times to equip Fulbright for greater service in the future.

Fulbright was teaching at the University of Arkansas when the president of the university died unexpectedly. To his own astonishment, Fulbright was elected president. However, after a mere three years, a vindictive politician maneuvered Fulbright's ouster.

Set back but not stopped, Fulbright took a former student's suggestion that he run for Congress against the very politician who had ousted him from the University of Arkansas. Fulbright won. Two years later he ran for the Senate and won. He held his Senate seat for thirty years. As he had done with Joseph, God guided Fulbright toward the highest and best use of his gifts and talents in spite of the painful loss of the university presidency.

While in the Senate, Fulbright introduced a resolution that led to the creation of the United Nations. Following World War II, he also created the Fulbright Fellowship program as a creative way for foreign countries to repay postwar loans. It was a brilliant move that enabled economically recovering nations to repay their debts in their own currency by funding tuition and living expenses for U. S. exchange students. Thousands of students have participated in this program, which fosters relationships across international borders. Fulbright spearheaded the John F. Kennedy Center for the Performing Arts in Washington, D. C., raising the money for its construction. Through Fulbright's effort, God's intentions for his people to be preservers of life wherever possible and to reveal his plans and promises in the world were fulfilled in great measure. Of Fulbright, an interviewer commented, "He met opportunities more than half way when they appeared and kept going even when he encountered obstacles."[15]

THE STORY OF MOSES

The key elements in the Moses story are:

1. *God's vision for Moses was to lead his people out of bondage, but first Moses had to confront the pain and failure of trying to fight oppression through violence.* The Moses story helps clients understand God's vision for their own future. From Moses they learn how God empowers people to change their world by confronting their own problems.

2. *After killing a brutal taskmaster, Moses left Egypt for the desert.* Isolation on the backside of nowhere provided Moses with protection, a new start, and a safe emotional distance from Egypt. In the desert, Moses thought he could gain relief from the powerlessness and guilt that had dogged his tracks in Egypt. Yet in the desert God's unmistakable voice called Moses from guilt to forgiveness, from powerlessness to a new hope, and from defeat to leadership. The Moses story enables clients to embrace the belief that God's power and presence is their only hope for realizing the personal changes they need.

3. *When Moses encountered God in the burning bush, their exchange was honest dialogue.* God needed a man, and Moses needed victory over his personal feelings of inadequacy. One by one God dealt with Moses' reservations. This Moses story encourages clients to understand they can choose to talk with God in an honest dialogue about their guilt, failure, fears, and desires. Not many have been dug out of a deeper hole than Moses and lifted to greater heights of leadership.

4. *Moses could have lived his life in royal comfort as the adopted son of Pharaoh's daughter, but instead he allowed God to use him, with all his human frailties, to lead the Israelites out of slavery into freedom.* The Moses story enables clients to see a God who leads individuals to become agents of transformation, not pursuers of success, in their world.

APPLYING THE LESSONS OF MOSES TODAY

The career-life journey of Moses fits the pattern researchers have identified as the "long growth curve and late bloomer." *Late bloomers* follow a career pattern that reaches its highest peak late in life. It is characteristic of these people to grow and rise to great usefulness at the age conventional wisdom assumes they should be winding down.[16]

As an African American growing up in segregation, Herbert Barksdale developed an early passion for justice and racial harmony. He did not, however, experience a conversion until later in life. At the age of seventeen Barksdale became a professional boxer for four years. Then he ran a numbers game in a black area of Washington, D.C. It was here, in the city, that he felt the horror of prejudice. After a stint in the Navy during the Korean War, he drove a cab for eight years in Washington, D.C.

There, through the influence of conversations with people in his cab, Barksdale made a commitment to Jesus Christ. Finally, Barksdale realized God's power and presence was his only hope for realizing the changes he needed in himself and in the world. He engaged in honest dialogue with God. This led him to pursue spiritual transformation. Through Christ he became a new creation.

Wanting to serve Christ, Barksdale became a counselor in a Methodist church for two years. In 1974, Barksdale became deeply involved in a mayoral campaign in Washington, D. C. He was in charge of distributing materials across the city. At that point, he became increasingly convinced that God was calling on him to impact public policy. God was empowering Barksdale to change his world by publicly confronting the very areas of personal bondage that had deeply troubled him. Five years later, he became an investigator in the Office of Paternity and Child Support Enforcement in Washington, D. C. In this role Barksdale was able to help the poorest and most needy members of society.

Barksdale also joined a prayer group that included the mayor of Washington, D. C., and heads of government departments who were "seeking to bring harmony and spirituality to the workplace through dialogue between workers and management."[17] God was clearly an agent of transformation in the personal life of Herbert Barksdale, therefore allowing him to become an agent for justice and racial harmony in the workplace. Barksdale was no longer a pursuer of personal success but God's agent for service and change in his small world.

APPLICATION EXERCISES

As clients work through the biblical narratives, Trautman provides exercises that assist them in applying the biblical lessons to their own career journeys. A sampling of these exercises follows.

Exercise 1: Getting in Touch with the Future I Hope to Realize. This exercise is designed to assist clients in applying the lessons from Abraham's story to their own career journeys:

1. Begin by taking a blank sheet of paper divided by a diagonal line. On one side of the diagonal write the words, "The future I want would bless me with . . ." On the other side of the diagonal write, "The future I desire would enable me to bless others by . . ."

2. Take time to identify what your best future would look like. First identify the blessings your future would bring into your life. Second, describe the ways you would be a blessing to others. Begin with expectations for your work life and then move into other important areas of your life.

For example, here is what I (Leslie) wrote when I first did this exercise. The future I want would bless me with:

an earned doctorate

opportunities to teach, counsel, and mentor college students

international travel—studies and short-term missions

a healthy marriage and three children

purchasing a home

close family relationships

learning gourmet cooking

deep friendships

contributing to a community of learners by developing an expertise for helping people improve their lives

learning, healing, and applying healthy faith and relationship principles in the lives of college students

creating an inspirational book that teaches biblical truth to children in simple ways loving and nurturing developing children

a marriage that sustains the demands of life with increasing strength for the blessing of my spouse and family and the stability of society.

3. Review the best future and identify one or two items that you desire to make progress on in the coming year. Indicate these by underlining the items.

4. Identify risks you may have to take during this next year if you are to realize the desired progress. These risks may include choosing the unknown over the known, saying "no" to an earned opportunity, alienating significant others, or trusting God with an important resource (tangible or intangible).

Here are some risks I (Leslie) might have had to take to realize my desire for earning a doctorate:

- *Choosing the unknown over the known.* I had no way of knowing what demands doctoral-level studies might place on me. Even if I knew others who were also working on a doctorate, my experience and how I responded to it might have been different. I also held my future open to the possibility of being accepted or not accepted. That was a giant unknown.

- *Saying "no" to earned opportunity.* If I pursued this doctorate, I would have to say "no" to a lot of other opportunities that came my way for the next few years. If a great opportunity for more responsibility at work opened up, I would have to defer until my school work was completed. If I had the chance to pursue some of my other future desires, such as international travel, I would have to defer until my graduate work was completed. Going for a doctorate meant giving up a lot of other things with the risk that I might never have those opportunities again.

- *Alienating significant others.* If I pursued this doctorate, not everyone would think I had made a wise decision.

Many people don't see the value in higher education nor do they welcome the sacrifices it takes to achieve an advanced degree. No one would be happy with me when I said "no" to them because I had to study. I would be undertaking something that was long delayed in gratification and required sacrifice for everyone in my circle of family and friends.

Exercise 2: Learning How to Release Control. Based on the story of Jacob, this exercise is designed to enable clients to identify the strategies of control they have developed in their families of origin that have now become their basic strategies for controlling life.

1. Take a few minutes to reflect on your childhood years (ages five to thirteen).
2. Divide a sheet of paper in half and over one half write the heading "Mom" and over the opposite half "Dad." Using a word or a brief phrase, write down four descriptions of these individuals (i.e., emotionally distant, talker and storyteller, busy doing everything, hard worker, hard to please, always giving advice).
3. As you reflect on these descriptive words, consider the following frequently used strategies for trying to control life. Check those that seem to apply to you.

Pleasing—Life is under control as long as I'm liked and appreciated.

Anticipating—Life is under control as long as I can outwit people and circumstances to get what I want.

Blaming—Life is under control as long as I know it's someone else's fault, so I don't have to change.

Avoiding—Life is under control as long as I don't have to face upsetting or discouraging situations or people.

Changing—Life is under control as long as I have another option to pursue.

Disciplining—Life is under control as long as I can maintain my schedules, eating habits, social patterns, savings level, etc.

Achieving—Life is under control as long as I am producing more results, better results.

Protecting—Life is under control as long as I can insure the proper treatment of the resources or people I value.

4. Once you have identified a few of your controlling strategies, think again your current heart's desire identified in the second part of exercise 1. Can you see how the strategies you have developed for controlling life in your family are hindering the advancement of this desire? If so, write down the connection you see.

5. Identify a specific response that would oppose the natural control responses you have developed in your life to advance this desire. List one or two.

Exercise 3: Identifying Personal Gifts and Talents (part A). Based on the story of Joseph, this exercise is designed to assist clients in applying the principle of perseverance in their career journey.

1. Take time to think back over the past decade of your life. Have there been demands placed on you by circumstances beyond your control and setbacks that have been unjust and unfair? However, in the midst of these unfair setbacks, have there been pockets of enjoyment where your unique strengths were released to give you a sense of personal satisfaction and accomplishment? List some of those personal accomplishments that come to mind. These accomplishments should not be measured by recognition received or by the magnitude of your effort, but by the personal sense of accomplishment you felt in the process.

2. Write a descriptive paragraph about each situation in your list of accomplishments. Focus on the *activity* you enjoyed that made this accomplishment happen. Then review the accomplishment descriptions and underline the key tasks you enjoyed most. For example:

Accomplishment: Talking a friend through a tough time.
What I did: Jill would call me to go out for coffee. I would ask her how things were going. She would talk in great detail

about a situation that had come up. I would <u>listen</u> for key issues, ask questions, make suggestions regarding what could be happening, always <u>encouraging</u> her.

Exercise 4: Identifying Personal Gifts and Talents (part B). From the Old Testament narratives of Abraham, Jacob, Joseph, and Moses, Trautman identifies four categories of vocational giftedness: contributor, influencer, manager, and director.

A *contributor*, like Abraham, prefers to spend time at work serving others through producing practical, technical, organizational, or aesthetic results. Every time God revealed himself to Abraham, he gave Abraham a result to produce (e. g., Gen. 12:1, leave Haran; Gen. 15:9–10, make a sacrifice; Gen. 17:9–23, circumcise his tribe; Gen. 22: 1–9, sacrifice his son).

An *influencer*, like Jacob, measures performance by the capacity to move others to action (i.e., exchange of resources), commitment (i.e., decision making), and results (i.e., growth and change). Jacob is most consistently involved in influencing others to respond (e. g., Gen. 25:29–34, influences Esau to obtain his birthright; Gen. 27:19–27, influences his father to get the blessing; Gen. 33:1–19, influences Esau to protect his family).

A *manager*, like Joseph, measures performance by how efficiently and effectively resources such as rewards, relationships, activity, or perception are managed to achieve the best results. The story of Joseph reveals the natural strengths of a manager (e.g., Gen. 39:4–6, managing Potiphar's household; Gen. 39:21–23, managing the prison; Gen. 41:33–40, managing famine relief for Pharaoh).

A *director*, like Moses, provides vision and direction by identifying and overcoming external threats, defining the nature of a community, and identifying large goals or projects that channel creativity of individuals within the community. A director provides vision or direction by launching something new, living out beliefs and ideas, achieving better results, and pursuing challenging interests. God inspired Moses to provide vision and direction for Israel (e.g., Exod. 5–12, overcoming the threat of Pharaoh; Exod. 20–24, instituting the Ten Commandments; Exod., 25–40, directing the building of the tabernacle and implementing worship for the community).

Review each of your tasks from exercise 3 and check which of the four roles of contributor, influencer, manager, or director are most clearly reflected in this task. Rank them from greatest to least in priority by placing the letters *C, I, M, D* in descending order.

Exercise 5: Barriers to Honest Dialogue. Based on the story of Moses, this exercise is designed to assist the client in engaging in honest dialogue with God. Two barriers to honest dialogue with God are the perceptions formed by your experiences with your parents or primary caregivers regarding (1) intimacy (usually Mom) and (2) authority (usually Dad).

1. Consider your reflections on your parents from exercise 2. You will recognize some assumptions that you developed at home regarding intimacy and authority that impact your communication with God.
2. Identify two of these assumptions that originate from your home rather than from the Bible.
3. Take time to write out an honest dialogue with God. Include any feelings, perceptions, questions, or disappointments. This is your time to be heard.

To this point we have been examining the big picture. After a lengthy view of the current work-quake, or jobs revolution, we moved on to discuss God's role in career choice and the extraordinary power of the family over young people making career choices. Finally, we have considered biblical principles and their application to career choices. It is time now to move on to specific career-development strategies.

NOTES

1. J. Bernbaum and S. Steer, *Why Work? Careers and Employment in Biblical Perspective* (Grand Rapids: Baker, 1986), 87.

2. L. Hardy, *The Fabric of This World: Inquiries into Calling, Career Choice and the Design of Human Work* (Grand Rapids: Eerdmans, 1990), 84.

3. Bernbaum and Steer, *Why Work?*, 80.

4. K. Farnsworth and W. Lawhead, *Life Planning: A Christian Approach to Careers* (Downers Grove: InterVarsity, 1979).

5. Ibid., 12–21.

6. Ibid., 29–24.

7. J. Shea, *Stories of God* (Chicago: University of Chicago, 1978); and J. Shea, *Stories of Faith* (Chicago: University of Chicago, 1980).

8. R. Rolheiser, "The Human Person as Understood by John Shea—The Biblical Perspective," (lecture notes, Institute for Theological Studies, Seattle University, 1 July 1992).

9. Intercristo is an outreach of CRISTA Ministries located in Seattle, Washington. Established over twenty-five years ago, Intercristo's purpose is to assist the Christian community to integrate faith and work through career counseling and an international Christian Placement Network.

10. J. Trautman, *How to Find Your Best Future: A Biblical Approach to Living Abundantly in a Turbulent World* (unpublished manuscript). For more information write to Intercristo, CRISTA Ministries, 19303 Fremont Avenue North, Seattle, Washington 98133, or call: 1-800-426-1342.

11. L. Brontë, *The Longevity Factor: The New Reality of Long Careers and How It Can Lead to Richer Lives* (New York: HarperCollins, 1993).

12. George Vecsey, "Norman Vincent Peale, Preacher of Gospel of Optimism Dies at 95," *New York Times*, 26 December 1993.

13. Brontë, *Longevity Factor*, 128.

14. Ibid.

15. Ibid.,169–70.

16. Ibid., 211.

17. Bernbaum and Steer, *Why Work?*, 72.

PART II

Specific Struggles

Chapter Five

Teenagers and Career Exploration

A<small>SHLEY, SEVENTEEN, IS AN ONLY CHILD</small> of divorced parents. She lived primarily with her father until she was sixteen, and then without a discussion with Ashley, her father quietly married a colleague from work, who moved in with him. Ashley was uncomfortable. She shuffled most of her things to her mother's home, but even this move was not settling.

Ashley's mother had dropped out of college and trained to be a hair stylist. She was good at her trade and had recently returned from a trip to Paris where she had received further training in the newest techniques. She had also just purchased a high-style salon in an upscale part of town. Excited, her mom talked a lot to Ashley about what it was like to own her own shop. She really enjoyed her work and tried to infuse Ashley with her enthusiasm.

On the other hand, Ashley's father had a Ph.D. in electrical engineering and seemed absorbed in vague projects at an avant-garde company. When Ashley asked her dad about his work, he was kind but noticeably distracted. Ashley was never able to understand exactly what her father did, and when Ashley asked her mother about his work, her mother just rolled her eyes.

Then Ashley took the SAT test. When her scores came back, she was at an astounding 99th percentile in math. This stirred up attention from her teacher, but Ashley brushed it off shyly.

Days later, while Ashley was filling in as a receptionist at her mother's shop (with her usual loathing) a customer innocently asked, "Ashley, what do you want to do when you grow up?" She mumbled something and rushed off on the pretense of an urgent task. But later, her eyes welled up and she quietly left the shop without telling anyone where she was going.

As she walked, Ashley's thoughts returned to the cherished dreams of her past. When she was a child, she had dreamed of becoming a ballerina. In middle school, she had gotten excited about becoming a jockey or horse trainer. She loved horses and had read every book she could find on horses in the school library. But now she was a lean five-foot, seven-inch, seventeen-year-old who had never been able to afford a horse of her own.

The next day at church she mentioned her confusion to a friend who said she knew a counselor who could help her think through her future and understand what she was good at. Tentatively, Ashley agreed to talk with the counselor at least once.

In the rest of this chapter we examine how to help adolescents like Ashley. We begin with (1) the developmental tasks every adolescent encounters, (2) the hazards that are likely to throw them off course, and (3) a number of strategies for helping teenagers explore career options.

DEVELOPMENTAL TASKS OF ADOLESCENCE

During World War II, Erik H. Erikson coined a phrase that stuck—*identity crisis*. He used it to describe the disorientation of shell-shocked soldiers who could not remember their names. Through the years, this phrase has broadened and become a useful tool to describe the struggle of growing up.

Achieving a sense of identity is the major developmental task of teenagers. Like a stunned soldier in a state of confusion, sooner or later young people are hit with a bomb called puberty that is psychologically more powerful than dynamite. Somewhere between childhood and maturity our bodies kick into overdrive, which fuels changes at an alarming rate. With this acceleration of physical and emotional growth, young people become strangers to themselves. Under attack by an arsenal of new motivational hormones, the bewildered young person begins to ask, "Who am I?"

While achieving a meaningful answer to this question may be a lifelong pursuit, it is the burning challenge of adolescence. According to Erikson, having an identity—knowing who we are—gives adolescents a sense of control that allows them to navigate the river of life.

However, the search for identity is scary. Somewhere between twelve and twenty years of age adolescents are forced to choose what their identity is to be. Suddenly, the playful question, "What do you want to be when you grow up?" causes anxiety rather then amusement. It signals the impending decision.[1]

In addition to guiding the overarching developmental task, a number of other significant tasks influence a career counselor's work with teenagers. Of special interest are:

cognitive development (forming ways of thinking)

moral development (forming ways of caring)

gender identity development (forming gender identity)

social development (forming relationships)

spiritual development (forming a faith)

career development (forming a path for the future)

FORMING WAYS OF THINKING—FROM CONCRETE TO ABSTRACT

Ashley was motivated and frustrated in her career exploration by a powerful new capacity—the ability to project herself, in her mind's eye, into the adult world of work. This emerging capacity tugged at her imagination as she tried to see herself in her mother's shoes. The fit was uncomfortable. She did not enjoy either the social or the artistic aspects of hairstyling. She also struggled to project herself into her father's shoes, a role she intuitively felt drawn to even though it remained shrouded in mystery.

Ashley's thought process mirrors the studies of Piaget, revealing a significant change in the cognitive abilities of adolescents. During adolescence, a young person's thought process moves from *concrete operational* thinking to *formal thought*. This shift allows the teenager to engage in abstract thinking rather than the literal, concrete ways of childhood thought.

Abstract thinking revolutionizes the thought life of an adolescent creating the capacity for self-analysis, introspective thinking, and the ability to project the self into the future in a realistic way.[2] Abstract thought is a high-tech psychological device that makes it possible to look at ourselves from outside ourselves.

FORMING WAYS OF CARING—FROM RULES TO RESPECT

Another important change occurs in adolescents when they realize their behavior must conform to social expectations without the constant guidance, supervision, and threats of punishment they experienced as children. To become adults, they must replace specific childhood rules with their own moral code.

According to Lawrence Kohlberg, during adolescence, teens reach a stage of moral development based on respect for others rather than on personal desires. While adolescents are intellectually capable of managing this change and creating their own moral code, the task is difficult. Every day adolescents see inconsistencies in moral standards. As they interact with peers from different religious, racial, or socioeconomic backgrounds, they soon see that people have different codes of right and wrong. Some fail to make the shift to an introspective adult moral code during adolescence and must finish the task in early adulthood, when the process is even more difficult.[3]

FORMING GENDER IDENTITY—FROM CHILDREN TO MEN AND WOMEN

No age group except preschool is as strongly influenced by gender-role stereotypes as are adolescents. Stereotypical gender roles are often more strongly held by adolescents than even by their parents or teachers.[4] While an increasing variety of role models are available for men and women, the work force still reveals some major gender-specific trends. In 1987, the U. S. Bureau of the Census discovered that 95 percent of nurses, 85 percent of librarians, and 67 percent of social and recreation workers were women. Only 18 percent of lawyers and judges and 19 percent of physicians and surgeons were women.[5] These statistics are the result of gender-role stereotypes.

During the turbulence of adolescence, girls are particularly torn between an identification with their mothers or with their fathers. Daughters of traditional mothers who attempt to move toward career aspirations more like their fathers may feel an intense abstract guilt over their "betrayal" of Mom. On the other hand, many fathers become more awkward with their daughters during adolescence because they face a level of discomfort with their budding sexuality.[6] Fathers often distance themselves from their daughters (in Ashley's case, through a second marriage and a preoccupation with work) just when daughters long to engage in more future-oriented discussions with them. A simultaneous increase in motherly attention can cause a variety of uncomfortable emotions.

The importance of this relationship between career and self-definition of both the mother and father was measured among students attending a northwest Christian college. For an undergraduate population, a significantly higher proportion of students believed that career is extremely important or somewhat more important to their father's self-definition than to their mother's self-definition.[7] This may cause confusion in the career exploration of adolescent men and women. The struggle for boys who do not identify with their father's career path may be even more intense during this period.

FORMING RELATIONSHIPS—FROM SIMPLE TO COMPLEX

While the biological changes of puberty are dramatic, they are rivaled by the social changes that also occur during adolescence. Between the sixth and eighth grades, the structure of school becomes different. Adolescents are likely to move from a relatively small neighborhood elementary school to a larger, more impersonal junior high school. This move has many social ramifications. It disrupts the old peer-group structure, exposes students to different achievement expectations, and provides new opportunities for different extracurricular activities.

Family relations also shift as boys and girls turn into teenagers. Family conflicts increase. Male adolescents become more dominant in conversations—especially with their mothers. Feelings of affection toward their parents also decline from the sixth to the eight grades. The decline is not necessarily negative; the change may be from very positive to less positive. The boy who admired his father's job as a fireman may shift his attitude in recognition of work status. Or a homemaker mother may be seen as less valuable than a mother who balances the responsibilities of home and a career.

FORMING A FAITH—FROM ACCEPTANCE TO QUESTIONS

Contrary to popular opinion, adolescents are genuinely interested in religion and feel it plays an important role in their lives. In *The Search for America's Faith,* George Gallup, Jr., and David Poling reported that 88 percent of today's teens say their religious beliefs affect their daily behavior.[8]

However, adolescence is a time when young people question the religious concepts and beliefs of their childhood. They may become skeptical of religious forms, such as prayer, and later begin to doubt the nature of God, but teens are definitely on a genuine spiritual quest. Parents may mistakenly interpret this as skepticism and doubt when, in reality, it is part of a sincere religious questioning. Adolescents investigate their faith to make it their own rather than that of their parents. They raise questions because they want to accept religion in a way that is meaningful to them. What they learn to believe about God, man, and salvation will guide their behavior on the job for the rest of their lives.

Forming a Path for the Future—From Fantasy to Reality

Ashley's lost childhood dream of becoming a ballerina is a classic illustration of the *fantasy stage* of career development. This stage, in which children imagine what they want to be without regard to any realistic consideration, occurs up to age eleven. This is the first of three stages of adolescent career development according to Eli Ginzberg. Ginzberg, an economist, worked with a psychiatrist, sociologist, and psychologist to gather a large body of research that culminated in a foundational career-development model widely accepted among professionals.[9]

According to Ginzberg, between the ages of eleven to eighteen, adolescents enter the *tentative stage* of career development. This stage has several distinct periods including:

1. *interest* period (ages 11–12)
2. *capacities* period (ages 13–14)
3. *values* period (ages 15–16)
4. *transition* period (ages 17–18)

The *interest* period (ages 11–12) is based on the likes and interests of the adolescent. For Ashley, the interest period was marked by a dream to be a jockey or a horse trainer. She loved horses, enjoyed riding them, and had an insatiable fascination for them.

The *capacities* period (ages 13–14) provides a new awareness of role expectations and of individual abilities necessary to fulfill them. By the time Ashley was in eighth grade, she realized that her lack of horsemanship and her lanky five-foot, seven-inch size excluded her from becoming a jockey.

Ashley had always whizzed through her math homework, and in ninth grade the teacher had appointed her as a peer tutor to help other classmates struggling with geometry. Even though she enjoyed math, Ashley discovered she did not really enjoy tutoring. She preferred to work independently to solve equations—the more challenging the better!

Although her mother attempted to train her in hairstyling so she could trim her friends' bangs for a little extra cash,

Ashley never seemed to get the hang of it. It was boring. Ashley had experienced the new self-awareness that buds in the capacities period.

The *values* period (ages 15–16) is the time for relating occupational roles to values. Ashley had just started to ask herself questions such as, "Is it better to make money or to help others? Is it better to get a college education or practical experience? Is my career important or unimportant to my self-definition as a woman?"

During this time of merging interests, capacities, and values with role requirements, there is an emergence of what counselors call *psychtalk* and *occtalk*. *Psychtalk* is talk about values, interests, abilities, and personality. "I am social," or "I love to solve challenging problems." Occtalk is shorthand for occupational talk. During the values period, teens merge psychtalk with occtalk as they move farther along the trail toward vocational choice. The statement, "I'd like to become a doctor," is occtalk that says, "I value helping people who suffer, being a professional, and investing myself in school" (psychtalk). Researchers Starishevsky and Matlin found that occtalk and psychtalk statements were interchangeable.[10] Understanding that beliefs about the self and personal values may be stated more comfortably through occtalk helps the counselor explore the vocational values of adolescents.

The *transition* period (ages 17–18) is characterized by a transition from tentative to realistic options. Frequently, the onset of this period is a response to pressures from school, peers, parents, and the circumstance of high school graduation. By seventeen, Ashley heard her peers talk about their college choices. One of them had a growing collection of catalogs from schools Ashley had never heard of. However, she was receiving unsolicited catalogs from all over the country because of her SAT score. One college contacted her personally. These pressures where forcing Ashley into the transition period.

The *realistic* period (18 and older) involves resolution of career decisions.[11] This developmental stage will be discussed in chapter 6, on "Young Adults and Career Decision Making."

HAZARDS IN TEENAGE CAREER DEVELOPMENT

Because the quest for identity is often fraught with anxiety and confusion, adolescents often lose their way. Preoccupied with unrestrained theorizing, caught up in extreme self-analysis, and plagued with a more-than-usual concern about the reactions of others, teenagers often fall victim to the development of pseudoidentity states.[12] Four such pseudoidentity states are:

1. negative identity
2. diffuse identity
3. identity foreclosure
4. psychological moratorium.

NEGATIVE IDENTITY

Perhaps the most commonly recognized adolescent pseudoidentity is the negative identity. A negative identity occurs when adolescents behave in ways that are in direct conflict with family and society. Most adolescents who experience an identity crisis pass through it with positive outcomes, but some adolescents get locked into this conflictual drama, maintaining this role over time. A negative identity is dangerous because it consumes the teenager's energy and squanders it on reactionary behavior, leaving little energy for the work of actually establishing personal autonomy.

Fifteen-year-old Tyler considered dropping out of school to join the Navy. His parents placed a high value on education and proximity of extended family. While talking with him about his plans, I asked Tyler what he would do if he were really angry with his parents and wanted to "push all their buttons." Tyler thought about it for a while and said, "I guess I would join the Navy. I can't think of anything they'd hate more." A glimmer of recognition flashed across his face. "I guess if I were choosing just for me, I would look into forestry or coaching. I'd really like something with adventure in it, but I don't really like the idea of living with all those rules they have in the Navy." Tyler, like many negative teenagers, was about to punish himself in a disguised effort to frustrate his parents.

IDENTITY DIFFUSION

Identity diffusion occurs when adolescents avoid decisions or commitments to values that would enhance their self-definition.

In his famous studies, Erikson encountered this state more frequently with adolescent girls who held open an empty space in their lives to be filled by a man who through marriage would give them a name, status, and self definition.[13] The subsequent work by Carol Gilligan revealed a tendency among girls to confuse identity with intimacy, defining themselves through relationships with others. This confusion is enhanced by the fear of appearing too smart, tall, assertive, or competent, which would reduce their chances of finding an intimate relationship with a spouse.[14]

Kelly, a bundle of energy at thirteen, seemed to have lost her spunk by age sixteen. She had always been a gifted sports enthusiast, but this year she didn't go out for any of the teams. When asked what she wanted to do with her life, she shrugged and smiled sweetly. Kelly longed for a good life; she just didn't know how to go about it. Also, her boyfriend, David, had plans for medical school. This prospect left her with a negative self-portrait behind a retail counter, a necessary way to put him through school. Her time, she thought, would need to come later. No wonder her enthusiasm was drained.

IDENTITY FORECLOSURE

Identity foreclosure occurs when an adolescent prematurely embraces his or her parents' values and even makes future plans by fitting into an occupational role controlled by the parents. These adolescents attempt to establish their identity without undergoing an identity crisis. Their plans and beliefs reflect their parents' wishes and ideas or those of other authority figures, but they don't have plans and ideas of their own.

Research shows that the adolescents who undergo identity foreclosure have a more vulnerable self-esteem than do identity achievers (teens who arrive at their commitments after passing through a crisis). They also tend to be more rigidly authoritarian in their attitudes.[15]

Jeff was bright, talented, and extremely helpful. He had already decided on a business major in college. He tried to take every business elective in high school. Already, Jeff was planning to join his father's marketing and advertising firm. But being around Jeff, as pleasant as he was, was not relaxing. There was an underlying anxiety he expressed by a compulsive drive to succeed and please. When one of his teachers suggested he might do better in a business career if he concentrated on writing and took more English classes, he immediately followed her advice. It was hard to put a finger on his problem, but somehow Jeff often seemed shallow.

Moratorium on Identity

Adolescents reach a state of psychological moratorium when they choose to hold their identity in abeyance while actively struggling to arrive at a career choice. A therapist working with adolescents states, "The struggle to gain a separate, clear, and positive self-image can also cause confusion and immobilization for adolescents and their families. New experiences in the world may subject them to anxiety, disappointment, rebuff, and failure."[16] Negotiating these painful and anxiety-laden experiences sometimes produces a quantum leap in deeper anxiety. Some adolescents get stuck in a crisis mode and are unable to move forward developmentally.

James had watched with awe as his older brother grew through his teen years. All those grown-up problems had seemed so cool to him then. Now it was his turn, and it didn't seem so great. After deciding to pursue law, he had tried out for the high school debate team, but failed utterly in his first debate. He could not remember his argument and made up some points that did not even make sense. After that, he was determined to forget his own idea of trying out for the school play, and maybe he should forget law. After all, it, too, was a performance, but with far more at stake. James, like many adolescents, had encountered life experiences that spun him into a period of identity moratorium.

Most seventeen-year-olds have spoken seriously to someone about their future plans, usually to parents and peers. Two-thirds of them feel their abilities and interests were effectively understood.[17] The following techniques are designed to help adolescents engage in a career exploration that deepens their self-understanding and clarifies their direction. These strategies provide adolescents with a solid foundation for mature judgments.

1. PINPOINT THE LEVEL OF CAREER MATURITY

At the beginning of vocational counseling with adolescents, it is good to assess their level of career maturity. This assessment can serve as a point of reference.

The Career Maturity Inventory (CMI) is the most widely used measure of career maturity. *Career maturity* refers to attitudes (decisiveness, involvement, independence, orientation, and compromise) and competencies (knowing yourself, knowing about jobs, choosing a job, looking ahead, and solving problems) needed for career exploration and development. The assessment takes about thirty minutes to administer and may be scored by hand or computer. The reading level is approximately sixth grade, and test norms are available for grades six through twelve. The CMI results in a profile (see appendix A) The scores for each competency scale may be used as counseling guides. They will help the counselor to concentrate time and energy on strengthening the most striking deficiencies. This instrument will also help decipher hidden needs. This inventory was created by John O. Crites in 1973 and is available through McGraw-Hill, Del Monte Research Park, Monterey, CA 93940.[18]

2. BE PREPARED FOR EGOCENTRIC ATTITUDES

Adolescents can become intoxicated by a sense of mastery, analysis, and introspection. They frequently become amateur philosophers and moral judges of social values and mores with a high propensity for questioning and challenging rules, standards, and opinions.[19] The other day I saw a carload of teenagers in an open Jeep with a bumper sticker that said, "Question authority."

This egocentrism may set up an adversarial relationship where the teen client is "right" and the counselor is "wrong."[20] Counselors can build trust by responding to criticisms with questions rather than personalizing the criticism and feeling threatened or attacked. Listening to teenagers' explanations and empathizing with their feelings is the surest method for developing a solid working relationship with adolescents.

3. AFFIRM THEIR NEED TO BE SEPARATE

The intensity of identity formation drives the adolescent to establish separateness from adults and all authority figures. They resist assignments in the counseling process. They may even feel the counselor is on trial, not themselves.

This attitude does not need to become a significant hurdle. The goal of vocational counseling is not to inform people. It is to provide a relationship within which people learn to discover themselves—a relationship in which people mature. True learning, the kind that significantly influences behavior, is for the most part self-discovered. The counselor's active listening helps struggling adolescents discover how they can best pursue their own career explorations. Active listening generates participation—people are motivated to act or follow through on decisions they have helped make. An adolescent's motivation to act on outside advice is minimal at best.

Adolescents encouraged to participate in decision making are more likely to be independent *and* to maintain a bond of closeness and affection with the parent or adult than those who are not.[21] The more adolescents participate in decisions about their vocational choice, the more progress will be made in the counseling relationship and in movement toward a self-confirming goal.

4. RECOGNIZE THE LIMITED TIME PERSPECTIVE

One of the frustrations of the vocational counselor is the limited time perspective of adolescents. Most teens find it difficult to picture themselves five or ten years into the future.[22] They live for the present and make decisions based on the here and now. Understanding this limited time perspective helps the counselor to work at the adolescent's level of career maturity.

5. HELP CREATE A PERSONAL COAT OF ARMS

Help adolescents understand that it is important to begin the vocational choice process by finding out who they are occupationally. Because they are likely to change as they mature, the momentary images they have of themselves are more like a frame in a motion picture than a snapshot. They will need an ongoing self-review process, but the Personal Coat of Arms is a fun exercise to get started.[23]

Personal Coat of Arms
for

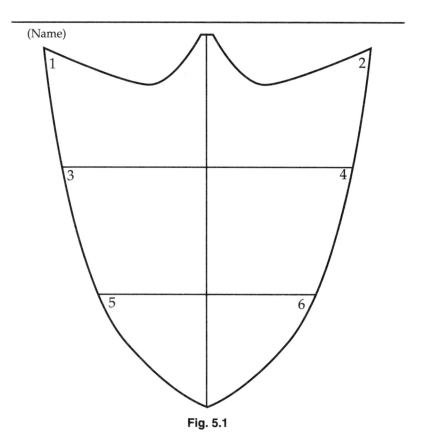

Fig. 5.1

In ancient times families created a coat of arms depicting significant family history, activities, and beliefs. Your client can use the Personal Coat of Arms to create his or her own coat of arms as an introductory bridge for you. A blank coat of arms is divided into six sections (see figure 5.1). Ask the teen to create a drawing in each section that expresses his or her thoughts in simple ways, following the instructions for each section listed below. Do not use words, except in section six.

1. Draw your own greatest personal accomplishment.

2. Draw your family's greatest accomplishment.

3. Draw one or two things that people who care about you have suggested you could do for a living.

4. Draw the thing you like most about being a student.

5. Show in a drawing what occupation you would ideally want to enter—if you had the time, money, and opportunity.

6. List the things you want most from work.

6. FACILITATE REALISTIC APPRAISAL OF ABILITIES

Realism is an important factor in career maturity.[24] Without an honest assessment of strengths and weaknesses, career goals are more fantasy than reality.

Avoid a candy-coated optimism because adolescents see through it and lose respect for the counselor. Remember the study mentioned in the introduction of this section. Although most seventeen-year-olds have spoken seriously to someone about their future plans, only two-thirds of them felt that their abilities and interests were effectively understood.[25] Facilitating a realistic appraisal of abilities is an important component in vocational counseling with teens.

However, the use of realism in vocational counseling can be dangerous. Inappropriate judging of realistic career choices can have a damaging effect on young people.

Sheri, age seventeen, went to a vocational counselor who gave her an abilities survey. When it was given back to her with little explanation, Sheri could only see that she would make an ideal nun. Those results were so traumatic that Sheri decided not to pursue a college education and worked, unhappily, as a secretary in her church office. Inaccurate predictions or poorly explained results can have a devastating impact on the career future of an adolescent.

One exercise suggests that the counselor have adolescents write a short paragraph on the subject of their personal strengths and weaknesses, including courses in which they do best and worst. From the two paragraphs, ask them to make two lists titled, "My Strengths" and "My Weaknesses." Once the lists are complete, instruct the teen to place a plus (+) beside each item that is energy-giving (refreshes the mind, is relaxing, and restores energy) and a minus (-) beside each item that is energy-getting (exhausts, depletes, and generally tires the teen out). Compare the strengths and weaknesses to see if there is a compatible match between energy-giving items and strengths. If not, explore. If so, brainstorm occupations that would involve these items.[26]

7. FACILITATE REFLECTION AND EVALUATION OF PERSONAL VALUES

Although teens can seem fickle, endlessly adjusting their personal style in pursuit of a true identity, research suggests that the values established in adolescence tend to remain fairly stable and endure over the life span.[27] Because the topic of values tends to be complex, it is important for counselors to define what they mean. *Values* often refers to the combination of personal beliefs (views about how the world operates), attitudes (the predisposition to like some situations or people but not others), and ethics (what one considers right and wrong).[28] More simply, our values are a reflection of, "the importance we attach to . . . events, people, and activities."[29]

One particularly effective values exploration exercise helps adolescents evaluate and reflect on (1) values that they held when they were younger, (2) values they have held but now question, and (3) values they hold now (see figure 5.2).[30]

Following each value on the list are lines for adolescents to use in rating the value along three dimensions. Ask them to place a check under the word *Younger* if they held that value in the past. If they question that value, place a check mark under *Questioning*. If they hold the value now and are not questioning

Personal Values

Younger *Questioning* *Now*

Achievement/Recognition/Status   Feeling satisfaction for a job well done or a challenge well met. Receiving approval or attention from those whose opinions you respect. Achieving status in line with your talents and achievements.   ___ ___ ___ ☐

Esthetic Considerations   Having the opportunity and time to appreciate the beauty in people, art, nature, surroundings, or whatever else you consider lovely and important.   ___ ___ ___ ☐

Challenging Opportunities   Having opportunities to use your creativity, your training, your intelligence, and your other talents. Facing a variety of challenges rather than the routine. Having the freedom to try new ideas or creative approaches.   ___ ___ ___ ☐

Health—Physical and Mental   Feeling good in a physical sense. Being relatively free of anxieties, hang-ups, and feelings of being harried that can hinder your peace of mind.   ___ ___ ___ ☐

Income/Wealth   Significantly improving your financial position. Obtaining those things that money can buy.   ___ ___ ___ ☐

Independence   Having the freedom to do your own thing either on or off the job. Having time flexibility. Having control over your own actions.   ___ ___ ___ ☐

Love/Personal Relationships/Family   Caring for, sharing with, and giving to those who are close to you, such as family and peers. Being generous, sympathetic, loyal, and helpful to those you love. Having the time to devote to personal relationships.   ___ ___ ___ ☐

Morality   Maintaining without conflict your moral, ethical, and/or religious standards whatever their source. Being able to accept the goals, values, and standards of your organization.   ___ ___ ___ ☐

Pleasure/Fun   Having a good time. Enjoying the company of others. Having the time to play. Making new friends.   ___ ___ ___ ☐

Power   The ability to influence or control others. Getting others to follow the course of action you prefer.   ___ ___ ___ ☐

Security   Feeling safe. Feeling free of continual concern about the dangers of unexpected and/or unpleasant changes. Having the essentials you need.   ___ ___ ___ ☐

Self-Development   Increasing your wisdom, maturity, learning, and understanding of life for their own sake. Becoming a more rounded person. Having the time to pursue intellectual interests.   ___ ___ ___ ☐

Service to Others   Being a useful member of the groups with which you identify. Knowing you have accomplished things that will benefit others.   ___ ___ ___ ☐

Fig. 5.2

Source: Milton Rokeach, *The Nature of Human Values,* (New York: Free Press, 1973). Reproduced by permission of Consulting Pscychologists Press, Inc. Palo Alto, Calif.

it, they should place a check mark under *Now*. Next, ask them to go back over the values checked *Now* and place a number (1–5) in the box at the end of the line to indicate how strongly they hold that value. (A 5 is very important, and a 1 is least important.) Then ask the adolescent to answer the following questions concerning each value: "What does this tell you about yourself?" "What does this value contribute to your picture of the ideal job?"

8. Encourage Practical Experience

Many teens hold part-time or summer jobs, but the job is usually for economic advantage, not to test fields of possible career choice. Counselors should help teens to seek work as a career-testing experience.

A fun variation on volunteer or paid work is to arrange for a shadowing experience. When one or several career interests have been identified, work with the adolescent in brainstorming possible contacts in that field. Networking resources are usually fairly easy. Identify possible work contacts including parents, parents' friends, adolescents' friends, parents of adolescents' friends, as well as church and school acquaintances. When a contact person is willing, the adolescent can arrange to shadow him or her throughout the work day. This allows a young client to participate in the daily work activities as an observer and to talk with working adults about their experiences on the job.

It may be helpful for the counselor to assist the teen in preparing a list of questions to ask. Sample questions include:

What do you like about your job?

What do you dislike?

How did you come to do this work?

What do you wish you had known about your career or another one when you were my age?

What advice do you have for me?

What is the entry-level position in this career?

Who is an ideal candidate for this position?

9. PROVIDE SUPPORT FOR IMMEDIATE DECISIONS

Jacqui was a senior in high school whose SAT scores rated her within the national merit scholarship range. She was from a small rural community in California and had little information about colleges. Confused about where to go, she finally chose a state school—following the lead of one of her less intellectually gifted friends. However, Jacqui did not know that this school had a bigger reputation as a party school than as a serious academic enterprise. After three weeks of misery, Jacqui dropped out, moved home, and enrolled in a community college that offered her even less academic challenge. Unfortunately, when Jacqui most needed help, the information she needed was not available.

It is imperative that vocational counselors for adolescents be able to provide ample resources at the level their clients need. Choosing a college, choosing a major, vocational training, and job availability are all decisions that require specific, current, and timely information. (See chapter 14 for more information on establishing a career resource center.)

10. HELP PARENTS SUPPORT THEIR ADOLESCENT'S DREAMS

It should be no surprise to parents that teens reject parental influence on matters of personal identity (music, clothing, hairstyles, language, and recreational activities) in favor of peer influence. What does surprise parents is to discover that when it comes to long-range plans, they actually do have the greatest influence on their teen.[31]

Parents often feel like they walk a tightrope. To establish a sense of identity, adolescents need to become increasingly more responsible for their own decision making, yet they also need to feel the security of parental guidance.[32]

Parents need to invest as much interest and energy as they can in listening and responding to their child's career dreams. They must take their child's ideas seriously—but not assume that the dream is *summative,* the culminating decision at the end of a process. Consider these dreams as *formative,* an intermediary step in the process of career decision-making.

When I (Les) was a teen, I announced my intention to be an architect. Since my father had no expertise in the field, he drew on outside resources. He scheduled an appointment for us to visit the dean of the school of architecture at a nearby university. When we arrived home from that meeting, I discovered a drafting table wrapped in a large red bow in my bedroom. I did not become an architect. However, the investment my dad made in my dream deeply impacted me and encouraged me on my ultimate career journey.

If there is a breakdown in healthy communication between the adolescent and his or her parents, family therapists suggest scheduling a meeting with the parents and their son or daughter. In this session the focus should be on the parents' adolescent years. Ask the parents questions such as:

What did you look like as a teen?

Where did you go to school?

Where did you work?

Who were your close friends?

Did you have a dream about what you wanted to become?

Was it a secret, or did you share it?

How did people react?—Mother, Father, teachers?

Did you realize your dream?

Did you have more than one dream?

Did you discover talents within yourself through school activities or studies?

Describe the day you graduated from high school.

Who participated?

Was there a celebration?

Were did you go next?

How did you decide to go there?

Were there times when you felt insecure?

Were there obstacles you couldn't overcome?

Did you ever try something and fail at it?

Allow the adolescent to participate in his or her own way, by listening or asking questions. The importance of this conversation is threefold:

1. Remembering their own adolescence gives parents a deeper empathy and a clearer picture of the present experience of their son or daughter

2. It reminds parents that the tensions they are now experiencing with their teen are neither endless nor permanent.

3. Hearing stories of their parents' past helps adolescents to see them as people, not just parents, and to find points of identification with them.

One unintentional outcome of this conversational exercise is that it frequently touches on moments of humor that become a shared experience for the family folklore.

Ashley, the teenager in this chapter's opening story, is like the majority of adolescents who make good career plans for their lives. She received valuable help from a professional counselor who understood young people and the puzzling world of work they face. Because of sound help in the beginning, Ashley is not likely to return to the counseling room after a tumultuous decade in the wrong career. Her future job changes are likely to be in line with her own personal and professional growth. This is the goal of every professional in vocational counseling.

NOTES

1. Some of the material in this chapter is adapted from L. Parrott III, *Helping the Struggling Adolescent* (Grand Rapids: Zondervan, 1993).

2. J. Piaget and B. Inhelder, *The Psychology of the Child* (New York: Basic Books, 1969); D. Elkind, "Cognitive Development in Adolescence," in *Understanding Adolescence,* ed. J. F. Adams (Boston: Allyn and Bacon, 1968); D. P. Keating. "Thinking Processes in Adolescence," in *Handbook of Adolescent Psychology,* ed. J. Adelson (New York: Wiley, 1980).

3. L. Kohlberg, *The Philosophy of Moral Development* (New York: Harper and Row, 1981).

4. M. McGolderick, "Women and the Family Life Cycle," in *The Changing Family Life Cycle,* 2d ed., ed. B. Carter, and M. McGolderick (Needham Heights, Mass: Allyn and Bacon, 1989.)

5. F. Rice, *The Adolescent* (Boston: Allyn and Bacon, 1990), 546.

6. McGolderick, "Women and the Family Life Cycle."

7. L. Parrott, III "Family Functioning and Career Decision-Making," (Ph.D. dissertation, Fuller Theological Seminary, 1993).

8. George Gallup, Jr., and David Poling, *The Search for America's Faith* (Nashville: Abingdon, 1980).

9. E. Ginzberg, "Toward a Theory of Occupational Choice: A Restatement," *Vocational Guidance Quarterly* 20 (1972): 169–176.

10. R. Sharf, *Applying Career Development Theory to Counseling,* (Pacific Grove, Calif.: Brooks/Cole, 1992); R. Starishevsky, and N. Matlin, "A Model for the Translation of Self-Concept into Vocational Terms," in *Career Development: Self-Concept Theory,* ed. D. E. Super et al., Research Monograph no. 4 (New York: College Entrance Examination Board, 1963), 33–41.

11. D. E. Super, "Career and Life Development," in *Career Choice and Development,* ed. D. Brown, et al. (San Francisco: Jossey-Bass, 1984). Developmental psychologist Donald Super also designed a career-development model that is frequently used with adolescents. Super's model of adolescent development is nearly identical to Ginzberg's although it lacks the values component. Super considered the formation of values to be too complex to be measured, and his model includes the fantasy, interests, capacities, and tentative stages. Both the Ginzberg Theory and Super's developmental model place the capacity stage after the interest stage. The developmental leap from interests to a realistic picture of capacities is an important step in career maturity. Super emphasizes that the time guidelines are not of central focus, and he believes there may often be a recycling of stages in adolescent career development. Subsequent research validates the need to relax the time line and expect adolescents to experience these stages at varied rates.

12. V. Zunker, *Career Counseling: Applied Concepts of Life Planning,* 4th ed., (Pacific Grove, Calif.: Brooks/Cole, 1994).

13. E. Erikson, *Identity: Youth and Crisis* (New York: Norton, 1980).

14. Carter and McGoldrick, *Changing Family Life Cycle,* 49.

15. A. Tan, et al., "A Short Measure of the Ericksonian Ego Identity," *Journal of Personality Assessment* 41 (1977).

16. N. G. Preto, "Transformation of the Family System in Adolescence," in *Changing Family Life Cycle,* ed. Carter and McGoldrick, 261.

17. Zunker, *Career Counseling.*

18. Sharf, *Career Development Theory;* Zunker, *Using Assessment Results for Career Development,* 4th ed. (Pacific Grove, Calif.: Brooks/Cole, 1994).

19. Preto, "Transformation of the Family System," 261.

20. Sharf, *Career Development Theory;* Zunker, *Using Assessment Results.*

21. Preto, "Transformation of the Family System."

22. Sharf, *Career Development Theory.*

23. This exercise is adapted from S. B. Simon, R. C. Hawley, and D. D. Britton, *Composition for Personal Growth: Values Clarification Through Writing* (Hart Publishing, 1973). It is modified in C. Carney and C. Wells, *Discover the Career Within You,* 3d. ed. (Pacific Grove, Calif.: Brooks/Cole, 1991).

24. D. E. Super, "A Life-Span, Life-Space Approach to Career Development," in *Career Choices*, ed. D. Brown et al.

25. Zunker, *Career Counseling*.

26. This exercise is adapted from Zunker, *Using Assessment Results*, and Carney and Wells, *Career Within You*.

27. L. V. Gordon, *The Measurement of Interpersonal Values* (Chicago: Science Research Associates, 1975).

28. Carney and Wells, *Career Within You*, 19.

29. P. Zimbardo, *Psychology and Life* (Glenview, Ill.: Scott, Foresman, 1979).

30. Carney and Wells, *Career Within You*, 76.

31. L. Larsen, "The Influence of Parents and Peers During Adolescence: The Situation Hypothesis Revisited," *Journal of Marriage and the Family 34* (February 1972): 67–74.

32. Carter and McGoldrick, *Changing Family Life Cycle*, 257.

Chapter Six

Young Adults and Career Decision Making

Mark, a college student majoring in philosophy and Christian education, sought career counseling. His hair fell around his collar at a carefree length, and his jeans and burkenstocks looked sufficiently broken in for maximum comfort. The first words out of his mouth voiced an apology: "I know I should have been here long ago." I later learned that Mark was a highly creative jazz musician and an avid sailor, but his yellow notepad and copious note taking throughout the session gave him a businesslike air that seemed incongruent with his appearance.

"I thought I was going to seminary, but now it just doesn't seem right. It's one week before graduation; I'm getting married to Madeline in a month; and I need to get a job. I have to support a family, and I don't even know how to create a résumé. Can you help me do what I need to do?" The anxiety was palpable.

Over the next six weeks I witnessed a striking transformation in Mark. As we worked together to craft a résumé, develop interviewing skills, and conduct a job search, Mark began a metamorphosis. He purchased a small wardrobe of well-tailored suits, cut his hair, and came to one session proudly sporting an expensive leather briefcase (filled only with copies of his résumé and other job-search materials).

After two months, Mark had landed the position he desired. He was a financial consultant with a nationally recognized firm. A flowering plant arrived in my office with a gracious note of thanks attached.

One year and one month later, I received a telephone call from Mark to schedule another appointment. This time he unfolded a story of both success and turmoil. He had a love-hate relationship with his newfound professional role. Mark's sudden, compulsive drive to establish himself in a stable situation had forced him prematurely into a job that was draining his spirit. His wife was supportive but concerned. His father-in-law had encouraged him to go back to his music. Even though Mark was miserable, his need for stability was so intense that the thought of a career change left him emotionally paralyzed.

In this chapter we examine how to support and enhance the career decision-making process of young adults like Mark. We begin with the developmental tasks of young adults, then the hazards that are likely to throw them off course, and we conclude with a number of strategies for helping young adults make good career decisions.

DEVELOPMENTAL TASKS OF YOUNG ADULTS

The phase of life that author Gail Sheehy has called "the trying twenties" includes finding a place of work. As adolescence ends and young adulthood begins, the focus shifts from the internal turmoil of adolescence—those haunting questions "Who am I?" and "What is truth?"—toward a new preoccupation with the external roles required in life.

The new problem is, "How do I put my aspirations into effect?" And young adults often ask those they respect, "How did *you* do it?"[1]

Researcher Kenniston similarly describes the college years as a unique stage of development focused on a central shift in identity from *preoccupation with self* to *fitting self into society*. This developmental passage is fraught with tensions that emerge between the desires of the young adult and the demands of society.[2] Managing these tensions is the business of young adulthood.

Largely compelled by *shoulds* and plagued by conflicting internal messages, young adults struggle with dictums such as:

I *should* get experience in a big corporation first.

I *should* work to change the system.

I *should* be married by now.

I *should* wait to get married until I've accomplished something.

I *should* help my people.

I *should* be running for president.

I *should* be free and try new things.

Whatever the specific list of *shoulds*, much of it has been defined for the young adult by family expectations, culture, and peers.[3]

A number of significant tasks influence a career counselor with young adults working to establish themselves. Of special interest are: (1) clarifying purpose, (2) achieving competence, (3) managing emotions, (4) becoming autonomous, (5) establishing identity, (6) freeing interpersonal relationships, and (7) developing integrity.[4]

CLARIFYING PURPOSE

One of the hallmarks of well-being is a life infused with meaning and purpose.[5] "Lack of something to feel important about is almost the greatest tragedy a man may have," said Arthur Morgan. The development of purpose occurs with increasing clarity and conviction in the domain of vocational aspirations, according to Arthur Chickering, a renowned developmental specialist on young-adult development.[6]

For Mark, his crisis was like a time-release bomb. His former lifestyle was no longer acceptable. Suddenly, the psychological weight of responsibility demanded his full attention. Career development is crucial to Mark and all other young adults. Successfully establishing a role in the world of work is one of the most prominent rites of passage in adult society.[7]

Developmental psychologist Donald Super has devised a model identifying two significant tasks in the career development of young adults.[8] The first, *exploration,* involves generating options, pursuing tentative choices, and reaching a decision about entry into an occupation.

The second task, *establishment,* is the career development task of young adults age twenty-five and older. The establishment stage is focused on creating a stable life structure through the development of advanced personal competency. Both stages are further broken down into three phases each.

The *exploration* stage includes: (1) crystallization, (2) specification, and (3) implementation. *Crystallization* is the stage that brings clarity to career goals. People decide what they want to do, learn about entry-level jobs in that field, and learn skills required for that job. *Specification* is the process of actually choosing the first full-time job, graduate school program, or specialized training. *Implementation* is the process of conducting a job search, applying to a program, or accepting a position.

The *establishment* stage incorporates the three tasks of (1) stabilizing, (2) consolidating, and (3) advancing.[9] *Stabilizing* is establishing a minimum commitment to a position to ensure a sense of permanence to meet job requirements. *Consolidating* is becoming a known, dependable, productive, competent, and reliable worker. Finally, *advancing* is moving into a position of greater challenge and responsibility. Taken together, these stages become a ladder that begins with clear career goals and continues through advancement on the job.

ACHIEVING COMPETENCE

All the expensive tailored suits, briefcases, and athletic club memberships could not erase Mark's anxiety. The field of financial consulting created too much pressure for him to absorb. Even if he landed a big account one month, he was afraid of the next month. For Mark, it was almost more excruciating to have a noticeably successful month then a bad one. In failure he felt he knew who he really was.

Young adults often suffer from what psychologists call the *impostor syndrome,* which is the lack of an inner assurance that one is as competent to meet the challenges ahead as are others.

According to Chickering, achieving a sense of competence—the belief that "one has in his (or her) ability to cope with what comes, and to achieve successfully what he sets out to do"—is a crucial developmental task of the young adult. Specific areas of competence to be achieved include intellectual, physical, and interpersonal skills.[10] The development of intellectual competency particularly influences the career decision-making process of young adults.

Achieving competence in career decision making for young adults is characterized by a movement from simplistic to complex reasoning. Four stages have been identified in this process:[11]

1. *Dualism* —the stage in which there is only one right career that must be found. This person's thinking pattern is simplistic, and he or she seeks answers from counselors, teachers, and parents.

2. *Multiplicity*—the stage that recognizes a range of career possibilities but looks outside himself or herself for the answers.

3. *Relativism*—the major shift from an external to an internal locus of control. At this point he or she begins to take ownership for the decision-making process and assume responsibility for the commitment.

4. *Commitment with relativism*—characterizes full responsibility for the career decision-making process, which ends with commitment to a specific career path.

MANAGING EMOTIONS

The ability to tolerate strong emotions is a character trait of an emotionally healthy adult.[12] Genuine emotional freedom exists when young adults know they won't go out of control. A healthy person does not need to avoid situations that might spark strong emotions or put up psychological walls to hold intense feelings at bay. In a healthy adult, emotions are free but behavior is under control. Management of emotions, then, is not a matter of practicing repression. Emotional management requires an increasing awareness of emotions and the skills required for effective self-expression.

According to developmental experts, the two major impulses that need to be managed most are aggression (or anger) and sex.[13] Anger is a tricky emotion for everyone, but is a particular struggle for young adults—especially those with a personal faith. Yet learning to express anger in constructive and creative ways is one of the developmental challenges facing every young adult. As they enter society through the world of work and marriage, they bring with them three common misconceptions that govern an inadequate management of anger. The three misconceptions are:

1. The belief that God does not want us to experience any anger.
2. The belief that angry feelings are best managed by hiding them.
3. The belief that the painful feelings of anger will vanish if ignored.[14]

Sexual impulses are more powerful than any time before and therefore require more emotional management. The task of the young adult in his or her twenties is to place limits on sexual behavior while simultaneously continuing to develop and integrate a maturing, Christian sexuality that is free from fear and anxiety.

BECOMING AUTONOMOUS

Most young adults have achieved some form of autonomy in their living situation. However, this new freedom is so unstable Chickering likens it to, "a hog on ice." Slipping this way and that, newly independent young adults often behave in a conspicuously random manner with little progress in any single direction.

To establish autonomy, the young adult must move from the dependency of youth to the interdependency of adulthood.[15] An interdependent relationship requires two people with self-respect and dignity who make a commitment to nurture their own and the other's spiritual growth.

Like a child, a dependent person desires happiness rather than personal growth. A dependent person is in need of continual reassurance, affection, and approval. He or she is far more interested in being nourished by parents or surrogate caretakers (i.e., professors, mentors, coaches, counselors, residence hall directors, supervisors) than in nourishing relationships. "Recognition and acceptance of interdependence is the capstone of autonomy," writes Chickering.

ESTABLISHING IDENTITY

Although achieving a sense of identity is the major developmental task of the adolescent, the quest for identity continues throughout the young adult years. Teenagers who have fallen victim to the development of a pseudoidentity as an adolescent (see chapter 5) must now grapple with the crisis of achieving true identity. Young adults whose identity is more fully formed, however, work to further clarify and define themselves against the backdrop of increasing personal awareness. Feelings, thoughts, and motives that have been unconscious break into awareness. Previously hidden, unknown, and blind aspects of the self come into the open and must be integrated into the young adult's identity.

FREEING INTERPERSONAL RELATIONSHIPS

Identity frees interpersonal relationships to become less anxious, less defensive, less burdened, friendlier, more spontaneous, warmer, and more respectful[16] This freeing process is so powerful that it leads to the formation of more lifelong friendships than in any other period of life. For the first time the young adult has the capacity to form friendships and love relationships that are strong enough to survive differences and disagreement. These relationships remain strong in spite of separation and noncommunication.

DEVELOPING INTEGRITY

Mark Twain once said, "Everyone is a moon and has a dark side that he never shows to anybody." In *A Pretty Good Person*, ethicist Lewis Smedes writes, "Integrity is about being people who know who we are and what we are, and it is about staying true to what we are even when it could cost us more then we should have to pay."[17] The young adult years are the time to bring unity to our values and behavior.

To summarize, the journey of the young adult toward full membership in society is complex and demanding. It involves clarifying purpose, achieving competence, managing emotions, becoming autonomous, establishing identity, freeing interpersonal relationships, and developing integrity. Each of these tasks has a significant implication in the career-life choice.

HAZARDS IN YOUNG ADULT CAREER DEVELOPMENT

Managing the tensions between the self and society can be an overwhelming burden. Three common hazards that young adults fall prey to are (1) premature stabilization, (2) dichotomous thinking, and (3) external locus of control.

PREMATURE STABILIZATION

The two tasks of exploration and establishment (discussed earlier in this chapter), by their very nature compete with each other. Exploration revolves around dreams and possibilities, while the establishment of a stable life structure deals with reality. Levinson's research reveals that beginning at about age eighteen young adults have a sense of urgency over what to do with their lives.[18] Sometimes this urgency creates an anxiety overload and leads adolescents to make premature commitments toward stabilization. Many young adults are taken in by the "maturity myth"—the belief that simply making a decision or commitment (of any kind) will bring happiness.[19]

Premature stabilization is an attempt to resolve a developmental stage by circumventing its accompanying crisis. The most frequent style of premature stabilization occurring in young adults is depicted in the characterization of the *family agent-decided* client.[20]

As discussed in chapter 3, family agent-decided individuals are low in personal distinctiveness or self-differentiation within their family of origin, but they are committed to a clear career goal. These persons may wholeheartedly seek to live out the values of their family of origin in order to gain a personal identity as an extension of the family system. This creates a premature identity formed without an authentic personal identity. These young adults are characterized by a quality of compulsive drivenness in the career-development process. The danger of premature stabilization is that it can cause young adults to be locked into commitments that later may become incongruent with their authentic self. At the extreme, this may result in a midlife crisis that dismantles their life structure.

Mark is a prime example of the emotional torment that may be created when premature stabilization occurs. Locked into a profession that gave him little satisfaction, Mark had already begun to see the future as drudgery.

DICHOTOMOUS THINKING

Young adults often become locked into dichotomous thinking that impedes their development. A common characteristic of these sidelined people is the belief that there is only one true course for their life to take.[21] Each decision is considered to be irrevocable and connected to an endless line of future decisions that will culminate in success or failure. Dichotomous thinking causes an inordinate amount of anxiety to surround even minor decisions. Not everything in life is black or white; much of it is gray.

EXTERNAL LOCUS OF CONTROL

The second stage of cognitive decision making is multiplicity. In this stage the young adult begins to recognize a range of career possibilities yet continues to look outside himself or herself for answers. Individuals who get locked into this stage of development have an external locus of control. A substantial body of research has been amassed on the negative relationship between external locus of control and vocational development.[22]

The two major components of locus of control are self-confidence and autonomous behavior (behavior independent of social pressure). Individuals with an *external* locus of control tend to believe that reinforcement is based on luck or chance, and they have little self-confidence and a great lack of autonomous behavior. Individuals with an *internal* locus of control believe that reinforcement is up to them. They combine a strong sense of self-confidence with autonomous behavior.[23]

Young adults seeking God's will often fall prey to the external syndrome, which forces them into dependent and confused decision-making styles (see chapter 2).

COUNSELING STRATEGIES

Young adults often feel an intense need for vocational counseling. In one study, 85 percent of college freshmen in a large university reported a need for career-planning assistance.[24] Another study at Cornell University found that vocational choice and career planning was considered the most relevant problem for graduate and undergraduate students. Career decision-making pressures ranked over the more immediate pressures of time management, study skills, and test anxiety.[25]

The following techniques are designed to help young adults negotiate the career-decision making process successfully. These strategies will also provide skills beyond the current decision to a lifelong process of job-related decisions.

PINPOINT CAREER DECIDEDNESS

At the beginning of vocational counseling it is helpful to assess the level of career decidedness already achieved. A careful assessment can serve as a point from which to initiate the counseling relationship and to measure progress in the future.

One of the most frequently used instruments to measure career decidedness is the Career Decision Scale.[26] The Career Decision Scale (CDS) focuses on measuring difficulties in making a career choice and is made up of two scales. The certainty scale measures the respondent's certainty of choice for academic major and career, and the indecision scale is designed to assess various aspects of career indecision.

The CDS is comprised of nineteen items that help determine the client's readiness and capacity to cope with the career decision-making process. Responses are recorded on a four-point scale that ranges from "not at all like me" to "exactly like me." Some sample items are:

> "Until now, I haven't given much thought to choosing a career. I feel lost when think about it because I haven't had many experiences in making decisions on my own, and I don't have enough information to make a career decision right now."

> "I'd like to be a _____, but I'd be going against the wishes of someone who is important to me if I did so. Because of this, it's difficult for me to make a career decision right now. I hope I can find a way to please them and myself."

> "I have decided on a career and feel comfortable with it. I also know how to go about implementing my choice."

The test is hand scored, and the test manual provides information for the use of the results in the context of the counseling relationship. Reliability testing conducted by investigators results in a .90 and .82 for the indecision scale and correlations in the .60 to .80 range for the certainty and indecision scales.[27]

One study of young adults discovered that differing levels of career decidedness are linked with anxiety, locus of control, and identity. Ranked into three categories by the severity of the career indecision,[28] the college students were characterized by:

1. career-decidedness—relatively free from anxiety with an internalized locus of control and a firm identity

2. moderate career indecision—internal locus of control but with increased anxiety, and in a state of psychological moratorium on identity

3. career indecisive—an external locus of control, a high level of anxiety, and a diffuse identity

In another study, five subtypes also emerged including those who were happy and work oriented, anxious and unclear on goals, undecided and limited in interest, caught in a dilemma as to work salience, or happy and playful.[29] But whatever the level of career decideness, the counselor must discern it in order to provide proper guidance and support.

CONSTRUCT A FAMILY GENOGRAM

One of the most helpful tools for vocational counseling with young adults is the family genogram. Because a career serves as a rite of passage into adulthood, the career decision-making process rings a warning signal that a change in the family system is imminent. In addition, parents watch the first forays of their children into the adult world as signs to measure their own success in child raising. Were their values and lessons incorporated or not? Launching the young adult from the family frequently causes a spike in family anxiety and intensifies the role of family. For some young adults these influences can be paralyzing.

Through the construction of a family genogram, Mark was finally able to examine and understand his own internal pressures with clarity. As we charted his family system over three generations, a striking pattern began to emerge. For three generations, every male member of his family (with the exception of one uncle) had worked as highly successful financial agents. An uncle had even been nicknamed "The Trader" by the *Wall Street Journal*. Incredibly, each one had worked for the same national firm that now employed Mark (albeit in another area of the country).

As a homework assignment, Mark telephoned the one uncle who was not a financial agent. It had been years since they had talked, and the uncle for vague and unnamed reasons was a marginal member of the family. To his surprise, Mark discovered that even the black sheep uncle had worked for the financial firm for ten years before making what he called "the big switch," starting his own photography company. They talked for nearly forty-five minutes, and Mark found him to be competent, successful, and creative. Mark also discovered he was the first family member to inquire about his uncle's career transition.

Suddenly Mark understood why he, a philosophy and Christian education major, had concluded that he had to work in financial management. The family genogram helped Mark understand family influence and take the first step in creating a vision of his own through personal awareness. (See chap. 3 for detailed instructions on creating a genogram.)

CONDUCT PERSONALITY, INTEREST, AND SKILLS ASSESSMENT

Career counseling is facilitated by the use of assessment tools. Young adults need tools that reveal aspects of their individual character traits (i.e., personality, interests, and skills) to ensure balance in their considerations.

Assessments of the emerging personality, interests, and skills can assist the career counseling process in three significant ways:

to *stimulate* exploration when the decision-making process stalls

to *broaden* exploration that is too limited and constrained

to provide *focus* to career exploration when needed[30]

Results from personality, interest, and ability inventories should be used carefully. Many have a naive tendency to place greater value in test results than they deserve. Thus, the vocational counselor needs to guard against the "test 'em and tell 'em" mentality and carefully present the results "as a mirror to help the individual examine his or her view of self."[31] Larry Burkett reports that only 80 percent of the information is directly applicable.[32]

For information about the most commonly used assessments in each of these areas, refer to chapter 12, "Assessing Personality, Interests, Aptitudes, and Abilities."

FACILITATE CAREER INFORMATION COUNSELING GROUPS

Research shows that group counseling with college-age young adults is equal to individual counseling interventions in strengthening and supporting career-development goals.[33] The most effective are structured groups that "impart information, share common experiences, teach people how to solve problems, offer support and help people learn how to create their own support systems outside of the group setting."[34]

Bonnie, a gifted minister to single adults, contacted a career counselor. Several members of the Twenty-Something church group were still struggling with job search and career issues several months after graduation. Some of them had even formed an informal weekly support group. However, Bonnie's fear was that they were "getting together and exchanging depressing stories."

The vocational counselor joined the group to answer questions, act as a job-search coach, and offer the latest information available about job-market trends in the region. The group became a meaningful place for young adults to examine career alternatives (in the face of stalled plans), brainstorm cost-saving strategies for temporary living situations, share networking contacts, and offer encouragement to one another. Each success strengthened the optimism of the group and served as a springboard for another.

DECREASE ANXIETY

In *The Power and The Glory*, Graham Greene wrote, "There is always one moment in childhood when the door opens and lets the future in."[35] Launching the first official job search signals the open door for many young adults. With their unknown future, the weight of personal financial responsibilities at hand, young adults in the career decision-making process are filled with anxieties.

Anxiety is a crippling emotional state that often causes a high level of avoidance, sometimes to the point of paralysis (being stuck), distraction (being nonpresent), or compulsiveness (being anxiously present and driven) in the career decision-making process.

Experts generally view anxiety as taking one of two forms. *State* anxiety is an intense discomfort to a perceived threat. *Trait* anxiety is a chronic, ingrained response of a person who has adopted an anxious lifestyle.

Anxiety is a powerful indicator of an unsuccessful career decision-making process.[36] Investigators have found that high anxiety is a primary predictor of career indecision. It sparks a destructive chain reaction. Those who experience high trait anxiety are not likely to be proactive in the career decision-making process. They are likely to experience high state anxiety and are, therefore, not likely to make a career decision.

Counselors can best alleviate anxiety by helping clients identify the inaccurate thoughts that make them anxious and by helping them develop more realistic ways of thinking that will generate positive influences on their feelings and behavior. Common myths that lead to anxiety can be dispelled.

One group of university students invited a vocational counselor to meet with them in their dormitory lounge. These students were so anxious about their career future that they avoided the career center completely. As they gathered into a large circle, their faces betrayed their fears. The counselor opened the group session with two simple questions. "What scares you about having a career?" and "What scares you about *not* having a career?" This was fuel enough for a two-hour session that allowed the students to acknowledge their fears and anxieties. In many cases they were able to release irrational myths or exaggerated expectations.

FOSTER A COMPELLING PERSONAL VISION

I (Leslie) accepted employment in an entry-level office position at Fuller Theological Seminary when I was only twenty years old, a recent college graduate, and a newlywed. Young, naive, and eager to prove myself, I was, nevertheless, lost vocationally. The zoology and psychology majors I had obtained from a liberal arts university did not seem to translate into any specific careers.

Walter Wright, a caring administrator with quick insight, asked me to construct a Ten Year Plan for myself. What poured onto the pages stunned me. Now that decade is almost ended, and many of the highlights I included are accomplished: running the 1989 Los Angeles Marathon, earning a master's degree and a doctorate, serving as a counselor and mentor to college students, several publishing projects, and so on. Also evident are the relational ties that were heartily affirmed through writing a personal mission statement. That intervention infused my life with a sustained level of energy and hope.

Throughout the twenties, young adults strive to shape a dream or vision of themselves that will generate enough energy and hope to carry them through life.[37] Organizational consultant Peter Block believes that vision drives people to make positive and courageous choices. According to Block, we know we have created a great vision when it has three qualities: (1) It comes from the heart; (2) it is uniquely ours; (3) it is radical and compelling. A vision dramatizes our deepest values and wishes. This makes it both radical and demanding. Block admonishes, "When our vision asks too much of us, we should begin to trust it."[38]

One of the most powerful interventions in vocational counseling of young adults is the assignment of a personal Ten Year Plan. The plan should incorporate dreams and goals for work-life, personal development and education, relationships, recreation and hobbies, experiences and adventures, and spiritual growth and development. It is helpful for clients to begin by creating personal mission or purpose statements for their life followed by goals for each area. A time-line for completion must be attached to give the plan muscle.

Creating a vision is difficult. Expect resistance. Block, in fact, identifies three reasons people find it threatening to construct a personal vision:[39]

1. In an implicit way, creating a vision signifies disappointment with what exists now.

2. The vision exposes the future that one wishes for and opens up an individual to potential conflict with the visions of others.

3. Articulating a vision of greatness forces a person to hold himself or herself accountable for acting in a way that is congruent with that vision.

What can the counselor do to help a young adult without a clear vision? Ask, " Suppose you had a vision of greatness, what would it be?" The element of imagination often allows enough space for the individual to create a vision in the face of ambiguity. If the client still resists, it may be helpful for the young adult to create a narrative scenario that focuses on fifteen to twenty years in the future. Longer range dreams are sometimes less threatening than those designed for the near future. Once a long-range scenario has been completed, establishing short-term goals can be a focus within the context of counseling.

HELP CLIENTS INITIATE MENTORING RELATIONSHIPS AND INTERNSHIP EXPERIENCES

Ralph Waldo Emerson said, "Our chief want in life is somebody who shall make us what we can be." Gail Sheehy considers finding a mentor one of the central developmental tasks for a young adult.[40]

The concept of *mentor* is an ancient one. In Homer's great epic *The Odyssey*, Mentor was Ulysses' wise old friend. Before embarking on a ten-year journey, Ulysses entrusted the education of his son, Telemachus, to Mentor. As a guardian, tutor, advisor, and even surrogate father, Mentor assisted the young boy to attain adulthood. More than two thousand years later, Mentor's name has survived and is now a symbol of a unique form of relationship.

Mentors help shape and share the dream of emerging young adults. They share a cherished perception of their latent potential. Mentors give their blessing by deeply understanding this unique dream and encouraging young adults to stretch beyond their current boundaries to contribute something excellent.

Such advisors also work to articulate their values clearly and live them out visibly, allowing the young adult an opportunity to observe and participate in their work through shadowing experiences. They serve as teachers of communication skills, organizational culture, and professionalism. Generally, mentors are eight to fifteen years older than the young adult or have negotiated a critical life passage that the young person is heading into (i.e., a long tenure in an organization, a seasoned career, a degree, etc.).

To encourage the initiation of mentoring relationships, ask young adults to:

1. Conduct a personal needs assessment. What kind of experience do they need? Who can provide this for them?

2. Take advantage of opportunities to interact with those already within their sphere of influence.

3. Pursue personal contact with authors who make a significant impact on them. If personal contact is impossible, encourage the use of biographies.

4. Ask persons who currently have a significant impact on their lives if they are interested in establishing a more formal mentoring relationship.

5. Network! Interview people they know, trust, and respect for potential mentors or internship supervisors.

6. Be willing to take on tasks that involve visible risks. Mentors often spot young people working on a demanding task and then are drawn to support their achievement.

Help Clients Develop Job-Seeking Skills

A colleague at Seattle Pacific University's Career Development Center coined a phrase, "Starting your career is the toughest job you'll ever have." In *Your Career in Changing Times*, Lee Ellis and Larry Burkett summarize the current situation job seekers face within the world of work: "Considering our shaky economy, the changes in corporate America, and the impact of new technology on the workplace, the next five years will see more people than ever looking for new jobs. With the competition for jobs increasing, knowing how to carry out a well-planned job search will be an essential skill in our society."[41] This situation is only amplified by the fact that young adults often compete with a host of more experienced and mature job seekers who are increasingly willing to accept entry-level positions with limited salaries. (Chapter 15 will address in detail the process of skill building and equipping for the job search.)

NOTES

1. G. Sheehy, *Passages: Predictable Crises of Adult Life* (New York: Dutton, 1974).

2. K. Kenniston, *Youth and Dissent: The Rise of the New Opposition* (New York: Harcourt Brace Jovanovich, 1971).

3. Sheehy, *Passages.*

4. Seven of the eight developmental tasks of young adults are adapted from A. Chickering, "The Young Adult: An Overview," in *Education and Identity* (San Francisco: Jossey-Bass, 1984).

5. G. Sheehy, *Pathfinders: Overcoming the Crises of Adult Life and Finding Your Own Path to Well-Being* (New York: Morrow, 1981), 12.

6. Chickering, "Young Adult."

7. D. Tiedeman and R. O'Hara, *Career Development: Choice and Adjustment* (Princeton, N.J.: College Entrance Examination Board, 1963).

8. R. Sharf, *Applying Career Development Theory to Counseling* (Pacific Grove, Calif.: Brooks/Cole, 1992).

9. Ibid.

10. Chickering, "Young Adult," 9.

11. V. Zunker, *Career Counseling: Applied Concepts of Life Planning,* 4th ed. (Pacific Grove, Calif.: Brooks/Cole, 1994).

12. T. Eaton and M. Peterson, *Psychiatry,* 2d ed, (Norwalk, Conn.: Medical Examination Publishers, 969).

13. Chickering, "Young Adult," 10.

14. Adapted from L. Parrott III, *Helping the Struggling Adolescent* (Grand Rapids: Zondervan, 1993).

15. Chickering, "Young Adult."

16. Ibid.

17. L. Smedes, *A Pretty Good Person* (San Francisco: HarperCollins, 1990).

18. C. M. Sell, *Transitions Through Adult Life* (Grand Rapids: Zondervan, 1985).

19. C. Carney and C. Wells, *Discover the Career Within You* (Pacific Grove, Calif.: Brooks/Cole, 1991) 65.

20. L. Parrott III, "Career Decision-Making and Family Functioning" (Ph.D. dissertation, Seattle University, 1993).

21. Sheehy, Passages.

22. K. Taylor, "An Investigation Of Vocational Indecision in College Students: Correlates and Moderators," *Journal of Vocational Behavior* 21 (1982): 318–29; K. Taylor and J. Popma, "An Examination of the Relationships among Career Decision-Making Self-Efficacy, Career Salience, Locus of Control, and Vocational Indecision, *Journal of Vocational Behavior* 37 (1990): 17–31; A. Trice, J. Haire, and K. Elliott, "A Career Locus of Control Scale for Undergraduate Students," *Perceptual and Motor Skills* 69 (1989): 55–61.

23. K. Corcoran and J. Fischer, *Measures for Clinical Practice: A Sourcebook* (New York: The Free Press, 1987).

24. L. Walters and G. Saddlemire, "Career Planning Needs of College Freshmen and Their Perceptions of Career Planning," *Journal of College Student Personnel* 20 (1979).

25. H. Kramer, F. Berger, and G. Miller, "Student Concerns and Sources of Assistance," *Journal of College Student Personnel* 15 (1974).

26. S. Osipow et al., *The Career Decision Scale,* rev. ed. (Odessa, Fla.: Psychological Assessment Resources, 1976).

27. S. Osipow, C. Carney, and A. Barak, "A Scale of Educational-Vocational Undecidedness: A Topological Approach," *Journal of Vocational Behavior* 9 (1976): 233–43.

28. D. Fuqua, C. Blum, and B. Hartman, "Empirical Support for the Differential Diagnosis of Career Indecision," *Career Development Quarterly* 36 (1988): 364–73.

29. M. Lucas and D. Epperson, "Personality Types in Vocationally Undecided Students," *Journal of College Student Development* 29 (1966): 460–66.

30. D. Prediger, "The Role of Assessment in Career Guidance," in, *Career Guidance and Counseling Through the Life Span,* 3rd ed., ed. E. L. Herr and S. Cramer (Boston: Scott, Foresman, 1988).

31. Herr and Cramer, *Career Guidance,* 320; L. Cronback, *Essentials of Psychological Testing,* 4th ed. (New York: Harper and Row, 1984).

32. L. Ellis and L. Burkett, *Your Career in Changing Times* (Chicago: Moody Press, 1993).

33. Herr and Cramer, *Career Guidance.*

34. G. Corey, *Theory and Practice of Group Counseling,* 3d ed. (Pacific Grove, Calif.: Brooks/Cole, 1990), 11.

35. G. Greene, *The Power and the Glory* (1940), quoted in *Familiar Quotations,* 5th ed., ed. J. Bartlett and E. Beck (Boston: Little, Brown and Co., 1982).

36. Corcoran and Fischer, *Measures for Clinical Practice.*

37. Sheehy, *Passages.*

38. P. Block, *The Empowered Manager: Positive Political Skills at Work* (San Francisco: Jossey-Bass, 1987).

39. Ibid.

40. Sheehy, *Passages.*

41. Ellis and Burkett, *Changing Times,* 247.

Chapter Seven

Midcareer Change

LINDA, A WOMAN IN HER EARLY THIRTIES, was a rehabilitation therapist in an outpatient clinic connected to one of Seattle's largest hospitals. The seed for this career decision was planted in her as a young child as she watched her brother struggle with cerebral palsy.

After earning her B.A., Linda soon joined a clinical team. As a fresh graduate she was aware of the field's latest techniques, and her older colleagues noticed. Linda's role was expanded as her skills increased. For six years she flourished as a clinic coordinator. But her seventh year was a new story. Her employer noticed that Linda's level of personal investment and enthusiasm was decreasing, and Linda admitted that she felt restless—even burned-out.

A bright and compassionate woman, Linda was actively involved in a church fellowship and had a close circle of friends. Although she enjoyed these relationships, Linda had expected to be married by now. At times the aloneness of her life seemed to stretch out as an endless plateau.

Empty and confused, Linda floundered. She phased in and out of minor depression for several months. After successful short-term therapy, she began to consider the field of psychotherapy. Discovering a master's program in counseling at a nearby university, she decided to apply.

For three years Linda worked part time at the clinic and pursued her studies. During this time she discovered the field of vocational counseling. Through an internship in a university career development center, Linda equipped herself for the transition. After a rigorous four-month job search, she landed an interim job at a community college. The position promised to integrate academic advising and career counseling. The setting sounded idyllic—a quiet community nestled on one of Washington State's San Juan Islands. In reality, the position called for the tedious and relentless analysis of academic transcripts. The quiet village was a lonely place.

Disillusioned and confused about the career transition she had launched three years earlier, Linda once again initiated a job search. Three months later she was offered a position as a full-time career counselor at a neighboring university in an active community. The position was just right for her.

Linda's two-year program had turned into a four-year journey that resulted in a qualitative difference in her career life. At last, she had a renewed sense of meaning and contribution. In harmony with Linda's story, this chapter is focused on how to support and enhance midcareer transitions.

DEVELOPMENTAL TASKS OF ADULTS IN TRANSITION

Contrary to conventional wisdom, adulthood is not a place of quiet waters following the white rapids of youth. Rather, it is a new period full of currents of change, continued growth, and evolution of self. Geothe declared, "Life belongs to the living, and he who lives must be prepared for changes."

Several foundational beliefs are crucial in effective vocational counseling with adults in transition.[1] Of these beliefs, four are specifically related to adult development:

1. Adulthood is full of conflict and choice. Adults can expect to experience the need for change in their lives.

2. Psychological development continues well into adult years. Personality development, character formation, and adaptation to the external environment and internal self are all factors in the adult journey.

3. As people grow older, they grow increasingly different from each other. Diversity increases with age.

4. Career development is just another factor in an individual's physical, emotional, and cognitive development. It does not function separately. It is connected to all aspects of life: leisure, education, values, motivation, lifestyle, and self-concept.

"The age of man resembles a book," said Edwards Parsons Day, "infancy and old age are the blank leaves; youth, the preface; and adulthood, the body or most important portion of life's volume." Typically, developmental theorists define the "body" of adult life as beginning during the mid-twenties and continuing through the sixties. Midlife is considered to start around thirty-four and continue throughout the forties.

Erik Erikson's life-cycle theory, with its eight stages, incorporates three developmental crises that beg resolution during the adult years: (1) Intimacy versus Isolation, (2) Generativity versus Stagnation, and (3) Integrity versus Despair.[2] Gail Sheehy, emphasizing the psychological and internal changes that accompany each of these transitions through adult life, has identified three similar phases of adulthood: (1) Rooting and Extending (early thirties); (2) Deadline Decade (thirty-five to forty-five); and (3) Renewal and Resignation (midforties and beyond).[3] By merging Sheehy's descriptive phases with Erikson's life-cycle crises, we can discern the developmental tasks of adulthood.

This chapter will focus on the two crises of adult development for those approaching and negotiating midlife transitions. The final passage of integrity achievement will be examined in chapter 8, "Postretirement Adjustment."

ACHIEVING INTIMACY THROUGH ESTABLISHMENT
AND SELF-EXTENSION

Sheehy considers this passage of life a time for "putting down roots and sending out new shoots."[4] In an attempt to secure and foster intimacy, adults earnestly invest their emotional and financial energy into building a home and career. The central task of this phase is the work of converting the life dream into the concrete goals that make the dream reality. Because adult development is sequential, patterns established in the twenties significantly influence the work of the thirties and beyond. Of particular interest from the vocational counseling perspective is the manner in which men and women have resolved (or not resolved) the dilemma of exploration and stabilization they were faced with in their twenties[5] (see chap. 6).

For men, the common patterns are:

1. *Transients*—established no firm commitments in their twenties

2. *Locked In*—established solid commitments in their twenties, but without any identity crisis or self-examination

3. *Wunderkind*—prone to generate and take risks designed to create dramatic success, believing that dream achievement will abolish personal insecurity

4. *Paranurturers*—committed to care for the family of humanity (i.e., clergy or missionary) or committed to fulfillment of the nurturing role in the family customarily filled by the wife.

The common patterns for women are centered more on the dilemma of career versus family responsibilities. These patterns are discussed in detail in chapter 10, "Women and Career Development."

Anxious adults work to gain balance in their attempts to foster intimacy while advancing toward their life dreams. They work toward mastery of the skills that, though they may have silently slipped through the cracks of their young adult lives, are beginning to cry out for attention, thus diverting their focus.

ACHIEVING GENERATIVITY IN THE SHADOW OF LIFE'S DEADLINES

At forty-two, Dante eloquently articulated the angst of midlife in the opening stanza of *The Divine Comedy:* "In the middle of the journey of our life, I came to myself within a dark wood where the straight way was lost. Ah how hard it is to tell of that wood, savage, harsh and dense, the thought of which renews my fear. So bitter is that death is hardly more."[6]

A change so dramatic characterizes this phase of life and seemingly alters reality for those who undergo it. Sheehy identifies the following dimensions in this radical change:

1. *The Nature of Time.* During this passage there is an internal jolt on recognition of time. It is forever changed. For most men there is a time panic. Time is running out. For most women, the new feeling of time is "Look at all the time ahead. What will I do with it?" The major task is to build into life what is most important *within the time left to live.*

2. *The Nature of Life.* Change in the nature of time reverberates as change in the nature of life. Sheehy states, "A distorted perspective foreshortens the future so falsely that it creates inertia."[7] Time suspension feels akin to boredom, but on a much more profound level. At this point the adult comes face to face with stagnation, with being consumed in the repetitive, daily activity, which tends toward meaninglessness. Trust and hope in the future become uncertain quantities.

However, stagnation may be the unseen motivation for resolving the crisis. Now is the time for revitalization. A renewed belief that, "Yes, I can change; it's not too late." This decision infuses the future with new energy and a redefined purpose.

The task of adults in this phase is to endure these losses while creating a renewed appreciation for the gift of life.

ACHIEVING INTEGRITY THROUGH RENEWAL

Achieving what Erikson calls *integrity*, the final stage of adult development, allows an individual to accept responsibility for his or her own life, to feel satisfied with the accomplishments, and to maximize its successes—in short, to give oneself a blessing.[8] This state of integrity is not won easily. The entropy of life pulls toward despair. At this juncture in adult life, "every loose end not resolved in previous passages will resurface to haunt us."[9] All of the characteristics that Jung has called our "shadow self," [10] submerged in our frantic efforts toward wholeness, goodness, and creativity, raise their ugly heads and demand to be known: selfishness, greed, competitiveness, fear, dependency, jealously, possessiveness, destructiveness. For perhaps the first time we are forced to seek the truth about ourselves. This process, for the courageous who are willing to take a risk, can lead to a deeper, fuller state of personal authenticity. But the same state of affairs can also drive a fearful person into despair.

The state of personal renewal is the gift of "riding out the down side"[11] and investing in the reintegration of our whole self. The fruit of this work is a renewed satisfaction in marriage and a reinvestment in life. This is a time of transcendence. As disappointments and disillusionments of the past are incorporated into life, the prospects of a good future become a grand and priceless treasure. Successful resolution of the previous passages fulfills time with renewed energy and delight.

ELEMENTS OF MIDCAREER TRANSITION

Midcareer transition must be understood for the elements of career transition to make sense. While most of us would like to think of a career as we would a trip—controlled, planned, and measurable—it is actually more like a journey, unfolding over time with unforeseen and largely uncontrollable experiences and less predictable results.[12]

PROBABILITY OF MIDCAREER TRANSITION

Whether or not the vocational client is on a fast track or a meandering path, one thing is certain: midcareer transitions will occur. Recent studies reveal that the average adult will experience between three to seven career transitions in a lifetime. This reality suggests that most adults could profit from vocational counseling as they negotiate the turbulence and complexity of the marketplace.

TIMING OF MIDCAREER TRANSITION

The term *midcareer change* is not limited to the worker ten to fifteen years short of retirement who is facing a single career change. In a landmark study of thirty million adults in career transition, the majority were between the ages of twenty and thirty-nine.[13] In the context of the new realities, a shift may be classified as a midcareer transition if the individual has (1) at least eight years of experience in an occupation, or (2) the equivalent of one year of career experience for each two-year period spent in graduate school.[14] For example, a school counselor who received a B.A. at age twenty-one, spent two years in a master's degree program, and then worked for seven years would be at midcareer by age thirty.

TYPES OF MIDCAREER TRANSITION

Career changes may be as subtle as a shift of key in a musical score or as dramatic as a transition from the flute to the trombone. Hiestand has conceptualized career change as either a forty-five or ninety-degree movement.[15] According to Hiestand, forty-five degree changes are those that cause minor discontinuity with the previous occupation, while ninety degree change involves major discontinuity with the former occupation. Neapolitan adds the third category of "radical job change," which is used to indicate a total break from an occupational history.[16] Vocational counselor Duane Brown summarizes, "Mid-life career change is a process in which an adult, usually between the ages of thirty-five and forty-five, enters a new occupation that may require mild, moderate, or extreme adjustments in training or experience."[17]

One researcher whose work focused primarily on educated males categorized career shifters into three types:[18]

> Type A—shifts that are directly connected to a major event that "impels the shifter to reformulate the meaning of life and personal goals"

> Type B—shifts that result from a restlessness and gradual disenchantment, boredom, or disillusionment of the previous career

> Type C—shifts based on a growing awareness of a new career that has the promise of more satisfaction and fulfillment, often as the result of an avocational interest that develops into a career.

The motivational component of a midcareer change may also come as a surprise. In a study of midlife career changers, ages thirty-four to fifty-four, it was found that many actually took salary cuts to move and change jobs. Only 11 percent indicated that salary conditions were important in their careers. Fifty-three percent of the respondents indicated that the transition into more meaningful work was the real reason for changing jobs. Increased meaning, then, is the most frequently identified factor in career change. In addition, 48 percent of the respondents indicated that their career change was motivated out of a desire to obtain a better fit between their values and their occupation. Other reasons respondents identified as motivators for change were increased time with family (26 percent), more recreation time (23 percent), and the opportunity for relocation (20 percent).[19]

In one survey,[20] the reasons people listed for voluntarily changing careers included, but were not limited to:

- initial career not person's own choice
- original aspirations not met by career
- purpose of first career accomplished
- desire to implement avocational interests
- inadequate outlet for creativity
- insufficient variety in work content
- coworkers divergent in values and lifestyles
- personality conflicts with supervisor or coworkers
- greener grass in another field

Whatever the reason, many adults are likely to seek vocational counseling at some point in their career journey. According to one researcher, "Almost every institution, whether public or private, has been affected by the reality that many people wish to shift career directions during a period when, according to accepted norms, they should be nearing the apex of their chosen career."[21]

THE HAZARDS OF ADULT MIDCAREER TRANSITIONS

Managing the complexity of midcareer transitions can be lonely and frightening for adults, especially if they fall into any of the four traps along the way: (1) ambivalence toward change, (2) job obsolescence, (3) single career orientation, and (4) the unfulfilled worker.

AMBIVALENCE TOWARD CHANGE

Lucius Cary said, "When it is not necessary to change, it is necessary not to change." It is not surprising that a large proportion of adults struggle with ambivalence over a possible career transition. Feeling burdened by unmet needs, frustrated by the realities of the current workplace, and tangled in a morass of overwhelming responsibilities immobilizes many adults. Most are well aware that the wrong kind of change may actually create more problems than it solves. Therefore, the entire process leaves them dragged down in ambivalence.

In *The Dance of Intimacy* , Harriet Goldhor Lerner, observed:

> All of us have deeply ambivalent feelings about change, we seek the wisdom of others when we are not making full use of our own and then we resist applying the wisdom that we do seek even when we're paying for it. We do this not because we are neurotic or cowardly, but because both the will to change and the desire to maintain sameness coexist for good reason. Both are essential to our emotional well-being and equally deserve our attention and respect.[22]

JOB OBSOLESCENCE

Job obsolescence [23] describes the condition that arises when workers fail to keep pace with job technologies, procedures, and practices that are essential to their field. The problem of job obsolescence is an increasing reality due to evolutionary changes in technology and the changing nature of business organizations in the last twenty years.

Your Career in Changing Times, by Lee Ellis and Larry Burkett, addresses the technological, economic, and governmental factors that have compounded to create today's marketplace. With a graph that goes back to A.D. 1400, Ellis and Burkett illustrate the reality of unparalleled change in the workplace from 1940 to the present. Both authors underscore the need for "well educated employees who can respond quickly to changing consumer demands." They go on to say, "In the future, workers must be willing to adapt—or be unemployed."[24] Workers who do not make a commitment to lifelong learning and skill building run a high risk of falling victim to job obsolescence. This is, however, a hazard that can be easily avoided with planning. Research with victims of job obsolescence has identified lack of motivation as the greatest single contributing factor to their problems.[25]

A SINGLE-CAREER ORIENTATION

Many equate the single lifetime career with the morality of the work ethic.[26] For these individuals, the idea of a career change and flexibility carries with it the stigma of failure or weakness of character. A large number of midlife workers seek job security and stability at the cost of all other job-related concerns. Unfortunately, these factors reduce career mobility more dramatically than any other.

THE UNFULFILLED WORKER SYNDROME

"Everyone thinks of changing the world, but no one thinks of changing himself." These words from Leo Tolstoy cut to the heart of the unfulfilled worker syndrome. The unfulfilled worker is on an endless quest for the job that will provide enough purpose to give meaning to his or her existence. The unfulfilled worker needs the tangible evidence of the right job to feel that he or she is significant. The unfulfilled worker is constantly on the search for a new challenge, deeper meaning, more fulfilling relationships, less conflict, more money, and so on. This revolving-door career pattern takes them from one job to the next as they search for the perfect opportunity. Some situations are remarkably better than others, but every job has its flaws and its pain. Workers who fall victim to the unfulfilled worker syndrome refuse to accept the realities of life.

COUNSELING STRATEGIES

The realities of the adult career journey indicate the need for career counseling that goes far beyond the point of a single career choice. Unlike the programs designed to aid initial career choice, vocational counseling for adults has specific components that meet exact needs. These strategies provide skills to resolve a current crisis and to enhance the lifelong process of career expansion and adjustment.

UNDERSTAND THE STAGES OF TRANSITION

Few people sail effortlessly through change. For most it is impossible to underestimate the impact of change—whether positive or negative. Hopson and Adams developed a seven-phase model of transition that career counselors have used for understanding adult career crises and the helping strategies.[27] The seven phases of transition include: (1) immobilization with despair or elation, (2) minimization, (3) self-doubt, (4) letting go, (5) testing out, (6) search for meaning, and (7) internalization.

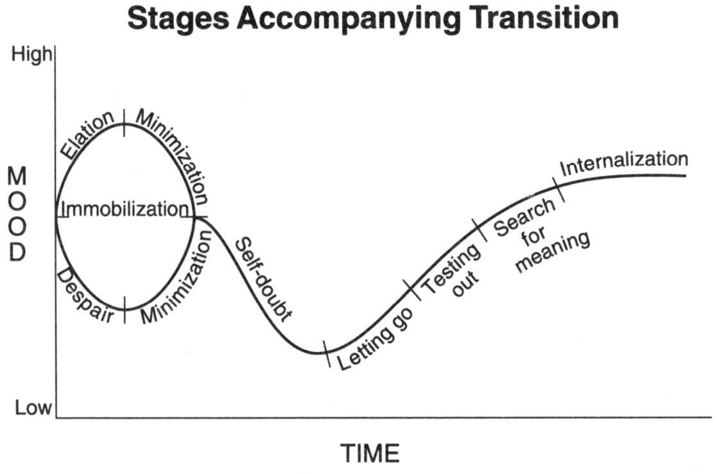

Stages Accompanying Transition

Fig. 7.1

Source: Reprinted by permission from J. Adams, J. Hayes, and B. Hapson, *Understanding and Managing Personal Change* (Newberry Park, Calif.: Sage Publications, 1977), 38.

Immobilization. This first phase may last up to a few days. In this stage the individual feels overwhelmed by events and is unable to respond realistically. A happy event such as a promotion or acceptance into an academic program can be the trigger. In these cases, the individual experiences elation. However, an unhappy event such as a layoff or a personal loss may also be the catalyst for immobilization, in this case with feelings of despair.

Minimization. After the cloud of immobilization lifts, a person tries to minimize the situation. Minimization is an attempt to make the change appear smaller than it is. Persons attempt to hold onto life as it was and to ignore the inevitable winds of change. In the worst cases, an individual may deny the change is taking place.

Self-Doubt. Minimizing and denial give way to a flood of new emotions. Anxiety, fear, and self-doubt take over. The individual may also begin to lose faith in his or her ability to negotiate the needed career change while keenly feeling the weight of responsibility to provide for self and family.

Letting Go. One of the tasks of transition is the ability to pull out of the negative situation and to distance oneself from it. Through detachment there is more capacity to look ahead and to plan the future. At this point the beginning of the upward curve in the transitional cycle begins. Hope and excitement begin to stir the air.

Testing Out. With a new burst of energy and a renewed sense of "I can handle it," individuals in the testing-out phase begin to move forward. They activate their networking channels if they are looking for a new position, and they begin to share their experiences with others who are experiencing the same problem. The focus is now on possibilities instead of losses.

Search for Meaning. From this new vantage point, the career shifter begins to extract meaning from the course of events that have occurred in the transition. If the transition was a forced one, this is the phase within which individuals discover a new capacity for empathy. They attempt to understand not only their own feelings but also the feelings and concerns of others who are involved. At this point individuals also seek more information for analyzing the situation.

Internalization. This final phase of the career transition is the incorporation of the spiritual, emotional, and cognitive results of experience into a new growth pattern. New skills are developed, and the crisis is integrated into the individual's life story.

CAPITALIZE ON READINESS AND MOTIVATION FOR CHANGE

When adolescents or young adults seek career assistance, they tend to be reluctant and sometimes unmotivated. The role of the career counselor in such situations is to create a sense of readiness for the career-development process. However, career-changing adults are different from young adults. Typically, the midcareer shifters come to the counselor with a high level of readiness and motivation.[28] The challenge, then, for the vocational counselor is to capitalize on this energy and motivation. Most individuals seeking midcareer change assistance are prepared to invest only in short-term counseling (about four or five sessions).[29] It is crucial, then, that the counselor work to maximize the impact of a relatively small window of time.

EXAMINE LIFE-ROLE CONFLICTS

Sometimes individuals find it difficult to identify the source of pain in their lives. For some, it is less threatening to admit personal unhappiness at work than at home. Sometimes individuals who express frustration and dissatisfaction with work are in reality grappling with unfulfilled needs in the family.[30] An effective vocational counselor will assist clients in a self-evaluation that enables them to become aware of and deal with the underlying source of pain in their lives whatever its origin.

Maintaining caring relationships and pursuing individual achievement may add conflict to a career transition. This conflict is true particularly for nurturers who have deferred achievement and are just now establishing a role in the workplace. Conflict can be just as strong in achievers who have deferred nurturing and are attempting to phase into a less demanding professional role that allows for increased family involvement. The needs of these individuals (usually women who have attempted to integrate marriage, career, *and* motherhood) may be the most complex of all. Each change will disturb the delicate balance of a highly complex system, often with un-controllable ramifications. Go slow and listen empathetically.

Evaluate the Current Career Circumstances

Many adults have difficulty in evaluating their current work situation. As a result, they develop misguided assumptions about their career future. Career specialists Carney and Wells have developed a set of questions for individuals who are confused over a possible career transition.[31] The more that specific issues can be identified, the more likely the career shift will serve as a further solution to the broader needs of the client.

The counselor can help clients explore their own thoughts through the following questions:

- Do you want more money? More or less responsibility? A new set of tasks? A different lifestyle?
- Have your career goals changed since you started your job? If they are changed, how do they differ from before?
- Are you a victim of the Peter Principle?
- How much of your dissatisfaction is due to your attitudes and behaviors? Which of those will follow you to any job you choose?
- Does your organization ask too much or give too little, leaving you feeling burned-out and unappreciated?
- Does your job have a negative effect on the other aspects of your lifestyle—your social life and avocational pursuits?
- Has your employer made comments about your work performance falling off, indicating that he or she also sees that you are less involved in your work than before?
- Is your employer supportive of your need for change, or is such change viewed as a threat to the status quo?
- Is there an unresolved conflict at work that haunts you from day to day?

Careful and honest responses to the above questions will aid in a relevant career-shift decision. An effective midcareer transition is multifaceted and complex. It defies simple solutions.[32] A good self-analysis will guard against rash changes that only result in continued dissatisfaction.

USE A COLLABORATIVE COUNSELING APPROACH

Counseling with midcareer shifters should be a joint venture between the counselor, the client, and all other existing supports (i.e., employee assistance programs, personnel services, clergy, professional associations, college or university services, city libraries, etc.). A pastor's involvement may be helpful in sustaining a fragile sense of optimism and hope.

PRESCRIBE A CLIENT AUTOBIOGRAPHY

Counselors must be aware of the tendency among adults to overlook their valuable assets from work and life experiences. These experiences provide rich sources of information not available to younger clients.

One of the most useful tools for gathering pertinent information on a client is the autobiography.[33] The autobiography can be loosely or tightly structured. The individual simply writes the story as he or she sees it. No guidelines are given. The assignment is open-ended. This allows clients to draw from experiences associated with work, leisure, family, and individualized lifestyles in a way that is meaningful to them with no preconceived constraints.

However, if clients are hesitant to see their history as useful in the career transition, it may be necessary to use a more structured approach. For a structured autobiography, the individual may be instructed to follow an outline or answer specific questions considered relevant by the counselor. One commonly used format calls for seven to ten significant life accomplishments from any arena of life (work, hobbies, family, volunteer activities, etc.).

Once completed, the client and the counselor can use the autobiographical sketch to assess values, identify interests, and maximize transferable experiences. They may also analyze the functional, adaptive, and technical skills that have surfaced in the writing of the story.[34]

DISSEMINATE SPECIFIC, CONCRETE INFORMATION

One study of midlife adults revealed that most career changers rely on their old decision-making styles based on limited alternatives and incomplete information.[35] Since realistic job information and placement assistance are crucial to career planning for adults, information dissemination is one of the vocational counselor's most significant responsibilities.[36] Career information hotlines, occupational libraries (see chap. 14), and job information seminars are effective resources for the vocational counselor serving adults in career transition.[37]

GUARD AGAINST AGE BIAS

Research has revealed that vocational counselors, especially young professionals, are vulnerable to age bias. Age bias, whether conscious or unconscious, can be extremely damaging to adults in midcareer transition. Three common types of age bias are:

1. *age restrictiveness*—setting up arbitrary or inappropriate age limits for certain behavior
2. *age distortion*—a misperception of the behavior or characteristics of any age group
3. *age-ism*—negative attitudes toward any age group.[38]

Researcher Lydia Brontë found that 85 percent of the 31 million people in the United States over age sixty-five are vital, active, and engaged in vocational or avocational pursuits.[39] Far from seeking retirement planning, many of these mature adults are launching new careers or allowing avocational interests to blossom into a vital new life work. It is next to criminal for any vocational counselor to discourage these adults because of age bias.

NOTES

1. S. Moore, introduction to, *Counseling Adults: Life Cycle Perspectives,* ed. D. Jones and S. Moore (Lawrence, Kans.: University of Kansas, 1985), vii–xii.

2. E. Erikson, *Childhood and Society*, 2d ed. (New York: Norton, 1963).

3. G. Sheehy, *Passages: Predictable Crises of Adult Life* (New York: E. P. Dutton, 1974).

4. Ibid.

5. D. E. Super, "A Life-Span Life-Space Approach to Career Development," in *Career Choice and Development: Applying Contemporary Theories to Practice*, 2d ed., ed. D. Brown et al. (San Francisco: Jossey-Bass, 1990).

6. Dante Alighieri, *The Divine Comedy*, quoted in G. Seldes, *The Great Thoughts* (New York: Ballantine Books, 1985).

7. Sheehy, *Passages*, 244.

8. L. Troll, *Early and Middle Adulthood*, 2d ed. (Pacific Grove, Calif.: Brooks/Cole Publishers, 1985).

9. Sheehy, *Passages*, 248.

10. C. Jung, *Psychological Types* (New York: Harcourt, 1923).

11. Sheehy, *Passages*, 250.

12. J. Trautman, "Vocation, Calling, and the Career-Life Journey," (lecture, Seattle Pacific University, 19 January 1994).

13. S. Arbeiter et al., *40 Million Americans in Career Transition: The Need for Information* (New York: College Entrance Examination Board, 1978).

14. J. Neapolitan, "Occupational Change in Mid-Career: An Exploratory Investigation," *Journal of Vocational Behavior* 16 (1980): 212–25.

15. D. L. Hiestand, *Changing Careers After Thirty-Five* (New York: Columbia University Press, 1971), quoted in Brown et al., Career Choice.

16. Neapolitan, "Occupational Change," 212–25.

17. Brown et al., *Career Choice*, 372.

18. W. Clopton, "Personality and Career Change," *Industrial Gerontology* 17 (1973): 9–17.

19. L. Thomas, "Typology of Mid-Life Career Changes," *Journal of Vocational Behavior* 16 (1980): 173–82, quoted in Brown et al., Career Choice.

20. D. Sinick, *Counseling Older Persons: Career, Retirement, Dying* (Ann Arbor, Mich.: ERIC Clearing House on Counseling and Personnel Services, 1975), 97.

21. Brown et al., *Career Choice*, 369.

22. H. Lerner, *The Dance of Intimacy* (New York: Harper and Row, 1989), 11.

23. H. Kaufman, *Obsolescence and Professional Career Development* (New York: American Management Association, 1974).

24. L. Ellis and L. Burkett, *Your Career in Changing Times* (Chicago: Moody Press, 1993), 18.

25. Kaufman, *Obsolescence*.

26. V. Zunker, *Career Counseling: Applied Concepts of Life Planning*, 3d ed. (Pacific Grove, Calif: Brooks/Cole, 1990).

27. J. Adams, J. Hayes, and B. Hopson, *Understanding and Managing Personal Change* (Newberry Park, Calif. :Sage Publications, 1977), 38, quoted in R. Sharf, *Applying Career Development Theory to Counseling* (Pacific Grove, Calif.: Brooks/Cole, 1992).

28. E. Herr and S. Cramer, *Career Guidance and Counseling Through the Life Span*, 3d ed. (Glenview, Ill.: Scott, Foresman, 1988).

29. Trautman, "Vocation, Calling, and the Career-Life Journey."

30. Zunker, *Career Counseling*.

31. C. Carney and C. Wells, *Discover the Career Within You* (Pacific Grove, Calif: Brooks/Cole, 1991), 191.

32. Zunker, *Career Counseling*.

33. Ibid.

34. Ibid.

35. J. Armstrong, "Decision Behavior and Outcomes of Mid-life Career Changes," *Vocational Guidance Quarterly* 29 (1981): 205–11.

36. A. Pascal, et al., *An Evaluation of Policy Related Research on Programs for Mid-life Career Redirection*, vol. 1 *Major Findings* (Washington, D.C.: National Science Foundation, 1975); A. Pascal, et al., *An Evaluation of Policy Related Research on Programs for Mid-life Career Redirection*, vol. 2 *Major Findings* (Santa Monica, Calif.: Rand, 1975).

37. Herr, and Cramer, *Career Guidance*, 362.

38. L. Troll and C. Nowak, "How Old Are You? The Question of Age Bias in the Counseling of Adults," *The Counseling Psychologist* 6 (1976): 41–44.

39. L. Brontë, *The Longevity Factor: The New Reality of Long Careers and How It Can Lead to Richer Lives* (New York: HarperCollins, 1993).

Chapter Eight

Postretirement Adjustment

W HEN RON STRONG, NOW SIXTY-NINE, retired from IBM four years go, he was financially ready. He even attended a company-sponsored seminar that covered pension benefits, Medicare, and Social Security. However, Ron sensed deeply that something was missing. He was haunted by stories about the emotional price tag of retirement. On the top of his agenda: "Nobody has prepared me for how to cope with what happens between my wife and me when I am suddenly at home twenty-four hours a day after being away at the office for thirty-five years. And what will I do with all my time?"

Ron is facing the great retirement transition. But he is not alone. According to statistics compiled by the U. S. Bureau of the Census, "By the year 2020, the number of people age 65 and older will exceed those under age 25."[1]

Turning sixty-five hasn't always signaled retirement. At the turn of the century, the administrator in charge of the social welfare system reportedly chose sixty-five as the official retirement age because he was advised that most workers wouldn't live long beyond that. He thought that setting the retirement age at sixty-five would allow costs to the government to stay at a minimum.[2] In the mid 1930s when Social Security became law, age sixty-five was chosen as the retirement time because few men lived past sixty-seven. Thus, the Social Security payout would be minimal. President Roosevelt sold the program to Congress and the nation on its wide benefits and minimal costs.

The results of the age sixty-five decision are ironic. First, the proportion of males over sixty-five who are retired has now risen to 75 percent and climbing.[3] The influx of baby boomers into the work force threatens to overwhelm the Social Security program by 2020, and the slowed economic growth has pushed many larger corporations to turn to early retirement incentive programs. In 1982 one survey found that 75 percent of those exiting the work force were under sixty-five and that the majority of retiring workers were age sixty-two.[4] About 15 percent of this group are too physically weak or frail for meaningful labor. The remaining 85 percent are considered healthy, active, and vital.[5] Many of them seem to be entering a second middle age with good health and a desire to work.

Economic and demographic futurists suggest that early retirement may soon be a relic of the past. There are several contributing factors, but chief among them is the expanding life span. Persons today can be expected to live, on the average, at *least* fifteen more years past sixty-five. According to researcher Lydia Brontë, there has been a net gain of about twenty-eight years in life expectancy from 1900 to 1991. In this century the ordinary American has lengthened his or her lifetime by 60 percent. Even the life expectancy increase from the days of ancient Rome to the year 1900 was not this great. Life expectancy has been increased more in the last one hundred years than it had in the previous two thousand. For the present generation, the amount of time spent in adulthood has literally doubled.[6]

Perhaps the most significant economic factor in changing the future retirement picture is the size of the baby boom cohort, who will pose a massive dollar challenge for the United States to support through Social Security and pensions.

Current retirement policies and practices in the United States have their critics. One recent article in the journal *Social Work* declared that, "retirement, whether mandatory, voluntary or forced, is a counterproductive social policy. Retirement needs to be flexible and optional."[7]

The bottom line is clear. Vocational counselors must reinforce their skills and become equipped to deal with the increasing numbers of individuals—many with long, healthy years ahead—who are engaging in postretirement planning.[8] Since the average length of retirement is extended to a fifteen- or twenty-year stretch, retirement has become a significant segment in a person's life. Retirement counseling is becoming a specialization, more and more in demand from vocational counselors.[9]

DEVELOPMENTAL TASKS OF OLDER ADULTS

Seneca, the Roman statesman and philosopher who lived during the time of Jesus, said, "As for old age, embrace and love it. It abounds with pleasure, if you know how to use it. The gradually declining years are among the sweetest in a man's life, and I maintain that, even when they have reached the extreme limit, they have their pleasure still."

Seneca's wise words about "embracing the *gradually* declining years" may have been more prophetic then he knew. Brontë states, "The period of life that was formerly the end of middle age (roughly fifty), and what is now the beginning of real, physical old age (some point after seventy-five) is a new stage in adult life—one that never existed before. This new stage occupies the third quarter of life."[10] Adults who are currently experiencing this *second middle age* are called "pioneers in time" by Brontë. These are the people who are redefining our ideas of adult development.

Many of us have reduced the older adult to a static image. We need to be reminded, however, that the life cycle differences between the 60s and 80s are at least as great as those between the 20s and 40s.[11]

The overarching developmental task of the elder is the achievment of what Erik Erikson calls *integrity*, the final stage of adult development. This stage allows an individual to accept responsibility for his or her life, to feel satisfied with the accomplishments it holds, and to maximize its successes—in short, to give oneself a blessing.[12] Integrity is coming face to face with the meaning of one's life in the shadow of one's death. This state of integrity is not won easily, but with much difficulty. The entropy of life is pulling one toward despair. At this juncture in adult life, "every loose end not resolved in previous passages will resurface to haunt us."[13]

The work of achieving integrity is accomplished through the addition of a new familial role—grandparenthood—and the acceptance and integration of three major losses: (1) retirement, the loss of one's work; (2) widowhood, the loss of a spouse; and (3) physical decline and dependency, the loss of health and independence. For our purposes, the focus will be on the process of achieving integrity through the retirement adjustment.

ELEMENTS OF RETIREMENT ADJUSTMENT

Retirement signals a process and a new role in life. Retirement constitutes the transition from worker to nonworker and signifies the withdrawal from the work role into the vaguely defined role of retiree. The individual who faces retirement is plagued by the question, "Is a person without work regarded as a person without wisdom?"[14] The challenge ahead is to find ways to integrate the wisdom they have gleaned from life into the new retirement role.

STAGES OF RETIREMENT ADJUSTMENT

Atchley describes several stages the retiree goes through in adjustment to this new career-life situation. First, there is a period of freedom, enjoyment, and fun, which is called the *honeymoon phase*. This fades over time and melts into a period of *disenchantment*, as the retiree faces the losses inherent in retirement as well as the differences between the dream of retired life and its reality. Then the retiree enters the *rebuilding* phase. This is a time when the individual works to confront and integrate fantasy and reality. With resolution of these tensions, the individual moves into the equilibrium of the *stable life* phase. This becomes the final phase of life.[15]

Emily Spruce, sixty-three, had served as a teacher in the public school system for over twenty years. She had pursued both her bachelor's and master's degrees through evening courses while her children were young and demanding. Widowed early, teaching had been her survival kit. When her San Antonio, Texas, schoolhouse became a refuge for non-English-speaking Hispanic children, she learned their language in order to teach them hers.

Emily's retirement brought her a sense of excitement not matched in those earlier, hardworking years. She packed up the belongings she had collected in her double-wide mobile home and moved to the midwest to be near her two daughters. That cross-country excursion was one of the joys of her life. The farewell from her colleagues and students had been touching, giving her a sense of closure on her life there. She was so glad to be away from it all—especially the faculty politics. (Older professionals like her were being phased out to incorporate more contemporary role models for the children; the administration had seemed overly eager to replace her.)

Her new situation on the Kansas prairies seemed ideal for a while. She was active in caring for her grandson. As the days wore on, however, the financial limitations became increasingly constricting. Her mind, which she tried to keep active through books and crossword puzzles, was craving a higher level of stimulation, and her social sphere did not include anyone in her peer group.

After only eight months of restless nonactivity, Emily returned to work. She accepted a position administering and scoring assessments in the addiction treatment center in the only hospital serving her small Kansas farming community. This part-time position eased her financial stress and kept her connected to a learning organization. Her life settled easily into a familiar routine. She found a small but friendly church where she taught the adult Sunday school class and agreed to teach an ecumenical Bible study on Wednesday evenings for those in her community who could not drive into the city to attend church. Life had restabilized. The imperfections were outweighed by the new sources of joy.

Not every retiree enters the stable life phase in the same way. Four distinctive styles have been suggested by gerontological researchers Walker, Kimmel, and Price: [16]

1. *reorganizers* —usually volunteer workers
2. *holding-on group*—those still engaged in paid work
3. *rocking-chair group*—those who choose to slow down to a very quiet, more disengaged pace
4. *dissatisfied group*—those who wish to be more engaged but are having trouble keeping busy

The *holding-on group* are a surprisingly dynamic cohort. The *Los Angeles Times* once printed a news release from London that listed the activities of some prominent people aged ninety years or over. It said in part:

- Pablo Picasso was still painting at ninety.
- Leopold Stokowski was still conducting at ninety.
- Pablo Casals was still playing the cello at ninety-five.
- Robert Stolz, friend of Johann Strauss, at ninety-one years of age was still getting out of bed at 7:00 A.M. to compose new songs.
- Bill Ricketts, chairman of Chappell's, the international music firm, was ninety.
- The gardening expert of British Broadcasting Corporation, Fred Streeter, was ninety-one.
- Playwright Melchor Lengyel was still working at ninety-two.
- King Gustav Adolfus VI of Sweden and President Eamon de Valera of Ireland were both in their ninetieth year.
- Titian was still painting "with incomparable steadiness of hand" when cut off by the plague at ninety-nine.
- Michelangelo was chipping away at a sculpture until a few weeks before his death in his ninetieth year.

Lydia Brontë's long-careers study, spanning the five-year period of 1987–1991, focused on 150 adults between the ages of sixty-five and one hundred one who, like their cohorts listed above, would fit the criteria for the *holding-on* category—those still engaged in paid work. A major goal of Brontë's qualitative study was to gain insights into how a long career differs from a career of conventional length in its positive impact on individuals over sixty-five.

From her research, conducted chiefly through interviews, Brontë suggested five long-career patterns: [17]

1. *Homesteaders*—those who stay in one career field all their lives, remaining captivated by their work.

2. *Transformers*—those who discover their dream job only after a major shift in their career path

3. *Explorers*—those who pursue growth and new opportunity, making many career direction changes throughout their lives

4. *Long Growth Curves and Late Bloomers*—those who do not reach a peak of vocational expression and excellence until later in life

5. *Retirees and Returners*—those who intended to leave work for permanent retirement but missed the challenge and activity and returned to their vocation

EMOTIONAL TASKS OF RETIREMENT ADJUSTMENT

With the 1961 publication of a book entitled *Growing Old*, Elaine Cuming and William Henry sparked the beginning of a new field in social theory. The authors called their ideas *disengagement theory*. Disengagement is the process of mutual withdrawal by the person and the society. This withdrawal often begins in late middle age but is especially prominent in retirement. Disengagement is "an inevitable mutual withdrawal or disengagement, resulting in decreased interaction between an aging person and others in the social systems he belongs to."[18]

The research of Cumings and Henry encompasses a survey of every culture and every historical period. Their conclusion is that the aging adults have prepared in advance for the ultimate disengagement of death through the mutual process of social disengagement. According to Cumings and Henry, the relationships of the older adult become qualitatively different—more emotionally charged and expressive, versus functional and active. Family and close friends become more and more important.

Social scientist Crawford worked with ninety-nine English couples in the process of disengagement. Through interviews he identified three retirement prototypes: [19]

1. An individual retires back to something he or she already has, for example, the family.
2. The retiree dreads retirement because of the loss of work and status.
3. The individual retires *for* something, looking forward to retirement for release from work pressures and the possibility of a different set of activities.

These retirement prototypes suggest that older adults who view retirement only as disengagement are deeply dissatisfied, while those who view retirement as reengagement to new roles are energized and fulfilled.

Benjamin Jowett said,

> Though I am growing old, I maintain that the very best part is yet to come—the time when one may see things more dispassionately and know oneself and others more truly, and perhaps be able to do more, and in religion rest centered in a few simple truths. I do not want to ignore the other side, that I will not be able to see so well or walk so far or reach so much. But there may be more peace within, more communion with God, more real light instead of distraction about many things, better relations with others, fewer mistakes.[20]

Whether or not the adult who seeks counseling in retirement planning looks forward to new opportunities or a peaceful path toward disengagement, there will be inevitable losses in life that must be recognized and faced.

In the literature on coping with losses and the grieving process, the work of Elizabeth Kubler-Ross is particularly useful. Kubler-Ross identified five stages to the adjustment process: (1) denial, (2) anger, (3) bargaining, (4) depression, and (5) acceptance. However, she suggested that there is no set schedule for these reactions, nor is there a one-way flow through the stages.[21]

Although the challenges of old age are great, so is the faithfulness of God: "Even to your old age and gray hairs I am he . . . who will sustain you" (Isa. 46:4).

HAZARDS IN POSTRETIREMENT ADJUSTMENT

It is no easy task to integrate the losses of old age—work, finances, physical and relational roles—with a renewed vitality and wholeness. There are a few common snares that drag some retirees toward despair. Chief among the snares are: (1) loss of a meaningful social network, (2) loss of a life purpose and direction, and (3) negative or ageist self-perceptions.

LOSS OF A MEANINGFUL SOCIAL NETWORK

Virtually every research finding in the field of gerontology confirms the vital impact of a social network. A strong social network is a support system against the most debilitating losses.

These support systems often center in the family, church, close friends, or neighbors. However, assessing an elder's social network can be difficult. There is the *invisibility* factor. Lack of a visible family sharing the household or living nearby does not mean the client is lacking in significant relationships. A common pattern for family systems is "intimacy at a distance." Emotional bonds can transcend geographic distance.[22]

An interview questionnaire that measures the different aspects of social support for adults after retirement is shown in appendix B. This questionnaire may be helpful in assessing the reality of an existing social network. Based on responses, appropriate assistance can be given to help the client reengage in retirement relationships, both old and new.

LOSS OF A LIFE DIRECTION OR PURPOSE

To maintain wholeness and health, individuals need to be linked with goals and purposes that transcend their own.[23] Maintaining a sense of purpose and direction is a key task in adapting to retirement, and one that many retirees fail to fully anticipate.

There is a landmark study that attempted to measure the comparative emotional health of *high-goal-directed* and *low-goal-directed* groups of early retirees. High-goal-directed retirees tended to be much more outgoing and involved in life, whereas low-goal-directed retirees were prone to be self-critical, dissatisfied with their lot, and solicitous of more emotional support. The characteristics evident in low-goal-directed retirees were similar with those associated with the narcissistic personality disorder (i.e., withdrawn, self-critical, dissatisfied, and solicitous of emotional support) as defined by psychologists Kohut and Wolf.[24]

Another type of narcissistic personality has a propensity toward shunning interpersonal contact. These people are avoidant; they do not mix well with others. These personality types suffer from isolation and are overly sensitive to personal rejection. The pattern of social withdrawal, directionlessness, and depression evidenced in the low-goal-directed retiree very closely resembles the neurotic contact-shunning personality type.[25]

As the self becomes consumed with self, the relational structures seem to implode, leaving the struggling older adult with fewer internal and external resources. A loss of goals that reach beyond the borders of the self is one of the most devastating snares of retirement adjustment.

NEGATIVE OR AGEIST SELF PERCEPTIONS

It is important that the vocational counselor be aware of a tendency in some older clients to apply ageist stereotypes to themselves, sometimes under the guise of merely being realistic. Prejudice is always damaging, but it is never more destructive than when it comes from within individuals who are prejudiced against themselves. Older adults may discount their abilities or see themselves as mentally slow, physically down, short of memory, less capable and adaptable—even when there is no supportive evidence for such realities.

How many times have you witnessed an older adult worrying about a forgotten telephone number or name of a casual acquaintance, believing it is symbolic of a weakening mind, when in reality it is not? Less frequent use, less attentiveness, and less concentration cause forgetfulness in people of all ages. These same retirees may fail to perceive the importance of their personal qualities, such as reliability, resourcefulness, stability, and sensitivity as *equally useful replacements* for any losses that may actually occur.

Empirical evidence is a powerful method for combating self-doubt. In working with elder clients who lack self-confidence, counselors must work to counteract devaluing misperceptions about aging.

The following facts gleaned from research sponsored by the National Council of Aging may dispel some common myths:[26]

- Physical strength seems to be maintained at its maximum level from the onset of biological maturity through the sixties.

- Maximum intellectual functioning appears to occur between the ages of forty-five and eighty.

- Available evidence shows little change in the ability to learn new skills and acquire new information between ages twenty and sixty-five.

- Vocabulary, information, and comprehension tests show little, if any, decline with age through the sixties.

- The functions of learning and memory, for the most part, are not significantly affected by aging.

- The middle-aged or older worker is primed to transfer learning from earlier experiences to new situations.

Perhaps the most powerful empirical evidence recently gleaned from research are findings of the Seattle Study, conducted by Dr. K. Warner Schaie, a psychologist at Pennsylvania State University. Dr. Schaie has spent over thirty years studying the development of mental processes in a group of adult residents of Seattle, Washington. The Seattle longitudinal study sample group was a randomly selected group of five hundred adults ages twenty-five to eighty-one. At age eighty, two-thirds of the group members experienced no decline but an improvement in their cognitive functioning abilities. Only one-third of the sample had experienced a moderate to large decline in overall mental abilities by age eighty. In most of these cases, decline was linked with specific illness.[27]

For retirees considering a new employment situation, the most convincing empirical evidence may be the attributes employers themselves have reported about older workers. According to the U. S. Department of Labor, employers have noted the presence of the following qualities in older adults when compared to the general work force: stability, steady work habits, less waste of time, greater reliability, less absenteeism, responsibility and loyalty, serious attitude toward job, less supervision required, less distraction by outside interests, greater inclination to stay on job.[28]

COUNSELING STRATEGIES

It is easy to forget that retirement is a significant part of one's career-life. Most of the anxiety revolves around the possibility that the loss of work will cause problems.[29] The following techniques are designed to help older adults successfully negotiate postretirement planning at a critical point in life's most tender passage of time.

ASSIST IN PLANNING

In the book *Pathfinders,* author Gail Sheehy describes the first phase of a healthy transition as *anticipation*—the work of imagining oneself in the next stage of life.[30] The transition to retirement raises planning issues around occupational pursuits, income sources, living arrangements, and possible limitations in physical capacity. All of these changes "can be met with sound and imaginative planning that makes the period of retirement as meaningful a part of the span of life as any other."[31]

Financial issues include:

social security and pensions

annuities and investments

assets and expenses

taxes

health insurance

wills and estate planning.[32]

Living arrangement issues involve decisions about:

downsizing

moving for climate

moving for family proximity

staying rooted in familiar territory

critical physical care

Financial and lifestyle decisions are directly related to occupational and vocational decisions. Since financial and lifestyle decisions are frequently charged with emotional intensity for the entire family of the retiree, discussing them with a neutral party is essential to the capacity for clear-minded planning.

Qualitative research with adults in their seventies has revealed two striking similarities in the cross section of happy and healthy elders: (1) They have prepared themselves to be engaged in activities that do not depend on anyone else's initiation to be accomplished. (2) They still practice strategic planning for at least five years into the future.[33] Happiness is sustained by the desire to learn, grow, and engage in life.

CLARIFY AFFECTIVE REACTIONS TO RETIREMENT

Individuals vary in their attitudes toward retirement. There is no universal reaction. Each retiree is to be understood on his or her own terms. Trauma, joy, anticipation, disengagement, reengagement, anger, disillusionment, depression, excitement, fear, and relief are all likely responses to the retirement transition.

ASSIST IN FINDING PART-TIME OR VOLUNTEER EMPLOYMENT

The idea of retirement as an extended vacation in not a helpful vision for most individuals. It does not take six months for endless leisure to wax and wane, leaving deeper human needs exposed. Over time the loss of old relationships and status and the absence of meaningful activity constricts personhood. Part-time volunteer work becomes a decompression chamber, releasing pent-up pressure by focusing on intentional activity. B. F. Skinner and his associate Vaughan wrote that it is not realistic to draw enough meaning from hobbies and avocational pursuits to remain fulfilled over time. They suggest *retiring from retirement* as a solution.[34]

The idea of retiring from retirement encourages elders to seek out a course of action among optional paths:

1. find new work
2. continue activities related to past work (e.g., the college professor who continues to write books although not associated with an institution)
3. become a volunteer

Criteria for choosing part-time employment are:

- committed time structure daily
- contact with people outside the nuclear family
- goals and purposes that transcend personal goals
- the work provides activity and identity[35]

MAKE APPROPRIATE REFERRALS TO COMMUNITY AGENCIES

There are a host of not-for-profit agencies that can provide activities, employment contacts, and a network of social support for older adults. One helpful resource for these agencies is the article entitled "Programs for Older Persons: A Compendium,"[36] which lists a wide variety of reputable organizations. These agencies include: the YWCA, YMCA, Forty-Plus Clubs, Foster Grandparents Program, Retired Senior Volunteer Program, Volunteers in Service to America, Peace Corps, Senior Companion Program, Service Corps of Retired Executives, U. S. Department of Labor's Senior Community Service Employment Program.[37]

ENCOURAGE INFORMATION INTERVIEWS WITH RETIRED ACQUAINTANCES

Other people in similar circumstances are the most powerful resources at *every* phase of career development—including retirement. Encourage your client to engage in a series of information interviews with people who have recently pioneered the territory of retirement. Richard Bolles suggests the following questions for sharing information.[38]

What are you enjoying the most about this period of your life?

What are you enjoying the least?

What do you wish someone had told you about retirement before you ever reached retirement?

What is the greatest problem that you face, or have faced- and how are you dealing or did you deal with that problem?

What resources and places for help, or what ideas, have you found the most helpful to you during this period of your life?

MINIMIZE THE USE OF TESTS AND ASSESSMENTS

Unlike other career clients, mature adults have a wealth of longitudinal data that are likely to yield more unique, specific, and realistic information about their skills, abilities, interests, and personality than tests and assessments. The use of their work experiences is far more productive and effective then objective testing.[39]

For some elders, the use of assessments is intimidating. They may already suffer from anxiety over the possible decline of their cognitive capabilities. Dynamics such as these will only become barriers to vocational solutions.

Conduct a Structured Life-Review

The use of a structured life-review with the whole family of the retiring adult is of great benefit to many individuals in later life. This treatment is particularly helpful for elders who are depressed over retirement or are recovering from an illness.[40]

A life-review extends the process of reminiscence into the acceptance of one's total life, including death. The involvement of significant family members can be a helpful experience for the entire extended family. Family albums, scrapbooks, genealogies, reunions, and sentimental journeys to old habitats are often therapeutic.

The resolution of later-life issues rests on the foundation of all earlier life stages. Conflicts or disappointments in earlier events may have resulted in cutoffs or frozen images that need to be seen from a new vantage point. Successive life phases need to be set in perspective of a whole life view. The transmission of family history to younger generations can be an additional bonus to such work.[41]

Richard Bolles suggests three possible mediums for the life-review.[42]

1. *A Written Review*. The written life-review serves essentially the same purpose as an autobiography. The client may relate comfortably to creating a life journal, diary, or personal history. A personal autobiography serves as a source of integrating all of one's experiences, preserving feelings and thoughts, and passing on family history to future generations.

2. *An Oral Review*. The oral review works best around a series of questions proposed by the counselor. The interview should be recorded. It is helpful for children, grandchildren, and other family members to participate in these interviews. For the sophisticated family, there is the possibility of making a video.

3. *A Graphic-Symbolic Review*. There are many ways to create a graphic-symbolic review. One is the genogram (described in detail in chap. 3), another is a life-line. This is a basic time-line that is divided into five-year segments. In chronological order,

place a dot and the date along the line for each significant decision or event. From that dot, draw a slanted line upward. On the slanted line, write about the significant event or decision.

An additional exercise with the life-line is to draw a slanted line downward for each decision or event. Then write what might have happened if you hadn't made that particular decision or experienced that event.

In *The Three Boxes of Life,* Bolles suggests a comprehensive list of questions that will aide the life-review.[43] The following is a sampling:

> What moment along your life-line stands out in sharpest detail in your memory?
>
> What faces from your past can you see most clearly? What voices can you hear most clearly? (family, classmates, playmates, colleagues, rivals, etc.)
>
> What were the events that moved you the most deeply?
>
> What were the scenes of your greatest sadness or your deepest joys?
>
> What decision do you regret the most or feel happiest about?
>
> What helped to preserve constancy in your life or brought about the most significant change?

In summary, there is life after retirement. It may be fulfilling or constricted by the attitudes, personal resources, and strategic plans and activities of the retiree. Billy Graham reminds us that the Bible does not mention retirement, but it has much to say about peace, love, and joy even into old age. "The righteous will flourish like a palm tree, they will grow like a cedar of Lebanon; planted in the house of the LORD, they will flourish in the courts of our God. They will still bear fruit in old age, they will stay fresh and green, proclaiming, 'The LORD is upright; he is my Rock, and there is no wickedness in him'" (Ps. 92:12–15).

NOTES

1. U. S. Bureau of the Census, *General Population Characteristics: United States Summary* (Washington, D.C.: U. S. Government Printing Office, 1980).

2. H. Sheppard and S. Rix, *The Graying of Working America: The Coming Crisis in Retirement-Age Policy* (New York: Macmillan, 1977).

3. B. Skinner and M. Vaughan, *Enjoy Old Age: A Program of Self-Management* (New York: Norton, 1983).

4. M. Bernstein and J. Berstein, *Social Security: The System That Works* (New York: Basic Books, 1988).

5. Statistics compiled by J. Siegel, C. Taueber, and A. Goldstein, quoted in L. Brontë, *The Longevity Factor: The New Reality of Long Careers and How It Can Lead to Richer Lives* (New York: HarperCollins, 1993).

6. Brontë, *The Longevity Factor*, xvi.

7. K. Perkins, "Psychological Implications of Women and Retirement," *Social Work* 37 (1992): 526–32.

8. J. Kieffer, "So Much for the Great American Dream of Retiring Early" *Generations* 6 (1982): 7–9.

9. J. Alder, *The Retirement Book: A Complete Early-Planning Guide to Finances, New Activities, and Where to Live* (New York: William Morrow, 1975).

10. Brontë, *The Longevity Factor*, 26.

11. Alder, *Retirement Book*.

12. L. Troll, *Early and Middle Adulthood*, 2d ed. (Pacific Grove, Calif.: Brooks/Cole, 1985).

13. G. Sheehy, *Passages: Predictable Crises of Adult Life* (New York: Dutton, 1974).

14. D. Sinick, *Counseling Older Persons: Careers, Retirement, Dying* (New York: Plenum, Human Sciences Press, 1978).

15. R. Atchley, *The Sociology of Retirement* (New York: Schenman, 1976).

16. J. Walker, D. Kimmel, and K. Price, "Retirement Style and Retirement Satisfaction: Retirees Aren't All Made Alike," *International Journal of Aging and Human Development* 12 (1980–81): 267–81.

17. Brontë, *Longevity Factor*.

18. E. Cuming and W. Henry, *Growing Old* (New York: Basic Books, 1961), 14.

19. J. Crawford, "Retirement and Disengagement," *Human Relations* 24 (1971): 255–78.

20. Quoted in D. Shelby Corlett, *Retirement Is What You Make It* (Anderson, Ind.: Warner Press, 1973), 8.

21. E. Kubler-Ross, *On Death and Dying* (New York: MacMillan, 1969).

22. F. Walsh, "The Family in Later Life," in *The Changing Family Life* Cycle, ed. B. Carter and B. McGolderick, (Boston: Allyn and Bacon, 1989).

23. M. Jahoda, "Work, Employment and Unemployment," *American Psychology* 36 (1981): 184–91.

24. H. Kohut and E. Wolf, "The Disorders of the Self and Their Treatment: An Outline," *International Journal of Psychoanalysis* 59 (1978): 413–25.

25. E. Payne, S. Robbins, and L. Dougherty, "Goal Directedness and Older-Adult Adjustment," *Journal of Counseling Psychology* 38 (1991): 302–8.

26. H. Grace, "Industrial Gerontology: Behavioral Science Perspectives on Work and Aging," *Industrial Gerontology: Curriculum Materials* (New York: National Council on the Aging, 1968), 1–84.

27. K. Schaie, "Intellectual Development in Adulthood," in *Handbook of the Psychology of Aging* (San Diego: Academic Press, 1990), chap. 17.

28. U. S. Department of Labor, *Counseling and Placement Services for Older Workers* (Washington D. C.: U. S. Government Printing Office, 1956).

29. *British Psychological Society Bulletin* 32 (1979): 309, 312–14.

30. G. Sheehy, *Pathfinders: Overcoming the Crises of Adult Life and Finding Your Own Path to Well-Being* (New York: Morrow , 1981), 100.

31. K. Close, *Getting Ready to Retire* (New York: Public Affairs Pamphlets, 1972), 3.

32. Alder, *Retirement Book.*

33. Sheehy, *Pathfinders.*

34. Skinner and Vaughan, *Enjoy Old Age.*

35. Jahoda, "Employment and Unemployment," 184–91.

36. B. Blai, "Programs for Older Persons: A Compendium," *Journal of Employment Counseling* 19 (1982): 98–105.

37. E. Herr and S. Cramer, *Career Guidance and Counseling Through the Life Span* (Boston: Scott Foresman, 1988).

38. R. Bolles, *The Three Boxes of Life: And How to Get Out of Them* (Berkeley: Ten Speed Press, 1981).

39. Sinick, *Counseling Older Persons.*

40. N. Westcott, "Application of the Structured Life-Review Technique in Counseling Elders," *Personnel Guidance Journal* 62 (1983): 180–81.

41. M. Lewis and R. Butler, "Life Review Therapy," *Geriatrics* 29 (1974): 165–73.

42. Bolles, *The Three Boxes of Life.*

43. Ibid., 360.

Chapter Nine

Surviving a Career Crisis

It was hard to believe that the woman before me was the same person whom I had met six months earlier. Last fall, when Anne Sinclair accepted the position that would move her from Cincinnati to Seattle, it was a monumental moment. As a competent, independent woman with a vibrant faith, Anne was intensely committed to her professional life. Now, she had the opportunity to apply her technical and managerial skills within a Christian organization. For her, this was the opportunity of a lifetime.

Anne's first day on the job was timed with the annual staff development retreat, which instantly drew her into the group and sealed her commitment to new colleagues, the organization, and the mission of her unit. Moving into her position of program management, Anne tackled her objectives with passion. She streamlined policies and procedures, improved customer service, established rapport with her administrative assistant, and took ownership for the vision and values of her unit. It was three and a half months later that the turbulence began when rumors started circulating that the institution was facing financial difficulties.

The unraveling of her position was dragged out over the next four months. Struggling to maintain her optimism and personal commitment, Anne continued to invest in her work. Desiring security, she clung to the reports that she was given at every level of the hierarchy that her job had a reasonable chance of being saved. Over time, Anne became increasingly distrustful and angry. She tired to push for answers. She sought advocacy where it could be found. The sense of powerlessness and betrayal were overwhelming. Enthusiasm in her job diminished daily, until finally, minutes before the organizational Christmas party, the letter arrived, delivered personally by the area vice president. Although her position had not been cut, *she had*. Since she was the last one hired, she was the first one fired in her department.

In the wake of this harrowing blow, Anne had the difficult work of launching a job search—not by choice, but by necessity. Her support network was back in Ohio. She was listless from months of false hope and denigrating fear. She was deeply discouraged and emotionally spent. Costs of relocating had emptied her bank account, leaving her financially vulnerable. Anne was experiencing a *career crisis*.

THE ANATOMY OF CAREER CRISIS

The word *career* in Latin is translated as "progress along a difficult road." In Greek, *crisis* is the "decisive moment."[1] Thus, a career crisis may be thought of as "a decisive moment on a long and difficult road."

A key distinctive between *career crisis* and *career transition* is the element of personal choice. In career transition, such as Anne's cross-country move, there is a strong sense of personal efficacy. Although the "decisive moment" may still be difficult, the move is made by the person from the will and desire for change. In a career crisis, someone else makes the decision. However, a voluntary career transition may result in an involuntary crisis. Anne's move from Cincinnati to Seattle was a career transition, while the subsequent layoff was a career crisis.

Investigative journalist Harry Maurer traveled across the country conducting interviews with a wide cross-section of people struggling with the fallout of job loss. Barry Glassner, chairman of the Department of Sociology at the University of Southern California, interviewed a group of 120 baby boomers who had gone through at least one career crisis. The interviews collected by Maurer and Glassner together create an oral history that gives much insight into the recurrent themes of depression, isolation, and self-blame that result from a career crisis.[2]

Perhaps the most debilitating and universal impact of career crisis is that of self-blame. Although individuals in career crisis feel that they have been treated unjustly, Maurer found they also, paradoxically, believe they have been the cause of their own injustice. Maurer states, "Unemployed people feel they have been robbed of something, yet on a deeper level they feel it was their fault."[3]

One managerial level professional whose job was eliminated in a layoff suggests that the very language used to describe career crisis manifests blame.

> Think about the implications of the most common statement of all, "I lost my job." In a time of touted and refuted recessions, how dare anyone be careless enough to "lose" a job? The phrase smacks of personal guilt; at the very least it hints of the onset of middle-age dementia, as in "Where did I leave my car keys?" and "Did I turn off the stove?" The unemployed haven't "lost" their jobs—they know where they are. The jobs are now overseas or they are one of the balls juggled and dropped in union-contract negotiations. Very often these lost jobs can be found listed proudly as "efficiency accomplishments" in the resumes of corporate executives.[4]

Moracco, Butchke, and Collins, a team of counselors from the University Alabama and University of Georgia who conducted research on career crisis state, "The only certainty about being fired is that it hurts."[5] These researchers discovered major similarities in nature and severity of struggles for the family of the terminated employee and the family of the terminally ill. Moracco, Butchke, and Collins identified high levels of financial difficulties, poor self-image, and negative emotions in families undergoing employment termination and terminal illness.

Dr. Greiff, a consulting psychiatrist to Harvard University's Health Service in Cambridge, Massachusetts, likens job loss to the humiliation that lurks in the proverbial nightmare about being found naked in a public place. "In our society, you are what you do, and that gets stripped from you when you get fired. You become, in a sense, vocationally naked."[6]

Who among us are likely to face a career crisis? The chances are great that you know or are related to one of the many hundreds of Americans whose job has been eliminated in recent years. Last year the U. S. Bureau of Labor Statistics reported that nearly 7.5 million people were unemployed, over 3.5 million of whom were laid off or fired. Business week has estimated that one million workers nationwide have lost their jobs in steady post-Reagan-era defense cuts alone.[7]

Barry Glassner, in his best-selling book *Career Crash*, states, "Career crashes have become a predictable crisis in many baby boomers' lives, as defining of their middle years as Vietnam or Watergate were for their youth."[8] Glassner compares the nostalgic career journey of the past generation to a calm drive in the countryside, and underscores that this is what most boomers may have anticipated for their own futures. What they actually find is that the career journey is more like a rollercoaster ride whose contours are shaped by economic turbulence, a penchant for change, and a basic anxiety—even despair—about the demands of life. According to Barry Glassner, this basic anxiety about life stands in contrast to the classic midlife crisis, which is fraught with anxiety about the encroachment of death.[9]

In addition to the overarching theme of a nonvoluntary transition with its resultant fallout of self-blame, there are a number of significant elements in a career crisis that should be understood. Of particular significance are:(1) types of career transitions, (2) types of unemployment, and (3) major impacts of unemployment.

TYPES OF CAREER CRISES

There are basically two types of career crises : (1) crises that are the result of unanticipated events and (2) crises that are the result of anticipated events that *do not* happen (nonevents).[10] Being fired, laid off, or transferred are unanticipated events. The promotion that does not occur or the desired transfer that is not approved are examples of anticipated nonevents. Some unanticipated transitions are voluntary, such as volunteering for an assignment that may or may not occur. For a transition to constitute a career crisis, however, in addition to being unanticipated, it is usually involuntary.[11]

Most people are more familiar with the type of crisis that follows a firing or a layoff than they are of the nonevent. Nonevents are often the catalysts to what author Barry Glassner has called "career crash." Sometimes a career crash may generate a genuine career crisis, but not always.[12]

According to Rantze and Feller, researchers who have focused on the experience of workers faced with a critical nonevent such as an unwanted career plateau, there are four possible responses:[13]

The Placid Approach. When Lindsey was overlooked for a coveted promotion, she told herself to accept it and to adjust. She worked hard to hide any signs of frustration and discontent. Placid responders do not express their disappointment or anger directly but continue on with business as usual. Workers who respond to a critical nonevent with the placid approach try to transfer their fulfillment to areas outside of the job situation. These placid responders may end up unwittingly creating a career crisis through passive-aggressive behavior at work.

The Hopscotch Approach. Individuals who take the hopscotch approach to resolving a career crisis remain in the organization but strive to make a lateral move. John felt the heavy hand of disapproval from his boss when he was pointedly overlooked to chair a key committee. Immediately, he began to scan the internal employee newsletter for open positions within the organization. Two month later he candidated successfully for a position in recruiting, vacating his parallel position in marketing. Hopscotchers attempt to escape the crisis by creating a different position, even if it is not a promotion. This practice is increasingly common in both the corporate and academic worlds.

The Change of Uniform Approach. After being out-promoted by a young recruit she had hired and trained herself, Jesse finally gave up and turned in her resignation to her new boss—the same employee she had supervised last year. It was time to try her hand with the competitor. Individuals who take the change of uniform approach leave the organization for a similar job in a different company with hope that the situation will provide them with more opportunity.

The Entrepreneurial Approach. When David lost his biggest account because he refused to fudge on productivity figures like the other middle mangers in his department, his decision was made. He would fix up the spare bedroom at home and start his own operation. This would allow him to maintain his own commitment to ethics and excellence in all situations. It would also provide more time with the kids. Workers who respond to a critical nonevent with the entrepreneurial approach trade their current disappointments for a new set of responsibilities, leaving the organization that initiated the crisis to start their own business or consulting firm. The entrepreneurial approach is a favored option for the baby boom generation.

TYPES OF UNEMPLOYMENT

A career crisis can occur at the personal level without being related to a companywide policy. Involuntary termination can happen as an isolated event or as a chronic, recurring pattern. It is important that vocational counselors understand the three major types of unemployment that sociologists have identified as involuntary.[14]

1. *Frictional Unemployment.* Frictional unemployment is a relatively short-term and situational state of joblessness. Frictional unemployment occurs when a worker is between jobs. About one-half to two-thirds of the unemployed fall into this category.

2. *Cyclical Unemployment.* Cyclical unemployment is job loss caused by a recession or another macroeconomic factor. This type of unemployment is the most deeply felt in manufacturing and construction industries based on the ebb and flow of supply and demand. Workers who face cyclical unemployment may be out of work for months or longer. Severe cuts in aerospace and defense that began in 1988 resulted in cyclical unemployment for 121,000 workers in Los Angeles County alone.[15]

3. *Structural Unemployment.* Structural unemployment is chronic, long-term joblessness that happens as a result of major changes in kinds of workers needed by the economy. This is unemployment caused by job obsolescence (see chap. 7). People who are replaced by new technology, imports, or geographical location (i.e., the relocation of workers hired from outside the U. S. in conjunction with NAFTA). These workers must be retrained or relocated to find employment.[16]

IMPACT OF UNEMPLOYMENT

Although the initial shock of job loss is traumatic, the long-term effects may be less devastating than is typically thought. Vocational counselors working with career crisis survivors frequently report that clients' personal stories are alive with recurring heroic images such as a phoenix rising from the ashes, the rebuilding of a war-torn city, or a successful artificial hip implant.[17]

While it would be much better not to have a crisis situation, it is also evident that most of those who face it and regain their footing through new employment see themselves as better for it.

One of the most positive impacts of career crisis is the window of opportunity it creates for career change. Loosing a job may give the license needed to consider opportunities that have only been dreamed about in the past. Lynne Dumas states, "When the umbilical cord of paychecks and employee benefits is cut, it's a good time to take the risk and go for it."[18]

Carol Hyatt, coauthor of the current bestseller *When Smart People Fail*, concurs: "Even if you did like your job, seeking out another opening forces you to reassess your goals and future options."[19]

Sociologist and UCLA professor Ralph Turner finds that people respond to life's challenges in either *institutional* terms or *impulsive* terms.[20] When faced with a job loss, those who emphasize their institutional self are focused on replacing the professional role that has been lost, while the impulsive responders are more focused on their desires for the future, unconstrained by the professional role they held in the past. It may be easier for the impulsives to use a career crisis as a window of opportunity for change than for the institutionally minded.

HAZARDS IN CAREER CRISIS ADJUSTMENT

The demands of a career journey deplete internal resources. When internal resources are not replenished, or when a person simply loses a job, a career crisis is inevitable. This section looks at (1) the impact of career burnout and (2) the damaging physiological and emotional costs of job loss.

CAREER BURNOUT

It was against the backdrop of the widespread disillusionment of the 1970s that a psychologist in a New York City clinic coined the term "burnout."[21] Today, *burnout* is used to describe the state of physical and mental depletion attributed to *excessive strivings to attain an unrealistic career goal* imposed by self, society, or the organization. Symptoms of burnout include a flatness in personality, loss of charisma, fatigue, headaches, sleeplessness, anger, suspicion, paranoia, and depression.

A client dealing with career burnout used graphic images to express how he felt: "I feel like a can of pop that has lost its carbonation. Nothing is left but a smooth, flat syrup that I tasted and poured out in disgust. It is only a matter of days before someone finds my empty shell of a can, flattens it with a crunch, and tosses it in the garbage."

Stress on the job is seen as the precipitating factor of career burnout. It is more prevalent in the helping professions, where dual pressures of devotion to helping and unrealistic expectations ultimately combine in burnout.[22]

Burnout is not to be confused with tiredness or even the state of exhaustion that accompanies adrenaline depletion after a demanding task. Burnout is not the result of a single difficult event; it is cumulative. The worker struggling with burnout may begin with barely noticeable changes that increase with intensity until there is a crisis. It may lead to chronic depression, substance abuse, or even suicide if left unresolved.[23]

Psychological and Physiological Costs of Job Loss

Advice in almost every popular article on coping with job loss emphasizes two messages: "Don't get down on yourself," and "Don't take it personally." There are also multiple warnings to the readers that they can expect to ride an emotional roller coaster of shock, disbelief, fear, anger, and—perhaps the most crippling emotion of all—shame.

Shame occurs with the loss of a job because the disapproval is from some authority with power to judge. When a worker has been fired, it feels as if everyone disapproves. Guilt comes from what I do. Shame comes from who I am. If I am fired, I must be an unworthy person.

Grace Keaton, a small, animated woman in her late thirties, was interviewed by Maurer after being fired from a job in publishing that she had held for fifteen years.

> It was the worst blow I ever had. I've been divorced. My father died a few months before I got fired. Both constitutionally and by event I've been through a lot of emotional upheaval in my life and I've never been through anything like getting fired. . . . For a while I was persuaded that I must be not only as bad as the company must have thought I was to fire me, but much worse than that. Probably the world's worst. Probably I didn't deserve to live. It doesn't simply take away your self-confidence. It destroys you. Utterly.[24]

Dr. Greiff, who coined the term "vocational nakedness" to describe the emotional cost of career crisis, has also documented that individuals in career crisis are far more susceptible to colds, headaches, and high blood pressure than the general population. On an even more serious note, Dr. Harvey Brenner, professor of behavioral sciences and health education at Johns Hopkins University in Baltimore, has discovered a statistical relationship between job loss and state mental health admissions, deaths from cardiovascular and renal disease, cirrhosis of the liver, and suicide rates. [25]

With the loss of structure it is common for people to let their physical standards deteriorate. Intense anxiety and pain are often accompanied by an exaggeration depending on the coping mechanisms each individual takes for granted in more normal times. Many overwhelmed individuals plunge into overindulgent behavior such as excessive eating or sleeping. Physical symptoms such as insomnia may also occur. Psychologist Marilyn Puder-Yost, who practices in the Wall Street area where there is a high rate of burnout, places a high premium on simply supporting the client in maintaining pre-crisis standards of health.[26]

COUNSELING STRATEGIES FOR CAREER CRISIS INTERVENTION

A knowledge of the following techniques designed specifically to help workers negotiate the devastated landscape of a career crisis may be effective. The goal is to help the suffering client move forward in the face of unwanted career transition with as much grace and savvy as possible.

PRESCRIBE A JOURNAL

Psychologists at Southern Methodist University and the outplacement firm of Drake Bean Morin (both in Dallas) asked forty-one recently fired, middle-aged, professional men to spend twenty minutes writing for five consecutive days.[27] About half were told to focus on the trauma of losing a job, while the others simply recorded their daily activities. A control group of twenty-two unemployed volunteers did no writing at all. Eight months later, the researchers found that *more than half of those who had written about their job loss had found new positions, while fewer than a quarter of the diary keepers and even fewer from the nonwriting group had done* so. All three groups had put similar efforts into their job searches.

The researchers concluded that not dealing with the hurt and anger that job loss causes can sabotage the job search process, particularly in the context of interviewing. The power of journaling as an intervention is twofold: (1) to assist closed individuals in opening up and getting their feelings on paper and (2) to allow expression of feelings surrounding the loss of the job, thus bringing closure to a traumatic experience.

Instruct the client to:

1. find a quiet place with no disturbances
2. write without censoring any content or paying attention to spelling or grammar
3. write continuously for about twenty minutes
4. repeat steps 1–3 for at least five consecutive days

Journals have also been used successfully to stave off the negative consequences of burnout.[28] One strategy for burnout is to create a daily log of stressful events. The log should be kept for about six weeks as a means for recording: (1) what events precede the feeling of stress, (2) when in the day the stress occurs, (3) what the feelings are like, and (4) what response results. Each day is rated by the client on a ten-point scale (1=disaster and 10=easy and enjoyable).

After the journal is analyzed, the next step is to apply coping techniques for the most debilitating stressors. Attention may be given to such things as communication deficits, work overload, role conflict or ambiguity, or training deficits.

PROVIDE SUPPORT IN DEALING WITH LOSS

Regardless of the specific context, job loss creates a wide range of intense emotions—shame, guilt, anger, self-loathing, denial, shock, relief. It is strategic for the vocational counselor to be well versed in the basic nondirective, client-centered skills.[29]

Carl Rogers' client-centered approach conceptualizes the counselor's use of self in the three therapeutic qualities[30] of

warmth—a nonpossessive, nondirective, but enthusiastic concern,

genuineness—a congruence in recognizing and sharing personal feelings with the client as it seems helpful

empathy—the ability to see the world through the client's eyes and understand its impact.

As the client begins to fully acknowledge loss, a void is often created in his or her life. Suddenly, pieces of the client's identity, cherished perceptions of self, and sense of life purpose and meaning, as well as a large piece of the social support network are missing. In the face of these losses, the vocational counselor is called on to serve as a psychic shoulder of understanding support for the client.[31] The client's self-worth, identity, and support systems have all been weakened. The client must be reassured about these losses. Time for mourning may be important.

Counselors need to help clients learn to work *with* rather than *against* the transition process brought on by career loss.[32] Before the client can move forward, he or she must first deal with the full impact of the loss. The foundation of comfort allows the emotional intensity to decrease, freeing new energy both for understanding what has happened and planning the future.

CREATE A NETWORK OF PROFESSIONAL SUPPORT

One of the most important buffers for persons in career crisis is the presence of social support that specifically provides reassurance. Persons who have lost their job need affirmation concerning their competencies and abilities.[33] Because this affirmation has been provided by coworkers and supervisors, a critical source of support is lost along with the person's job— precisely at the time it is needed most.[34] Although friends and family may be valuable in providing other types of support, research shows that affirmation from sources outside the work setting are less effective than those from people at work.[35]

Finding alternative sources of emotional support may be a key to helping unemployed workers gain their equilibrium. Many job-search counselors begin with some sort of self-assessment of skills and experience. If these assessments are conducted in a small group of job-search clients, they may become the foundation for much-needed new support. This technique is commonly used in outplacement counseling. Self-assessment exercises, when shared with a group of trusted peers, may become a useful way to provide reassurance of professional worth and support.[36] The clients can become a new reference group of "coworkers," who are capable of validating the self-worth of one another.

HELP MAINTAIN PREUNEMPLOYMENT ACTIVITY AND DAILY STRUCTURE

Because work meets so many important human needs, it is important for attention to be given to helping clients maintain a positive structure in their daily lives. It is crucial that unemployed persons continue to participate in their regular activities.

Additionally, it is important to help unemployed clients generate equivalent work experiences until employment is available. Job seekers are timid about engaging in activity that is not a part of their job search. One of the least-known job-search techniques is to serve as a volunteer in the same industry or company in which employment is sought. An unpaid internship can be helpful if increased experience or contacts in a *new* field are needed. Developing opportunities for volunteer work of any nature, as well as involvement in new leisure activities, will boost the morale of a client.

Men need to relax gender-role stereotypes within the home that inhibit them from taking a more active part in the daily care of the family. These roles will provide the fuel clients need for maintaining a growing and productive stance in the season between jobs.

HELP THE CLIENT OVERCOME LEARNED HELPLESSNESS

In the midst of career crises, many people fall prey to what researcher Dr. Martin Seligman has called "learned helplessness."[37] Researchers discovered the condition of learned help-lessness by accident in an experiment planned to measure something altogether different.

A group of dogs in a divided box were given a warning so they could escape a slight electric shock by jumping over the narrow divider. (The shock was the same type of jolt you might feel from touching a doorknob on a dry winter day.) In one case, the dogs were accidentally obstructed when they tried to escape. Researchers discovered the error and corrected it. But the dogs had learned from their experience that they couldn't escape, so they just stayed in the box and took the shock when there was easy access for escape.

It was not long before Seligman discovered that you do not have to be a dog to fall victim to learned helplessness. People who fall victim to learned helplessness look at life in *personal* terms. If something bad happens to them (such as losing a job), it is all their fault. They also see bad events and experiences as *permanent*. It is not just this situation that is bad, but their entire careers have gone down the tubes, and they assume they probably will never recover. Persons who are faced with a career crisis often feel stuck. Time is frozen, and there will never be progress again. They also see a crisis in *pervasive* terms. Not only are they defective in their careers, but they are overall failures as people. The career crisis experience will color everything they try to do in the future because they now see themselves as helpless.

People need optimism to cope with crisis. Therefore, it is important for the counselor to help them see that their problems are not all personal. Help them account for all the external factors that were beyond their control. Help them see that the situation is not permanent, nor is it pervasive—the one crisis will not take over life for all time. As one sage taught us, "This too shall pass."

ESTABLISH LINKS WITH COMMUNITY RESOURCES

While the vocational counselor cannot fill the roles of a financial counselor and social worker, it is important to become personally acquainted with the human and financial resources available to individuals in job crises. Many counselors rely heavily on services offered by the United Way, consumer credit counseling bureaus, and others. Counselors should become familiar enough with available community resources to make referrals comfortably when specific outside assistance is needed by a client.

SUSTAIN COMMITMENT UNTIL THE CLIENT IS REEMPLOYED

Often the most crucial time for the client is *after* the crisis, when the pain has been sorted through, a new direction has been made, a resume has been crafted, and job-search training has taken place. Armed with new enthusiasm, hopes are often dashed when that first job offer does not come as anticipated. During these dry and discouraging periods in the job search, the assistance of a career counselor becomes essential in controlling damage to the client's fragile self-esteem.[38] Timely and effective resolution of the client's self-doubt is crucial to sustaining the confidence that is attractive to potential employers. Research shows that positive self-perception and self-confidence do impact the job search, leading to an increase in job search activity and greater opportunities for reemployment.[39]

There is no way to escape the pain of a career crisis or job loss, but there are ways to survive and recover. That is the business of the vocational counselor who knows how to contain self-damage, rebuild lost confidence, open new horizons, and then stay the course until the unemployed person is happily working again.

NOTES

1. E. Jennings, *The Executive in Crisis* (New York: McGraw-Hill, 1965).

2. B. Glassner, *Career Crash: America's New Crisis and Who Survives* (New York: Simon and Schuster, 1994).

3. H. Maurer, *Not Working: An Oral History of the Unemployed* (New York: Holt, Reinhart and Winston, 1979), 5.

4. M. Purcell, "Really, I'm Fine—Just Ask Me," *Newsweek,* 20 November 1992, 12–13.

5. J. Moracco, P. Butche, and M. Collins, "Professional Career Services: An Exploratory Study," *Journal of Employment Counseling* 28 (1991): 21.

6. L. Dumas, "You're Fired," *Health* 20 (July 1988): 38–40, 74.

7. E. Schine, "From Hughes to Hell—and Back," *Business Week,* 18 October 1993, 76–78.

8. Glassner, *Career Crash*, 16.

9. Ibid., 32.

10. N. Schlossberg, *Counseling Adults in Transition* (New York: Springer, 1984).

11. B. Hopson and J. Adams, "Towards an Understanding of Transitions: Defining Some Boundaries of Transition," in *Transition: Understanding and Managing Personal Change*, ed. J. Adams, J. Hayes, and B. Hopson (Montclair, N.Y.: Allenheld and Osumun, 1977): 1–19.

12. Glassner, *Career Crash*.

13. K. Rantze and R. Feller, "Counseling Career-Plateaued Workers During Times of Social Change," *Journal of Employment Counseling* 22 (1985): 23–28.

14. P. Kelvin and J. Jarrett, *Unemployment: Its Social Psychological Effects* (Cambridge: Cambridge University Press, 1985).

15. Schine, "From Hughes to Hell—and Back," 76–78.

16. M. Weinstein, "A Primer on Unemployment," *Occupational Outlook Quarterly* 23 (1979): 24–27.

17. E. Herr and S. Cramer, *Career Guidance and Counseling Through the Life Span* (Boston: Scott, Foresman, 1988), 379.

18. Dumas, "You're Fired," 38–40, 74.

19. Hyatt and Gottlieb, *When Smart People Fail*.

20. R. Turner, "The Real Self: From Institute to Impulse," *American Journal of Sociology* 81 (1976): 989–1016.

21. H. Freudenberger, "Staff Burnout," *Journal of Social Issues* 30 (1974): 159–64.

22. H. Freudenberger and G. Richelson, *Burnout: The High Cost of High Achievement* (Garden City, N.Y.: Anchor Press, 1980).

23. Herr and Cramer, *Career Guidance*, 383.

24. Maurer, *Not Working*, 19.

25. Dumas, "You're Fired," 38–40, 74.

26. Ibid.

27. D. Willensky, "Writing Off the Unemployment Blues," *American Health* 12 (June 1993): 35.

28. J. Cedoline, *Job Burnout in Public Education: Symptoms, Causes, and Survival Skills* (New York: Teachers College Press, 1982).

29. J. Burdett, "Easing the Way Out: Consultants and Counselors Help Terminated Executives Strategically and Psychologically," *Personnel Administrator* 33 (1988): 157–66.

30. C. Rogers et al., *The Therapeutic Relationship and Its Impact* (Madison: University of Wisconsin Press, 1967).

31. R. Mirabile, "Outplacement as Transition Counseling," *Journal of Employment Counseling* 22 (1985): 39–45.

32. Ibid.

33. B. Mallinckrodt and J. Bennett, "Social Support and the Impact of Job Loss in Dislocated Blue-Collar Workers," *Journal of Counseling Psychology* 39 (1992): 482–89.

34. R. Weiss, "The Provisions of Social Relationships," in *Doing Unto Others*, ed. Z .Rubin (Englewood Cliffs, N.J.: Prentice-Hall, 1974).

35. J. House, *Work, Stress and Social Support* (Reading, Mass.: Addison-Wesley, 1981).

36. D. Steinweg, "Implications of Current Research for Counseling the Unemployed," *Journal of Employment Counseling* 27 (1990): 37–41.

37. M. Seligman, *Learned Optimism* (New York: Alfred A. Knopf, 1991).

38. S. Guinn, "Outplacement—Separating the Myths From the Realities: What Professional Outplacement Should Include," *Organizational Development Journal* 6 (1988): 58–61.

39. R. Kanfer and C. Halin, "Individual Differences in Successful Job Searches Following Layoff," *Personnel Psychology* 38 (1985): 835–47.

Chapter Ten

Women and
Career Development

JANICE IS A FORTY-TWO-YEAR OLD WOMAN who is married to a skilled carpenter. She has two teenage children in school. For the past three years, Janice has been attending classes at a local community college. She now wishes to go to a four-year liberal arts college but is wavering on the choice of a major. Janice is basically struggling to choose between education and business. She has a slightly higher interest in teaching but is afraid that the education major will take an extra year since some of her credits will not transfer to the new college. She is also afraid that it will be more difficult to find a teaching job near her home. Janice has limited emotional support for her career journey. Her husband tolerates this pursuit of a college degree but complains about her lack of attention to the children.

Some days Janice feels deflated by her husband's pressure, the kids' demands, and her school deadlines. She can hardly wait to graduate so she will not have to deal with school-home problems anymore. However, she really enjoys her classes and is an excellent student. Her self-image has changed for the better, and Janice has grown to believe that she is a competent, capable person with creative ideas.

By the year 2000, one of every two American women will be employed.[1] Janice will be one among the women who will constitute 47 percent of the work force. Her experience will be shared with many of her friends, who will also be working outside the home. In a twenty-year time span, from 1970 to 1990, the number of women in management jobs climbed from 24 percent to almost 40 percent.[2] Although women are entering the work force, their dreams for career success are not necessarily parallel to men. Unlike men, whose career dreams focus largely on career growth and success, women's dreams seem to uniquely incorporate both career and family.[3]

DEVELOPMENTAL TASKS FOR WOMEN

Few issues spark more passion than whether females are equally productive with men in the world of work. Research suggests few important differences among men and women in job performance. No consistent male-female differences in problem solving, analytical skills, competitive drive, motivation, leadership, sociability, or learning ability have been substantiated.[4] However, no one denies the physical superiority of the muscle system in men.

TRADITIONAL STAGE MODELS OF ADULT VOCATIONAL DEVELOPMENT

According to Erik Erikson and many others, men and women are similar in achieving intimacy, generativity, and integrity (see chap. 7). In the late 70s Daniel Levinson wrote a landmark book, *The Seasons of a Man's Life.* According to Levinson, vocational development is lifelong and is experienced differently through distinct stages.[5]

1. *Growth*—ages 0 to 14. This is a formative time, with an unfolding self-concept and a growing awareness about the meaning of work in life.

2. *Exploration*—ages 15 to 24. This is a time to reach an occupational decision.

3. *Establishment*—ages 25 to 44. The development of competence occurs during this stage This is a time to reach an occupational decision.

4. *Maintenance*—ages 45 to 65. This period is marked by wisdom, continuity, and a sustained vocational commitment.

5. *Decline*—ages 65 and over. The stage for completion and letting go.

Although this five-stage model is based on male research groups, vocational counselors have made the transition to the vocational development of women.

GENDER DIFFERENCES IN LIFE ORIENTATION

Experts on gender agree, however, that the sexes develop strikingly different orientations to life. Men define themselves through goal-oriented and assertive activity, while women define themselves through interdependent, nurturing relationships.

Men assess their worth by comparing their achievements against those of others. Advanced education, financial security, prestige, and power are common male paths toward personal definition.[6] In contrast, women are more likely to gauge the quality of their lives—including their work lives—by the tone of their relationships with other people.[7] For women, a sense of community at work is a crucial element for their fulfillment. Meaning in a women's career is often gained through enhancing the development of those who are close.[8]

From the time boys emerge on the playground at elementary school they are likely to compete in team sports. These games often demand knowledge of two things: (1) how to play *with* those whom they dislike, and (2) how to compete *against* those whom they like. This style, incorporating competition and conflict, is carried over into the workplace, especially in the traditional corporate culture.

Girls, on the other hand, have generally grown up avoiding conflict and competition with friends or foe. Girls choose games based on achieving a personal best rather than on direct competition. Research shows that girls will almost always choose to end a game if conflict breaks out. They subordinate the game to the relationship.[9]

There is strong evidence that these feminine habits carry over into the organizational setting. One study designed to measure women's internal responses to success in the workplace found that success anxiety was present only in women whose success was won at the expense of another's failure. Thus, once again, early patterns of relating in competition and conflict become evident in the interpersonal context of work.[10]

Overall, there is much evidence to support the notion that women enjoy more social support from their relationships than men. However, they may also experience higher stress from giving more support than they receive from others (especially men).[11]

What consequences do these gender differences have in the workplace? Sociologist Carol Gilligan believes women have difficulty incorporating both self-care and care for others into career identity. Trying to merge these two spheres often results in a meandering career pattern.[12]

VOCATIONAL PATTERNS OF WOMEN

As women seek to combine love and work in their pursuit of intimacy, generativity, and integrity, they choose one of the following patterns:

1. *Caregivers.* These women are established in a commitment to their domestic role from their early twenties.

2. *Nurturers Who Defer Achievement.* These women postpone career efforts to marry and start a family with the intention of developing a career later.

3. *Achievers Who Defer Nurturing.* These women postpone motherhood and/or marriage to spend six or seven years completing their professional preparation. However, women who choose to establish careers before mother-

hood may feel out of synchronization with peers whose children are older.

4. *Integrators.* These women attempt to combine marriage, career, and motherhood all at once, usually beginning all three roles in their twenties. Women with this career-life pattern may find it difficult to watch promotions and prized assignments go to coworkers who are free from the added restrictions of marriage and motherhood.[13]

5. *Single Servers.* These women are often committed to serving as a caretaker for the family of humanity in such roles as missionary, clergy, or social worker.[14]

WOMEN'S VOCATIONAL PATTERNS VERSUS THE TRADITIONAL STAGE MODEL

Many developmental specialists suggest that women have different developmental patterns than men. In a chapter entitled "The Seasons of a Woman's Life," J. Bardwick examines the experiences of women as they move through the stages of adult life.[15] It is helpful to compare these observations about women's vocational development with Levinson's life and vocational stages based on the experiences of men.

Levinson characterizes the *establishment* stage as a time for stabilizing oneself in a career. Bardwick suggests that career women between the ages of thirty and forty are concerned with their delay in having children. Also, career women at this stage are concerned about balancing their emerging professional role with their femininity. For some women, professional success brings a turning point toward dependence rather than concern for individual accomplishment. This kind of career journey fits the pattern of Achievers Who Defer Nurturing.

The June 1987 issue of *Business Week* featured an article entitled "Corporate Women: They're About to Break Through to the Top." Diane Folzenlogen Stanley, a financial wizard who was among the top one hundred corporate women in 1976, explained her transition from career to family. Diane was treasurer of Electronic Data Systems Corporation (EDS) and slated for a brilliant, high-profile career. As she began longing for a family, however, her motivations changed, and the corporate world lost its magnetism. Diane walked away from her career to start a family. [16]

Levinson describes the *maintenance* stage as a time to consolidate one's gains and update career skills. Bardwick believes that women between the ages of forty and fifty (late-establishment and early-maintenance stages) are just starting to develop more autonomy and become more independent. By this time, those who gave up careers to raise children may now return to a career. This type of career journey fits the pattern of the Nurturers Who Defer Achievement.

According to Bardwick, women over fifty can make substantial career accomplishments. Their husband's retirement or death may open up more career demands and opportunities. *Caregiver* women often have careers that blossom unexpectedly after the loss of their husband.

The journeys of men and women do not parallel. Men choose a career and then follow a linear progression up their institutional ladder, reaching a plateau. They may stay at this plateau until retirement. In contrast, women's careers are more complex, with more interruptions, lateral moves, and transitions—a pattern similar to that of a patchwork quilt.[17]

Because of the complexities of women's careers, recent studies question the appropriateness of any stage models for women.[18] In the place of stages, there are four central themes in women's development.[19]

1. Women experience intense role confusion early in their development.
2. Women are more inhibited in their self-expression.
3. Women tend to defer career aspirations to family responsibilities.
4. Women's developmental patterns are individualized and unique.

Mary Catherine Bateson, daughter of the famous anthropologist Margaret Mead, characterized the stage-defiant career-family journeys of women as a model of artistry, likened to a jazz ensemble, composed extemporaneously. She says, "The arts of improvisation involve recombining partly familiar materials in new ways, often in ways especially sensitive to context, interaction, and response. . . . Jazz exemplifies artistic activity that is at once individual and communal, performance that is both repetitive and innovative, each participant sometimes providing background support and sometimes flying free."[20]

HAZARDS IN WOMEN'S CAREER DEVELOPMENT

Managing the complexity of the career journey can be extremely challenging for a woman. Three unique struggles women encounter on the road are: (1) dual roles, (2) the identity tension line, and (3) the glass ceiling.

DUAL ROLES

Counselors have identified five areas of stress common to couples who are both pursuing full-time careers and have at least one child:[21]

- *Overload Dilemmas.* These are the daily stresses and strains that arise from the management of a household and child-rearing activities over and above work demands.

- *Personal Norm Dilemmas.* These are the conflicts arising from the tensions between what the dual-career parents personally consider a proper lifestyle and what is the stereotypical proper lifestyle. Caught in these tensions, couples often question their own values and judgments.

- *Dilemmas Of Identity.* These are the conflicts associated with the role of each individual. The dual tasks often leave the individuals wondering "Who am I?" "Am I a good parent?" "A good worker?"

- *Social Network Dilemmas.* These are the conflicts associated with the availability and support of relatives, friends, and other associates. Issues of discretionary time, increased support needs, and lifestyle conflicts add to these dilemmas.

- *Role Cycle Dilemmas.* These conflicts are associated with family life cycle changes that produce career stress. The demands of an infant are different from those of a toddler, and the demands of a school-age child are different

from those of an adolescent. Each stage of child development calls for different responses and makes unique
demands on the parents.

Role-cycle dilemmas are the reason women periodically
leave and reenter the workforce. Upon the birth of a child,
some women may take a standard maternity leave that allows
them to reenter their position after a matter of weeks. However, others may elect to stay out for a longer time and forfeit
their position. These women often find that returning to the
career they left behind is no longer a fulfilling prospect. In any
case, reentry into the workplace can be traumatic. Counselors
need to be sensitive to the inevitable fluctuations in self-esteem
that accompany reentry after a woman has been immersed in
her home.

THE IDENTITY TENSION LINE

Darlene was employed in a Christian college as a vocational
counselor—a role that she thoroughly enjoyed. The professional
challenges were invigorating. After a few years, Darlene's desire to expand and grow professionally motivated her to
pursue a doctorate. She tackled her studies with enthusiasm,
enjoying the enhancement of new ideas and theories in her
work.

However, the scholastic activities had an unanticipated impact on Darlene's life. The combination of work and school had
tipped a delicate balance, and Darlene gradually experienced
a loss of self-steem. She began to crave feminine activities such
as cooking, decorating, and spending time with children. The
sense of her own femininity plummeted, and she experienced
a general loss of professional motivation.

Crossing the *identity tension line* is one of the most difficult
impediments women face in their careers. The identity tension
line is that invisible point beyond which the demands of career
call for behavior that is uncharacteristic of their gender—either
male or female.[22] Many women who are attempting to balance
the demands of work and home are stretched beyond their ability to adjust. Pushing their husbands into traditional women's
work in the home as well as taking on professional roles that

require more masculine traits causes them ultimately to lose their sense of themselves as women.

The work situation may not allow a woman to express the characteristics she considers to be the heart of her feminine identity. Characteristics such as responsiveness, accommodation, and nurturance may make it difficult for her to project authority in the workplace. Women feel uncomfortable in relinquishing these feminine traits or allowing the emergence of other traits that have been characterized as masculine. Some research suggests that women generally become more anxious after asserting themselves, whereas men generally experience a sense of relief after asserting themselves.[23]

The conflict generated by the paradoxical needs of a women for competence and success and the comfort of a socially sanctioned role and style is the dilemma of the identity tension line. There is a risk to self-esteem and a loss of affirmation from others when familiar styles of relating are relinquished for uncharted adventure.

THE GLASS CEILING

Recent evidence suggests that discrimination against working women continues. It is often subtle and indirect, but it is there. In a longitudinal study on gender and power in organizations, Ragins and Sundstrom provided a convincing analysis of how women are systematically blocked from real power in organizations.[24] A subtle, transparent, yet strong barrier called the *glass ceiling* keeps women stuck in jobs with little authority and lower pay than their male counterparts.[25]

The glass ceiling is an impenetrable barrier that allows women to hold positions just one step away from upper management. They are held in a position that never really affords them the opportunity to advance into top management with its rewards and responsibilities.[26]

Many women in executive positions leave their jobs after they become disenchanted with a culture that holds them back. In surveys over a ten-year period, *Fortune* magazine found that nearly a third of the women studied had resigned from their jobs, but not because of the conflict between work and family. Instead, they departed because of a perception that they could go no further in their organization.[27]

In her book *Breaking Through the Glass Ceiling,* Morrison, president of the New Leaders Institute in San Diego, found that women who were vocal about their gender were more likely to have their careers derailed. According to Morrison, "They were seen as wanting too much for themselves or for other women."[28] When this disillusioning effect is added to the responsibilities for home and family that women frequently assume and compounded by fewer opportunities for mentors and informal relationships with work colleagues, women professionals encounter a different work environment than do their male peers.

COUNSELING STRATEGIES FOR WOMEN

The following techniques are designed to help women tackle the unique demands and challenges of a career and to enjoy the rewards of the feminine career journey.

SUPPORT CLIENTS IN MANAGING DUAL ROLES— HOMEMAKER AND WORKER

Any counseling models that fail to address how women blend the two domains of work and family do not represent women's reality accurately. Counselors need to be aware of a variety of styles for blending the roles of work and nurturing, depending on whether the counselee is married or single, intending to have children or not.[29]

Four suggestions for effective vocational counseling with women regarding their need for combining childbearing and work can serve as a guide.[30]

1. *Help women who are planning to assume full-time caregiving roles to be more satisfied with their choice by carefully assessing their options for an eventual return to employment.* Also, consider ways for maintaining their professional competence while they are unemployed.

Carol, a labor and delivery nurse, had invested much time and energy into her career. Her love for patients had motivated her to pursue special training in grief-work that allowed her to serve parents with loss through miscarriage, stillbirth, and other complications. She had extraordinary tenderness and effectiveness. Like most nurses, Carol had put in several years working evenings and weekends before she earned the convenient schedule she now enjoyed working four ten-hour days each week. Carol was expecting her first child and had a strong desire to take a leave from work for the baby's first year.

Before resigning, Carol decided to meet with a career counselor. The counselor helped Carol to look realistically at the turbulence of the healthcare industry and to design several optional scenarios for her return to work. First, Carol decided to continue her activity in the hospital on an informal basis as the leader of a parents support group. While this was not a formal paid position, it would keep Carol current in her specialization and would provide uninterrupted relationships with her colleagues. This would also allow Carol to monitor the changes in her field firsthand.

After carrying out her plan, Carol eventually decided not to return to the hospital setting but, instead she transitioned into a position making home visits to convalescing mothers and their infants. If Carol had not continued her informal involvement in the hospital, most likely she would have attempted to return to her old position only to find herself overwhelmed by renovations in hospital management. She would not have been prepared for the new pressures for productivity, increased patient numbers, and management driven by the bottom line.

2. *Help women to combine career and family roles by assessing the availability of substitute child care, the possibility of flexible work hours, part-time employment, and employment that does not involve separation from small children.* A careful evaluation requires an examination of needs and feelings as well as brainstorming and researching multiple options.

Cindy and Paul had full-time positions in two different educational organizations. Prior to the birth of their baby, they sought the assistance of a career counselor to explore options for their future. After assessing their situation, Cindy approached her employer about a part-time position. To accomplish this, she had to step out of an administrative role and move back into a professional direct-service role. When their baby girl arrived Cindy was able to maintain a high level of involvement with her baby—she worked two and a half days and stayed home two and a half days.

Paul also approached his employer about flexible employment arrangements. His strategy was different. After outlining his daily commuting time and other factors related to the nature of his work, Paul negotiated one day a week of full-time work in the home without compromising his position. With the addition of a fax and a modem, a spare bedroom was transformed into a working office in Paul and Cindy's home. Childcare was arranged for the additional day and a half a week, and emergency backup plans were covered by extended family.

3. *Encourage women to seek out other women who have made similar choices for nurturing family and pursuing a career.* As was mentioned previously, people in similar circumstances are useful resources at *every* phase of career development. Encourage your client to engage in a series of information interviews with people who have already tried the dual roles. The following questions may serve as a catalyst for the exchange of information.

What are you enjoying the most about this period of your life?

What are you enjoying the least?

What resources and places for help—or what ideas—have you found the most helpful to you during this period of your life?

What do you wish someone had told you about this transition before you made your decision on how to handle it?

What is the greatest problem that you face or have faced as a parent? With dual roles? How are you dealing with that problem?

4. *After the woman chooses how to divide or delegate career-home responsibilities, the counselor must help each marriage partner deal with the pressures inherent in that choice.* Careful attention must be given to:

- asking each other for assistance and suppport
- realistically limiting the number of additional obligations taken on at any one time

- clarifying expectations, goals, and needs with each other
- establishing time schedules (especially time for being alone and together)
- making decisions about outside help for domestic, maintenance, and childcare needs
- taking time to get away together to relax
- planning for emergencies—having backup plans for situations that are not a part of the schedule (e.g., sickness, trip out of town).[31]

5. *The support of the husband is crucial in adjustment to maternal employment.* The effective vocational counselor will help each spouse understand the implications of personal choices for each other. Even though it is difficult, the counselor needs to explore the emotional hot buttons that are likely to emerge before final decisions are made. This process calls for *each spouse to be present.*

DESIGN STRATEGIES FOR COMBATING HARASSMENT

Amber had always enjoyed working with her supervisor, an amiable and gifted worker who had treated her with respect and appreciation. That is why she was shocked by their recent encounter. It occurred casually, while they were enjoying their first cup of coffee for the day with several colleagues, who had gradually disappeared into their offices. Amber had turned to go when her supervisor looked at her with a quizzical smile. "You'll never guess what I dreamed about you last night." Expecting a lighthearted story, Amber asked what he had dreamed. "If you want the sordid details, you'll have to shut the door first," he countered. Suddenly, an internal alarm signaled and her knees felt weak. "Actually, I'm running late for a meeting; better take off." "Okay, but all I know is, I'll never look at you the same way again."

Amber tried to brush the uncomfortable incident aside. She tried to convince herself there was nothing to it. But later that day, her supervisor dropped another suggestive innuendo. Amber knew her comfortable, collegial relationship was now severely threatened.

Counselors with women need to take the gendered context of the work environment seriously in preparing their clients. It is not alarmist to teach women how to recognize and deal with experiences that range from subtle to extreme in sexual discrimination and harassment. There are several ways to educate and prepare women to deal with the uncomfortable problem of sexual harassment.

One effective counseling technique is role-playing. However, the process must include making the client aware of: (1) boundaries (i.e., "If you mean what I suspect you mean, now is the time to stop."), (2) a network of support, and (3) the legal steps to take against discrimination and harassment (i.e., personnel officer, ombudsman, trusted supervisor, regional lawyer known for sensitivity and specialized skill in these issues, etc.).

Finally, educate women to be proactive, swift, and confident in seeking justice. Five escalating levels of sexual harassment have been defined to help women assess their experiences.[32]

Level 1: Gender Harassment. This level of harassment includes verbal remarks or nontouching behaviors that are sexist in nature. Examples include suggestive stories or rude, sexist remarks.

Level 2: Seductive Behavior. This level of harassment includes inappropriate sexual advances. These advances may be verbal or physical.

Level 3: Sexual Bribery. This includes requests for sexual favors in return for some kind of reward. Often offered by a superior, this kind of harassment could include the offer of a higher grade, a raise in pay, or a promotion.

Level 4: Sexual Coercion. This approach is the opposite of sexual bribery. An individual is coerced into sexual activity by threat of punishment. For example, when a woman is told that if she does not engage in sexual activity she will fail a course, lose a job, or be demoted, she is being coerced. The perpetrator intentionally threatens a woman's career.

Level 5: Sexual Assault. This kind of behavior includes forceful attempts to touch, grab, fondle, or kiss.

The trauma of sexual harassment depends on several factors: the personality and needs of the individual, the power of the harasser, the level of harassment, the nature of the situation, the duration of the harassment, and the presence or lack of support from colleagues and superiors.Whatever the level of sexual harassment your client faces, the role of the counselor as advocate should not be underestimated.

WORK TO UNCOVER ROLE MODELS

The absence of role models and mentors for women in many career fields is a documented fact. In 1989, less then 16 percent of the state legislators, 12 percent of mayors, 10 percent of judges, 5 percent of the members of the United States House of Representatives, and 2 percent of the Senators were women. In 1984 there were 16,000 men on major corporate boards, whereas there were only 400 women. Despite the dramatic influx of women in the corporate world, barely 5 percent of middle and 1 percent of top management are women, and few women are full partners in law firms or hold major banking positions.[33]

Career counselors should encourage women to join organizations that can provide association with other professional women. Most specialized fields have multiple professional organizations including a women's association. Most major cities also offer an association for Christian business women.

REDEFINE SUCCESS

Career counselors can help women realize that popular definitions of success based on rugged individualism represent only one possibility. New definitions of success that incorporate interdependent values may better fit the realities of women's (and men's) lives. Help your client articulate a personal statement of purpose. It will help her sort through the ambivalence and nagging guilt that saps the energy of a woman trying to go upstream in the work culture.

HELP WOMEN DEVELOP AND VALUE INDEPENDENCE

For centuries women have learned to achieve vicariously rather then directly. This is done by "measuring their success by the success of individuals to whom they are related, with whom they identify, and to whose success they have contributed."[34] Women may be fulfilled through successful family members. "That's my son," may be said with deep pride. Balancing these indirect contributions with direct personal achievement is no small task.

Many women reject assertiveness and ambition for themselves because of the negative or masculine image it conjures. Appearing too aggressive produces intense internal conflict in many women. It is the counselor's responsibility to point out the distinction between assertive, nonassertive, and aggressive behavior for women.

In their excellent book entitled *Boundaries: When to Say Yes, When to Say No to Take Control of Your Life,* Henry Cloud and John Townsend identify myths that keep people from setting appropriate boundaries or practicing healthy assertiveness in the workplace.[35] Among the most distressing and common myths are:

- Boundaries are selfish.
- Boundaries are a sign of disobedience to God.
- Setting boundaries will cause me to be hurt by others.
- Boundaries are an expression of anger.
- When others set boundaries, it injures me.
- Boundaries cause guilt feelings.
- Setting boundaries is like burning a bridge in a relationship.

The consequences for not setting boundaries in the workplace can be damaging for women. Among the negative consequences are: (1) getting saddled with someone else's work; (2) putting in too much overtime; (3) taking work-related stress home; and (4) remaining in a job you dislike because it fits someone else's expectations for you. Women who take responsibility for themselves at home and in the workplace enjoy the freedom to be more loving and self-affirming.

GUARD AGAINST GENDER BIAS

Research shows that women who are ambivalent about choosing a career goal that is not traditionally feminine may find career counseling to be unhelpful or even harmful.[36] All counselors are gender biased to some extent, in the sense that individuals (including counselors) typically use gender stereotypes to simplify the world and make it more predictable. It is more helpful to assume this bias is a natural result of living in a world with two different genders than to assume it is somehow sinful or politically old-fashioned, as many current experts suggest. It is extremely important that counselors ask themselves what they assume to be true of others because of their own gender bias and how counseling from this perspective can distort the life possibilities open to their clients.

HELP WORKING WOMEN DEAL WITH STRESS

There are many unique pressures women feel as a result of working outside the home.[37] Frequently, the family is seen as a support system for the male worker; yet women who choose to work are seen as depriving their families by working. The family is not a refuge for working women as it frequently is for men.

This lack of a refuge is highly significant. Women frequently serve in service positions (such as nursing, teaching, and secretarial work) with enormous psychological demands that drain the spirit. Also, women in the workplace often have little power or control over their working situations. This combination creates a particularly stressful situation for women—often exceeding the levels of stress men may carry.[38] In addition, many women are caught in the guilt trap over their track record as a less-than-perfect mother and a less-than-perfect worker. Therefore, relaxation and stress reduction is a legitimate need for women seeking assistance from a vocational counselor.

NOTES

1. S. Sullivan, "Is There a Time for Everything?: Attitudes Related to Women's Sequencing of Career and Family," *Career Development Quarterly* 40 (1992): 235–43.

2. C. M. Solomon, "Careers Under Glass," *Personnel Journal* 69 (1990): 96–105.

3. P. Roberts, and P. Newton, "Levinsonian Studies of Women's Career Stages," *Psychology of Aging* 2 (1987): 154–63.

4. P. Chance, "Biology, Destiny, and All That," *Across the Board* (July/August 1988.): 19–23.

5. D. J. Levinson, *The Season of a Man's Life* (New York: Ballantine Books, 1978).

6. J. O'Neil, "Male Sex Role Conflicts, Sexism, and Masculinity: Psychological Implications for Men, Women, and Counseling Psychologists," *Counseling Psychologist* 9 (1981): 61–80.

7. J. Grossman and N. Chester, eds., *The Experience and Meaning of Work in Women's Lives* (Hillsdale, N.J.: Erlbaum, 1990).

8. Ibid.

9. J. Block, "Psychological Development of Female Children and Adolescents," in *Women: A Developmental Perspective*, ed. P. Berman and E. Rainey (Washington D.C.: Department of Health and Human Services, Public Health Service, National Institute for Health, Pueblo, Colo., 1982).

10. G. Sassen, "Success Anxiety in Women: A Constructivist Interpretation of Its Sources and Its Significance," *Harvard Educational Review* 50 (1980): 13–25.

11. E. Worthington, J. McLeod, and R. Kessler, "The Importance of Life Events for Explaining Sex Differences in Psychological Distress," in *Gender and Stress*, ed. R. C. Barnett, L. Biener, and G. K. Baruch (New York: Free Press, 1987), 144–56.

12. C. Gilligan, *In a Different Voice* (Cambridge, Mass.: Harvard University Press, 1982).

13. P. Voydanoff, *Work and Family Life* (Beverly Hills, Calif.: Sage Publications, 1987).

14. G. Sheehy, *Passages: Predictable Crises of Adult Life* (New York: Dutton, 1974).

15. J. Bardwick, "The Seasons of a Woman's Life," in *Women's Lives: New Theory, Research, and Policy*, ed. D. McGuigan (Ann Arbor, Mich.: University of Michigan, Center for Continuing Education of Women, 1980).

16. L. Baum, "Corporate Women: They're About to Break Through to the Top," *Business Week*, 22 June 1987, 72–78.

17. M. Stoltz-Like, "The Working Family: Helping Women Balance the Roles of Wife, Mother, and Career Woman," *Career Development Quarterly* 40 (1992): 243–56.

18. S. Ornstein and L. Isabella, "Age vs. Stage Models of Career Attitudes of Women: A Partial Replication and Extension," *Journal of Vocational Behavior* 36 (1990): 1–19.

19. A. Spencer, *Seasons* (New York: Paulist Press, 1982); and I. Sanguiliano, *In Her Time* (New York: Morrow, 1978).

20. M. Bateson, *Composing A Life: Life as a Work in Progress—The Improvisions of Five Extraordinary Women* (New York: Plume, Penguine Books, 1989).

21. U. Sekaran, *Dual-Career Families: Contemporary Organizational and Counseling Issues* (San Francisco: Jossey-Bass, 1986).

22. R. Rapoport and R. Rapoport, "The Dual Career Family," in *Career Development and the Counseling of Women* , ed. L. S. Hansen and R. S. Rapoza (Springfield, Ill.: Thomas, 1978).

23. C. Dunbar, et. al., "Successful Coping Styles in Professional Women," *Canadian Journal of Psychiatry* 24 (1979): 43–46.

24. B. Ragins and E. Sundstrom, "Gender and Power in Organizations: A Longitudinal Perspective," *Psychological Bulletin* 105 (1989): 51–88.

25. A. Morrison and M. Von Glinow, "Women and Minorities in Management," *American Psychologist* 45 (1990): 200–208.

26. D. Schultz and S. Schultz, *Psychology and Work Today: An Introduction to Industrial and Organizational Psychology,* 6th ed. (New York: Macmillan, 1994).

27. S. Robbins, *Organizational Behavior: Concepts, Controversies, and Applications,* 5th ed. (Englewood Cliffs, N.J.: Prentice Hall, 1991).

28. A. Morrison et al., *Breaking the Glass Ceiling: Can Women Reach the Top of America's Largest Corporations?* (Reading, Mass.: Addison-Wesley, 1992).

29. E. P. Cook, "The Gendered Context of Life: Implications for Women's and Men's Career-Life Plans," *The Career Development Quarterly* 41 (1993): 227–37.

30. M. Zaslow and F. Pederson, "Sex Role Conflicts and the Experience of Childbearing," *Professional Psychology* 12 (1981): 47–55.

31. M. Parker, S. Peltier, and P. Wolleat, "Understanding Dual Career Couples," *Personnel and Guidance Journal* 60 (1981): 14–18.

32. R. Sharf, *Applying Career Development Theory to Counseling* (Pacific Grove, Calif.: Brooks/Cole, 1992), 213.

33. C. Nadelson, "Professional Issues for Women," *Women's Disorders* 12 (1989): 25–33.

34. J. Lipmen-Blumen, "Emerging Patterns of Female Leadership in Formal Organizations: Must the Female Leader Go Formal?" in *The Challenge of Change,* ed. M. Horner, C. Nadelson, and M. Notman (New York: Plenum Press, 1983), 61–91.

35. H. Cloud and J. Townsend, *Boundaries: When to Say Yes, When to Say No to Take Control of Your Life,* (Grand Rapids : Zondervan, 1992).

36. A. Thomas, and N. Stewart, "Counselor Response to Female Clients with Deviate and Conforming Career Goals," *Journal of Counseling Psychology* 18 (1971): 352–57.

37. C. Piotrkowski and R. Repetti, "Dual-Earner Families," *Marriage and Family Review* (1984): 73–74.

38. G. Baruch, L. Biener, and R. Barnett, "Women and Gender in Research on Work and Family Stress," *American Psychologist* 42 (1987): 130–36.

Chapter Eleven

Special Populations and Career Development

WHILE AMERICA'S ETHNIC POPULATION has become increasingly diverse, equal opportunities for American minorities are still unbalanced. People of color, for example, receive less pay than white men for equal work and are often denied access to jobs most likely to lead to advancement and higher pay. The median yearly income of full-time workers is lowest for black women and highest for white men. Conversely, the unemployment rate is lowest for white men and highest for black women.

The job market has been equally challenging for individuals with disabilities. These individuals are frequently the victims of considerable prejudice by potential employers as well as bias by counselors. Deep rooted attitudes place a stigma on individuals with disability. [1]

In this chapter we focus on support for these special populations. We will disucss specific problems and needs of American minorities, quality counseling interventions to help overcome the workplace barriers faced by minorities, and specific problems and needs of individuals with disabilies. We will conclude with a number of counseling interventions to assist disabled individuals in crafting a meaningful and challenging career.

VOCATIONAL COUNSELING WITH MINORITIES

Five folding chairs were placed in an intimate circle in the corner of an empty Sunday school room. The echoing voices and footsteps in the hallway had faded minutes ago, but this group showed no signs of slowing down. Joseph, a soft-spoken American minority person in his thirties, had quickly won the hearts of everyone in the job-search support group with his professionalism and spiritual dedication. Now, as he confided yet another failure to be selected for a position that fit his qualifications completely, the group was dumbfounded. The knowledge (an inside bit of information) that the applicant selected for the position fell far short of Joseph in his level of experience and education compounded their frustration. It was the first time most members of this group had seen so clearly the injustice of the constant roadblocks and barriers faced by American minorities in the job market.

The barriers and roadblocks for individuals of minority cultures do not begin with discrimination in the workplace—they begin on the playground. As children, they had limited access to career role-playing and dreaming that leads to career maturity. The number of minority persons completing high school and college in the United States has been steadily rising over the past twenty-five years. However, most minority youth are concentrated in large, urban areas. Twenty-three of the twenty-five largest school systems in America are dominated by minority students.[2] Yet high school students from lower socioeconomic families and from small schools in rural areas are also unlikely to have access to career guidance.[3] Children from these backgrounds who are encouraged to dream and explore are later overwhelmed by the limited educational and occupational opportunities available to them.[4] This is especially true for third-generation welfare families.[5]

When clients realize they face prejudice, social barriers, a sense of isolation, and helplessness due to their culture-related differences, the challenges in career development seem insurmountable. However, the counselor who provides effective support for minority clients can make a significant difference in their lives and in the lives of all those who follow them. For instance, a first-generation college student not only helps himself or herself but all the generations that follow him or her. The barrier has been broken.

SPECIFIC PROBLEMS AND NEEDS OF AMERICAN MINORITIES

The special problems and needs of American minorities discussed in this section should be considered representative and not exhaustive. The intensity of an individual's identification with his or her culture of origin should not be assumed before assessing his or her values and motivations. However, there are several significant cultural groups about whom the vocational counselor should be knowledgeable.

African-Americans. The largest racial minority in this country are Black Americans. Black families have come to the United States from many different countries over the last four centuries. By far the largest group of Blacks in America are of African origin whose ancestors were brought here directly as slaves.[6] Blacks comprise approximately 11 percent of the American population.

Racism and oppression have made it extremely difficult for the majority of Black people to enter this country's mainstream. The long-lasting effects of poverty and oppression have caused many to feel broken by the system; most of them are disillusioned and frustrated. However, Black Americans have shown an amazing ability to survive in the face of impossible conditions. This survival has been attributed to strong kinship bonds, flexibility of family roles, and a high value placed on religion, education, and work.[7]

Many African Americans face a double bind in their career development. While they are encouraged to go out and seek education and work opportunities, those who move too far away may be perceived as rejecting their families and friends, even their culture.[8]

In a moving portrait of the Black American worker, based on recent research, the specific vocational needs of many in this culture become vivid. "The profile of the Black individual as portrayed in the research cited is a portrait of a vocationally handicapped person. According to the studies examined, the average Black, if one can speak of average individuals of any racial group, is one who may lack positive work role models, does not manifest a lifetime commitment to a career as a way of life, is work-alienated, and places a greater priority on job security rather than self-fulfillment in an occupation. Moreover, he tends to have a negative self-image which fosters identity foreclosure and a rigid closing out of self and directions. His aspirations are high, but his expectations of achieving his desired occupational goals are low. He has limitations placed upon his occupational mobility because of his racial membership, evidences interests that are more person than thing oriented and is vocationally immature."[9]

Counseling strategies designed for the specific needs of African Americans include:

- focusing on building self-esteem and developing a healthy self concept
- strengthening the internal locus of control
- providing a wide variety of information about possible job opportunities
- restoring hope that has eroded into low expectations and fear of failure
- dealing with ambivalence toward white persons.

When white counselors are dealing with African American clients, they need to be able to handle suspiciousness, rejection, and challenge to authority in a supportive and nondefensive style.[10]

Asian-Americans. Asian-Americans represent a culturally diverse ethnic group including Cambodians, Chinese, Filipinos, Indians, Japanese, Pakistanis, Thai, and Vietnamese. As a group, Asian-Americans have the lowest rate of unemployment.[11] This culture generally values industriousness and education. Asian-Americans have demonstrated a high level of willingness to assimilate to a new culture,[12] and many have taken advantage of higher education —especially in math, science, and technology. However, the stereotype of the Asian-American as being "good in sciences but lacking in verbal skills" is damaging and can serve to limit their careers.

Limitations in career development are intensified for first-generation Asian-Americans. Career counselors assisting these clients must be prepared to guide them in

- learning English
- recognizing the importance of their transferable skills
- understanding the American structure of career ladders
- locating information for unemployment benefits
- recognizing the importance of résumés and interview training in the job-search process.

Counseling for Asian-Americans is not easy. Most of them make use of counseling resources only as a last resort and are much more likely to advocate solving their problems on their own rather than risk the potential stigma that is associated with asking a professional for help.[13]

Specific concerns for working with Asian-Americans in vocational counseling include these factors:

1. Asian-Americans are sensitive about verbalizing personal problems, especially in group encounters.
2. Asian-Americans tend to be inexpressive when asked to discuss personal achievements and limitations.
3. Asian-Americans may misinterpret the role of counseling and not identify with the benefits.

4. Asian-Americans may be perceived as passive and nonassertive with authority figures, while in reality they are only conforming to a cultural norm that discourages them from being perceived as aggressive.

5. Asian-Americans may strongly resist suggestions to modify unassuming and nonassertive behaviors in the job-search process.[14]

Hispanic Americans. The second largest minority group in the country, Hispanic Americans compose about 5.6 percent of the United States population. The largest subgroup of Hispanics are Mexican Americans (over 7 million legal workers in America), followed by Puerto Ricans (about 2 million), Cubans (approximately 1 million), and 2.5 million Hispanics from Central American, South America, and Spain. The majority of Mexicans living in the United States were either born in Mexico or born to parents who are Mexican-born.[15]

While it is not a good idea to overgeneralize, research reveals that the behavior of Hispanics can be characterized as less mobile than other ethnic groups, primarily because of their strong family ties. They are the least Americanized of the ethnic groups because traditionally held values are passed on to subsequent generations. The strength of this cultural identity is aided by the proximity of Mexico, which allows trips to and from their native land. On these trips home, they renew ties, maintain a reference group, activate their support system, and reaffirm their ethnic identity.[16] The American citizenship of the Puerto Ricans also allows them to travel frequently, strengthening rather than weakening their cultural connectedness.

An article by M. Ayres in the *Occupational Outlook Quarterly* entitled "Counseling Hispanic Americans" suggests that Hispanics may be exposed to a limited variety of occupations and, consequently, may make vocational decisions with very limited information. Ayres believes they are in need of encouragement, motivation, and reinforcement to pursue occupations and opportunities not traditionally considered reachable by Hispanics.[17] In addition, they may not have basic job-seeking skills (i.e., filling out applications).

The counseling relationship is strengthened with a Hispanic American client when the therapist takes on a less direct form of communication, stepping into the role of a philosopher of life through storytelling, anecdotes, and humor. The use of analogies, proverbs, and popular songs is also an effective and culturally congruent method of communication.[18]

Native Americans. One of the most influential factors in the career development of Native Americans is their preference not to adopt the dominant cultural values. Native Americans may be thought of as being caught between two cultures. Feeling misunderstood, isolated, and resistant to cultural assimilation, Native American youths have difficulty in identifying with career roles in the dominant society. About 50 to 60 percent of all Native American children drop out of the educational system before they finish high school.[19]

Native American societies view life from a different perspective than the dominant American culture. Therefore, their dropping out of school has often been misunderstood. Native Americans are not generally motivated to acquire possessions—attaching little value to material goods—and do not measure success by wealth or power. Native Americans are oriented to the present (not the future), have a nonlinear concept of time, and disapprove of individual initiative designed to accomplish personal occupational goals (valuing instead shared working conditions).[20]

About half of the Native American population (more than 1.5 million) live on reservations where many are involved in farming, ranching, fishing, and lumber production. Many Native Americans value working with their hands more than mental exercise or paperwork.[21] Some tribes are engaged in bingo and lottery enterprises as well as motel management.[22]

Several strategies have been suggested to help Native Americans maintain their cultural heritage and at the same time introduce concepts of career development within the dominant society.

1. Use parents and relatives as counseling facilitators. The rationale for this approach is embedded in the strong family ties of Native Americans.

2. Use Native American role models, who can assist in helping to break down resistance to counseling objectives; Native Americans will react more favorably to other Native Americans.

3. Emphasize individual potential in the context of future goals. Identity conflicts make it difficult for Native Americans to project themselves into other environments, including work environments.

COUNSELING INTERVENTIONS FOR MINORITIES

To build a helping relationship across ethnic cultures, the counselor must first and foremost posses all of the basic skills and abilities required for any counseling relationship. However, research findings suggest special strategies for effective counseling intervention with the cultural minorities.

Examine Personal Bias. Counselors must be willing to recognize their own personal values and attitudes that can make a damaging impact on minority clients. Unconscious biases can cause the vocational counselor to influence the client unwittingly. The college advisor who suggests an introductory class in chemistry rather then one in interpersonal communication to his Asian advisee may believe that he is affirming a strength in the student, when in fact he or she is revealing personal bias. The high school advisor who pushes the idea of a four-year college degree onto an adolescent Hispanic, whose family values call for him to become equipped with mechanical skills and join the family business, is also operating on a personal bias that may be damaging to the client. Effective counseling across ethic lines demands objective self-judgment and humility.

Cultivate Empathy with Optimism. The effective counselor needs to cultivate an understanding of the historically unfair impact of the American sociological and economic system on minorities. However, this understanding must not come across as pessimism that places the client in the role of a powerless victim. Deficits in career development among minorities are often consequences of life in a deprived socioeconomic class, which is also the result of life in a specific racial or ethnic group. Help the client sort through the realistic career options and then make choices that are most likely to bring long-term success.

Find the Right Workplace. Malcolm S. Forbes, a third generation member of the Forbes family to serve as publisher of *Forbes*
magazine, once commented that the secret of his career success was choosing the right grandparents. American minorities
were unable to choose the "right grandparents," and they have
been discriminated against generation after generation. It is left
to the next generation to overcome barriers in the workplace.[23]
Harvard Business School professor, Roseabeth Moss Kanter,
responds to Forbes's quip by saying, "Since that option (to
choose the right grandparents) is not available to most minorities in American business, they have to do the next best thing:
choose the right company."[24]

In his book *The Best Companies for Minorities,* Lawrence
Graham profiles the Fortune 500 and other large companies
who genuinely promote diversity in their employment practices. These are the companies that offer career advancement
and invest their money and energies in charities, scholarships,
and training programs for minorities. The Graham book is the
result of research conducted in 625 private and public companies over a two-year period. Under consideration were:

annual revenues

percentages of minorities in the company's overall work
force and within the management pool

salary scale

minority members on the board of directors

minority internships

recruiting programs at colleges

contributions to minority organizations and causes

honest evaluations by current minority employees.

The eighty-five companies profiled represented a cross section
of American industry. Minority clients should be encouraged to
utilize resources such as the Graham book (printed character
references) to study companies where they are interviewing.

Work to Keep a High Level of Involvement. Discouragement is
hard on motivation for job seekers. Some minority clients have

a low tolerance for the detail work needed in a job search. Interviewing requires careful preparation and consumes a great deal of time. Many become bored by the process. When discouraging results dampen hope, it is important to be the client's encourager and guide. If possible:

1. Find shortcuts.
2. Enlist the help of others.
3. Take the initiative to set up interviews.
4. Provide materials for the client to read.

In short, do whatever is necessary to maintain the client's hope.

Be Selective in Using Assessments. Because many of the popular career assessment tools have been used primarily with English-speaking, Caucasian subjects, the processes and results may be biased and misleading. Before using a standard assessment tool with culturally different clients, refer to the following checklist of questions: [25]

1. Is the sample representative of my client?
2. Does the sample include enough cases of similarity?
3. Does the sample group consist of the sort of person with whom my clients can be compared?
4. Is the sample appropriately subdivided?

The rehabilitation and research International Center for the Disabled of New York City has developed a vocational evaluation called *Micro-Tower*.[26] *Tower* is an acronym for Testing, Orientation, and Work Evaluation in Rehabilitation. The Micro-Tower is based on work samples that measure aptitudes for a number of unskilled and skilled occupations including: *motor*—electronic connector, assembly, bottle capping and packing, lamp assembly, clerical perception; *zip*—coding, record checking, payroll computation; and *verbal*—want-ad comprehension, message taking. The test, designed at a fourth-grade reading level, is assessable to a wide range of individuals. However, the individual must understand English. One unique feature of the

Micro-Tower system is the involvement of clients in group discussions designed to explore interests, values, lifestyles, and so forth. Discussion groups are also used before the test to make the testing situation as nonthreatening as possible.

Refer to a Counselor of the Same Culture. The mark of an experienced counselor is the wisdom to refer a client who may be better helped elsewhere. When the client is not able to progress toward his or her career aspirations, or when he or she remains disengaged from the counseling relationship, it may be important to refer the minority person to a counselor of the client's own culture, or to invite a trusted friend, minister, or teacher of the client's own culture to serve as a cocounselor.

Vocational Counseling for Individuals with Disabilities

Mike was distraught. All of his life he had wanted nothing more than to be a high-school math teacher. However, the envelope in his hand contained a rejection letter from a college of education even though he had respectable grades. Mike was devastated. Following a serious head injury in junior high, he had always struggled to contain his emotions and control his impulses. He tended to talk, eat, and feel in extremes. When the faculty had called in a neurologist for a consultation before recommending admission to the education program, doubts had surfaced about his ability to work well with children or adolescents. In the end, the faculty had voted against his continued training in education. Now, it seemed to him, the only dream he had ever dared to sustain was crumbling.

The great poet Milton, who grappled with the vocational limitations imposed on him with the onset of blindness, wrote:

> "When I consider how my light is spent
> Ere half my days, in this dark world and wide,
> And that one talent which is death to hide,
> Lodged with me useless[27].

Mike had joined the likes of Milton in one of the most painful of human dilemmas—disability.

It is estimated that approximately 10 percent of the United States population have chronic physical, mental, or emotional conditions that limit their activity sufficiently to make a substantial career difference. The Americans with Disabilities Act (1990), states, "An individual with a disability is a person who has a physical or mental impairment that substantially limits one or more 'major life activities.'"[28]

Although each situation and disability is unique, there are several guidelines that can facilitate vocational counseling with individuals who have a disability:[29]

1. *Personal history, especially previous work history, is a good predictor of future work potential for an individual with a disability.*There is a tendency for individuals in the difficult passage of adjustment to a disability to treat the pretrauma past as if it has no relevancy to the future. On the contrary, there is often a strong need for the client to remain active in work similar to his or her previous job and in association with the old and familiar network of colleagues and professionals in his or her field.

2. *Provide continual and sustained support.* The wide variety of challenges—from traveling to the job, using specially structured instruments, developing new levels of personal competence, maintaining a consistent presence, to sustaining hope and optimism—require as great an investment by the vocational counselor *after* placement as before. This continued support is a key factor in counseling with this special population.

3. *Use a step-by-step, systematic approach.* The counselor must work with subtle external and internal barriers. Creating small victories with each step builds strength and confidence for the client adjusting or readjusting to the world of work.

4. *Focus on building vocational skills, not on diagnosing the disorder of the client.* Focusing on the new limitations can overwhelm the client and generate hopelessness. A strong focus on existing skills, the redevelopment of familiar skills, and the acquisition of new skills is essential.

5. *Understanding and assessing self-esteem and ego strength are better predictors of the future work adjustment than more psychological tests.* The stereotypes faced by individuals with disabilities are extremely challenging. The interpersonal and social aspects of the workplace are difficult for all workers (nondisabled included). Understanding and strengthening the self-concept and ego strength of the client is excellent preparation for entry into the workplace.

SPECIFIC PROBLEMS AND NEEDS OF INDIVIDUALS WITH DISABILITY

The special problems and needs of disabled individuals discussed in this section should be considered as representative examples from a diverse population. The range and intensity of physical and mental limitations that impact career choice and development is exceedingly broad. However, there are two predominant patterns of disability that place unique demands on the vocational counselor.

Childhood (Congenital) Disabilities. Individuals who have dealt with a disability from childhood must overcome two unique dilemmas that can seriously hamper and delay their career development: (1) overprotection and (2) limited exposure.[30] The overprotective syndrome is a common result of childhood disability. It is easy to understand how the deep sympathy of family members can unwittingly rob the disadvantaged individual of the opportunity for work. The necessary independence and assertiveness have been blocked. Without intervention from supportive specialists, families may find it difficult to determine whether to foster an acceptance of limitations in functioning or to provide motivation toward independence. Make the most of every opportunity to consult with the parents concerning the career development of their child. They are the ones who can do the most in encouraging the development of self-awareness, decision-making skills, and experiences that can nurture a broad range of interests.

Early onset of disabilities often influences career choice by creating unnecessary limitations in career options. In some cases, the client has been robbed of the self-esteem, confidence, and self-understanding that are gained by mastering a variety of childhood tasks. This lack of childhood successes is an impediment in appraising interests and abilities needed for a career.

Disabling Physical Trauma. The major vocational task of those who undergo physical trauma leading to disability is to find new ways to satisfy their career aspirations. Vocational counselors in the 1960s coined the term "career redevelopment" to describe the basic concept of this work.[31] The task of modifying the self-concept to include new limitations is a demanding one. Many will experience shock, depression, and denial before accepting and adjusting to their disability.[32]

Career changes initiated by sudden disability may be described within the context of the transition model presented in chapter 7. Ultimately, however, the process of vocational redevelopment is shaped by the pretrauma experiences in career, personal, and social circumstances of the individuals and the posttrauma adjustments that must be made. Some disabilities require only subtle changes similar to those described by Hiestand as a forty-five degree turn.[33] Forty-five degree changes cause only minor discontinuity with the former occupation. A teacher who discovers she has insulin-dependent diabetes, for instance, may limit her teaching to half days and arrange for a teacher's aide to be present at all times in case of an insulin reaction. These changes will require adjustment and some loss, but they are things a person can live with.

Vocational changes brought on by severe physical trauma resulting in a disability may be as dramatic as a ninety-degree change involving *major* discontinuity with the former occupation. This kind of trauma resolution requires a total break from the occupational history of the individual.[34]

Bill was a church youth minister who was deeply fulfilled in his work. Driving home late after a New Year's Eve all-nighter, Bill a was hit by a drunk driver. The accident resulted in severe injuries, including head injury. After several months of recovery in the hospital, Bill was able to work part time as the custodian for a local junior high. He was not strong enough to return to his former ministry.

The disillusionment that results in this more severe change may interfere with motivation to seek rehabilitation and any new employment. Failure to accept the new personal limitations leaves the individual stuck in a nonproductive mode.

COUNSELING INTERVENTIONS FOR INDIVIDUALS WITH DISABILITY

The following techniques are designed to help individuals with disability tackle the unique demands and challenges of a new career journey.

Emphasize Interpersonal Skills. Persons with disabilities often have restricted social lives. The constant rejection, sick labels, and being completely overlooked can create a poor self-image. One lonely, articulate young man said it well: "When I ride by in my wheelchair, people either stare at me or look away, it's a rare person who just looks me in the eye with the natural ease I observe between others." Another observed, "The terms of our visibility are created by those who see what they want to see rather than what is there."[35] Yet the lack of friendships outside the disabled community often become a vocational limitation. Specialists have suggested that interpersonal skills be given greater attention than the strategies of work when counseling the disabled.[36] Helping persons cope with a disability by building a wide range of healthy relationships is an important career counseling goal.

Uncover Hidden Career Options. Clients who have little experience and knowledge in the world of work might need to begin by creating a wide list of job possibilities, which can be narrowed down as a future starting place for career exploration. Psychologists Yost and Corbishley suggest that clients engage in the following exercise as a way of overcoming the obstacle of limited career exposure:

1. Work with the client to create a list of thirty to fifty different jobs performed by his or her relatives, neighbors, friends, or members of the client's church.

2. The client then selects the *least aversive jobs* on the list and eliminates the others (no more than half of the jobs). You might want to use categories of "would not choose," "might choose," or "in question" to help in the selection.

3. Discuss what the client finds attractive about each job.

4. Help the client get information on each of the selections.

5 For each job researched, an additional, related job should be added to the list.

This technique is particularly helpful for clients who are un-aware of the wide range of possibilities available to them. [37]

Individualize Career Assessment. Counseling individuals with disability (just as with nondisabled clients) will involve assessment of interests, personality, aptitudes, and values. While assessment is important, specialists suggest that the assessment process be individualized to fit the unique needs of each disabled client. The following suggestions can serve as a guide for implementing effective assessment for this population:

1. Give individual, rather than group tests.

2. Use timed tests carefully, providing rest periods and multiple testing sessions to accommodate special needs.

3. Use work samples as an assessment tool for vocational skills.

4. Use the counseling interview to discuss interests, values, and needs rather than relying heavily on inventories designed to gather similar information.

Provide Guidance for Successful Career Choices. One of the most delicate situations for the vocational counselor is the sense that the client is choosing a career that is unrealistic or inappropriate. The counselor must guide a disabled person who wants to pursue a career that requires an unrealistic level of ability. The situation can be extremely sensitive because of the potential conflict between the client's need for freedom of choice and the counselor's responsibility to provide a framework of expectations that will enable him or her to succeed. If most of the client's options seem to be unrealistic in some way, it is important to intervene quickly, before the client has made an emotional investment in any of the options. If you voice your concern, be sure that your reservations are not from personal biases or stereotypes surrounding disability.

It is possible that you will be wrong in your judgment. Motivation and effort are as important as ability. Some clients will choose careers that are unrealistic because they underrate their own capabilities. Career choices that do not provide challenge probably will not fulfill the client for long. Helping clients realistically assess their strengths and weaknesses bolsters self-confidence and opens the door to better career choices.

Serve as a Workplace Advocate. Employers tend to believe lots of myths against adding an individual with a disability to their payroll. Some of the most entrenched beliefs are that sick leave will be frequent, health insurance rates will skyrocket, and safety on the job will be a problem, requiring costly modifications in facilities. These fears, which stem from stereotyped views of individuals with disabilities, often result in discrimination. Career counselors can serve clients by working hard to build positive attitudes in employers as well as clients.[38] One of the most effective tools for advocacy in the workplace is to provide examples of a job redesign for the employer that allow him or her to see exactly what is involved in accommodation. Vocational counselors working with disabled clients need to take an active role as educators of employers.

Although disabled persons require great patience and understanding, marvelous results occur from helping these persons to make a successful entry into the world of work. There is joy in seeing the eyes of a reluctant employer glisten as he or she tells the story of a disabled worker's success. It is enough to warm the heart of any vocational counselor.

NOTES

1. Special populations are defined as those individuals whose career development needs are out of the mainstream of opportunity in American life. C. McDaniels and N. Gysbers, *Counseling for Career Development: Theories, Resources, and Practice* (San Francisco: Jossey-Bass, 1992).

2. Carnegie Forum on Education and the Economy, *A Nation Prepared: Teachers for the 21st Century* (Washington, D.C.: CFEE, 1985).

3. V. Lee and R. Ekstrom, "Student Access Guidance Counseling in High School," *American Educational Research Association Journal* 24 (1987): 287–310.

4. E. Smith, "Issues in Racial Minorities' Career Behavior," in *Handbook of Vocational Psychology*, vol. 1, ed. W. B. Walsh and S. H. Osipow (Hillsdale, N.J.: Erlbaum, 1983).

5. J. Axelson, *Counseling and Development in a Multicultural Society*, 2d ed. (Pacific Grove, Calif.: Brooks/Cole, 1993).

6. P. M. Hines and N. Boyd-Franklin, "Black Families," in *Ethnicity and Family Therapy*, ed. M. McGoldrick, J. Pearce, and J. Giordano (New York: Guilford Press, 1982).

7. R. Hill, *The Strengths of Black Families* (New York: Emerson Hall, 1972).

8. Hines and Boyd-Franklin, "Black Families."

9. E. Smith, "Profile of the Black Individual in Vocational Literature," *Journal of Vocational Behavior* 6 (1975): 41–59.

10. V. Zunker, *Career Counseling: Applied Concepts of Life Planning*, 3d ed. (Pacific Grove, Calif.: Brooks/Cole, 1990), 422.

11. Smith, "Racial Minorities."

12. R. Sharf, *Applying Career Development Theory to Counseling* (Pacific Grove, Calif.,: Brooks/Cole, 1992).

13. S. Shon and D. Ja, "Asian Families," in *Ethnicity*, ed. McGoldrick, Pearce, and Giordano.

14. E. Kaneshige, "Cultural Factors in Group Counseling and Interaction," in *Understanding and Counseling Ethnic Minorities*, ed. G. Henderson (Springfield, Ill.: Thomas, 1979).

15. J. Hernandez, L. Estrada, and D. Alvirez, "Census Data and the Problem of Conceptually Defining the Mexican American Population," *Social Science Quarterly* 56, no. 4 (1973): 671–87.

16. M. Carlos and L. Sellers, "Kinship Structure and Modernization in Latin America," *Latin America Research Review* 7(1972): 95–124.

17. M. Ayres, "Counseling Hispanic Americans," *Occupational Outlook Quarterly* 23 (1979): 3–8.

18. C. J. Falicov, "Mexican Families," in *Ethnicity*, ed. McGoldrick, Pearce, and Giordano.

19. V. Parrillo, *Stranger to These Shoes*, 2d ed. (New York: Wiley, 1985).

20. G. Henderson, "American Indians: Introduction," in *Ethnic Minorities*, ed. Henderson.

21. Sharf, *Career Development Theory*.

22. Axelson, *Multicultural Society*.

23. J. Vondracek and E. Kirchner, "Vocational Development in Early Childhood: An Examination of Young Children's Expressions of Vocational Aspirations," *Journal of Vocational Behavior* 5 (1974): 251–60.

24. R. Kanter, forward to *The Best Companies for Minorities*, ed. L. Graham (New York: Penguin Books, 1993).

25. V. Zunker, *Using Assessment Results for Career Development*, 4th ed. (Pacific Grove, Calif.: Brooks/Cole, 1994).

26. Ibid.

27. J. Milton, "On His Blindness" (1962), quoted in G. Seldes, *The Great Thoughts* (New York: Ballantine Books, 1985).

28. U. S. Department of Justice, Civil Rights Division, *Coordination and Review Section* (Washington D.C.: U.S. Government Printing Office, 1991).

29. E. Herr and S. Cramer, *Career Guidance and Counseling Through the Life Span: Systematic Approaches*, 3d ed. (Boston: Scott, Foresman, 1988), 183.

30. J. J. Stone and C. Gregg, "Juvenile Diabetes and Rehabilitation Counseling," *Rehabilitation Counseling Bulletin* 24 (1981): 283–91.

31. J. McDaniel, "Disability and Vocational Development," *Journal of Rehabilitation* 29 (1963): 16–18.

32. D. Cook, "Impact of Disability on the Individual," in *Rehabilitation Counseling*, ed. R. Parker and C. Hansen (Boston: Allyn and Bacon, 1981).

33. D. Hiestand, *Changing Careers After Thirty-Five* (New York: Columbia University Press, 1971) quoted in *Career Choice and Development*, D. Brown et al. (San Francisco: Jossey-Bass, 1984).

34. Ibid.

35. L. Kriegel, "Claiming the Self: The Cripple as American Male," in *Disabled People as Second Class Citizens*, ed. M. Eisenberg, D. Kriggins, and R. Duval (New York: Springer, 1982).

36. M. Fine and A. Asch, "Disability Beyond Stigma: Social Interactions, Discrimination, and Activism," *Journal of Social Issues* 44 (1988): 3–21.

37. E. Yost and M. Corbishley, *Career Counseling: A Psychological Approach* (San Francisco: Jossey-Bass, 1987.

38. W. Neff, *Work and Human Behavior*, 2d ed. (Chicago: Aldine, 1985).

PART III

Special Issues

Chapter Twelve

Assessing Personality, Interests, Aptitudes, and Abilities

I T WAS IN THE FIFTH CENTURY B.C. when the Greek physician Hippocrates theorized that the body contained four basic fluids or humors—blood, phlegm, black bile, and yellow bile— each associated with a particular personality temperament. An individual's personality depended on which humor was predominant in his or her body. Hippocrates believed people would be basically quiet, sad, brooding, excitable, aggressive, and so on, based on the composite of their body fluids.

Thousands of years after Hippocrates laid down his theory of personality assessment, a Harvard professor named William Sheldon related physique to temperament. He assigned people to three categories based on their body builds: endomorphic (fat, soft, round), mesomorphic (muscular, rectangular, strong), or ectomorphic (thin, long, fragile). Sheldon's typology specified relationships between each physique and particular personality traits, activities, and preferences.[1]

Considering its rather interesting past, psychological assessment has come a long way. There are currently over 74 achievement batteries, 245 intelligence and academic aptitude tests, 487 vocational tests, and 576 personality inventories.[2] However, assessment tools designed to measure complex constructs such as personality, interests, aptitudes, and abilities must still be considered "objective checks of subjective opinion."[3]

Adam, a twenty-seven-year-old man, found himself seriously discontented with his career in electrical engineering. A graduate of a well-respected engineering college, Adam had excited his professors and provoked envy among his friends when he was hired by a high-profile company before graduation. Now, five years into his career, Adam was restless and contemplating a career change. A meticulous and intentional person, Adam consulted several career counselors for help in the process.

The psychologist Adam was referred to by the Employee Assistance Program at his workplace recommended that Adam take a battery of abilities assessments to determine whether his basic skills were being applied in his current job. After the assessments were interpreted, the psychologist concluded that Adam was unhappy because his social abilities were not being used sufficiently. He recommended that Adam consider a management position in the electrical engineering field to incorporate his strongest abilities and revitalize his career.

A psychotherapist who specialized in career counseling recommended that Adam take a battery of personality assessments to help him "discover the deeper causes of his unhappiness." The feedback session with the therapist focused on the fact that Adam was clearly an extrovert who could never expect to enjoy a solitary and introverted field such as electrical engineering. The therapist advised Adam to consider a career change, moving toward a more "people-intensive" position.

Adam also went to a career counselor in the career development center of the college from which he had graduated. This counselor sensed that Adam was lacking motivation for his work. Focusing on this aspect of his dilemma, the counselor asked Adam to embark on a battery of assessments that were designed to "discover what he *really* wanted to do." Results from the interest assessments seemed to indicate clearly (to the counselor) that Adam's career and interests were not congruent. His recommendation was fairly vague, that Adam "seek a career in the social services/sciences arena of the world of work."

Which of these counselors was right? In part, each was right. Important information was gleaned from each counselor's assessment of abilities, personality, or interests. However, none was helpful in enabling the client to move through his career dilemma toward a workable solution. Rarely, if ever, is the entire source of discontentment in a career identified by a cursory assessment of abilities, personality, or interests alone. Effective counselors rely on assessments as tools for fostering career exploration but not as determiners of choice. One psychologist describes assessment results as "a series of candid camera shots, if you will, which, when put together, give a composite picture of the individual."[4] The process of career decision making is complex and unique to each person. Assessments are helpful but not final.

Decisions about how, when, and where to use assessments in counseling are joint decisions to be shared by the counselor and the client. Consideration should be given to the following factors:

- Can assessment results provide the information sought?
- Is that information relevant for the decisions that are to be made by the client?
- Are these test results being given with discretion?
- Are these assessments designed for the unique needs of this client?
- What is the most strategic time in the career decision-making process to introduce assessment?
- What are the alternatives the individual is considering?
- Does the information provided by the test correspond to the requirements of the jobs or training programs under consideration?

In this chapter we address the task of assessment in vocational counseling. We will deal individually with the assessment of personality, interests, and abilities. Finally, we will focus on providing interpretive feedback to the client as well as the construction of written reports that facilitate self-understanding and aid the career development process.

ASSESSING PERSONALITY

Paul said, "Having then gifts differing according to the grace that is given to us, let us use them" (Rom. 12:6 NKJV). Personality assessments have been created precisely for the purpose of identifying and using our best gifts. Although much of the work in personality assessment has focused on personality dysfunction, many assessments have been designed as descriptive instruments that identify personality strengths and weaknesses. Three prominent measures of personality that give insight into vocational selections are the California Psychological Inventory, the Edwards Personal Preference Schedule, and the Myers-Briggs Type Indicator.

CALIFORNIA PSYCHOLOGICAL INVENTORY

The California Psychological Inventory (CPI) attempts to assess personality by measuring the kind of everyday variables that ordinary people use in their daily lives. These variables, (i.e., independence, sociability, and self-control) are called "Folk Concept Scales." There are twenty Folk Concept Scales that provide the underlying structure for the CPI in assessing personality:

Dominance	Capacity for Status
Sociability	Social Presence
Self-Acceptance	Independence
Empathy	Responsibility
Socialization	Self-Control
Good Impression	Communality
Sense of Well-Being	Tolerance Achievement via Conformance
Achievement via Independence	Intellectual Efficiency

Psychological-Mindedness   Flexibility
Femininity/Masculinity

In addition to the twenty Folk Concept Scales, three structural scales have been created, based on clusters of the Folk Scales. The three structural scales are:

Internality—introversion/extroversion

Norm-Favoring—questioning or conforming to the norm

Self-Realization—capable and well-integrated or vulnerable and not actualized

There are two special purpose scales that are particularly relevant to the vocational counselor: the Managerial Potential Scale and the Work Orientation Scale.

An analysis of the vector scales creates a model of four personality types entitled *alpha, beta, gamma,* or *delta*. A final analysis of the three vector scales provides a five-level developmental classification (ranging from level three, "below average integration and realization of potential," to level seven, "superior integration and realization of the positive potential of the type"). These classifications provide insight for the test takers on the "degree of which the positive potentiality for the personality type has been realized." To obtain this assessment, contact Consulting Psychologists Press, Inc., 3803 E. Bayshore Road, Palo Alto, CA 94303.

Administering the California Psychological Inventory. The CPI has 462 true or false items and is largely self-administering. Answers are recorded on a sheet that can be hand scored with templates or returned to Consulting Psychologists Press for computer processing. Administration of the test takes forty-five minutes to one hour. This assessment is appropriate for individuals age thirteen and older.

Scoring the California Psychological Inventory. There are two scoring options for the CPI—by hand or by computer. To hand score is a simple process involving the use of templates for each scale, which provide a raw score tally. Once the raw score is indicated on the profile sheet provided, it is automatically converted to a standard score. There are several choices for computer scoring through Consulting Psychologists Press, including a special "narrative" option, which provides an in-depth interpretation of the test taker.

Interpreting the California Psychological Inventory. In the Administrator's Guide, Harrison Gough, developer of the CPI, suggests a three-step process for interpretation. First, the profile should be examined for reliability by noting the Good Impression, Communality, and Well-Being scales, which in terms of standard scores should all be at or above 35. The Good Impression scale should be no higher than 65. Second, analyze the Structural Scales, which provide the personality classification and level of functioning. Finally, examine each of the scales separately to determine the unique profile of the test taker.[5]

EDWARDS PERSONAL PREFERENCE SCHEDULE

In the 1930s Henry Murray developed a theory that individuals strive to meet certain manifest psychological needs, establishing different personality preferences.[6] The Edwards Personal Preference Schedule (EPPS) scales and descriptors include:

Achievement—a need to accomplish tasks well

Deference—a need to conform to customs and defer to others

Order—a need to plan well and be organized

Exhibition—a need to be the center of attention

Autonomy—a need to be free of responsibilities

Affiliation—a need to form strong attachments

Intraception—a need to analyze behaviors and feelings of others

Succorance—a need to receive support

Dominance—a need to lead

Abasement—a need to accept blame for problems and confess errors

Nurturance—a need to assist others

Change—a need for variety

Endurance—a need for completion

Heterosexuality—a need to be associated with attractive members of the opposite sex

Aggression—a need to express opinions and criticize.

To obtain the Edwards Personal Preference Schedule contact, The Psychological Corporation, 555 Academic Court, San Antonio, TX 78204.

Administering the Edwards Personal Preference Schedule. The EPPS is not timed but does take approximately forty minutes to complete.

Scoring the Edwards Personal Preference Schedule . Results from the test are recorded in percentiles, which may be compared with the norms for college students, general adults groups, and separate gender groups.

Interpreting the Edwards Personal Preference Schedule The results of this instrument can be used effectively in career counseling to explore current needs and preferences that serve as a driving factor in career decision making. Combinations of needs can provide straightforward insight about career fit. It is important for the counselor to remember that an individual's needs do not always have the same priority but are dynamic and changing over the life span.[7]

MYERS-BRIGGS

The Myers-Briggs Type Indicator (MBTI) was designed as a result of the work of Carl Jung in the 1920s and Katherine Briggs and Isabel Myers in the 1940s. Jung developed a theory of psychological type that dealt with three sets of bipolar personality dimensions; Myers and Briggs added a fourth:

1. Relating to the world:

extroversion—focusing one's attention and energy on the world outside self	introversion—focusing one's attention and energy on the world inside self

2. Perception:

sensing—using the visual and auditory processes as well as smell, taste, and touch to collect information and make detailed observations	intuition—seeking meaning, possibilities for the future, and relationships in an indirect, abstract, and imaginative way

3. Judgment or decision making:

thinking—the objective use of logic to make decisions	feeling—the subjective process of using values to make decisions

4. Lifestyle orientation:

judging—organized, planned, and orderly	perceiving—flexible, spontaneous, and open-ended

Jung's theory postulates that every individual has the capacity for each of these processes—introversion and extroversion, sensing and intuition, thinking and feeling, judging and perceiving. However, we each experience a preference for one side of each pair (much like being right- or left-handed). Different combinations of preferences act in concert with each other to create sixteen different personality types. The MBTI provides information about each of the preferences as well as the overall type. To obtain the MBTI, contact Consulting Psychologists Press, 3803 E. Bayshore Drive, Palo Alto, CA 94303.

Administering the Myers-Briggs Type Indicator. Several MBTI instruments are available including the MBTI Expanded Analysis, offering five subscales for each of the four dimensions; two standard forms (166 or 126 items); and an abbreviated form containing fifty items. The MBTI is not a time-limited test, but it takes about thirty minutes to complete. The MBTI is appropriate for high school students through adulthood.

Scoring the Myers-Briggs Type Indicator. The MBTI can be hand scored using stencils or computer scored by Consulting Psychologists Press. Numbers are assigned to each preference indicating the strength of the preference. Low scores indicate there is little or no difference between preferences.

Interpreting the Myers-Briggs Type Indicator. The profile presents brief descriptions of psychological types and combinations of types including examples of frequent occupational choices made by each type. There are numerous interpretive tools for use in career counseling. Among these, one particularly relevant resource is *An Introduction to Type in Organizations,* by Hirsh and Kummerow, which focuses on the most fitting contexts for each type at work through describing the leadership style, most significant contributions to the workplace, environmental needs, and areas for personal development for each type.[8]

Assessing Interests

Interest inventories are used to provide an objective measure of the likes and dislikes of a person in a variety of contexts. The most common use of interest inventories in counseling is vocational choice or academic direction. The three most widely used interest assessments are the Kuder Occupational Interest Survey, the Strong Interest Inventory, and the Self-Directed Search.

Kuder Occupational Interest Survey

The Kuder Occupational Interest Survey (KOIS) was created by measuring the interests of successful and satisfied people in an occupation to develop a scale that compares the interests of these individuals to the interests of those who are unsure of their career choice. Interest scales, when compared with those happily in their occupation, tend to predict occupational success and satisfaction decades after the test was taken. The KOIS yields 119 occupational scales, forty-eight college major scales, a verification scale, and eight experimental scales. The KOIS may be obtained by contacting CTB-Macmillan/McGraw-Hill Book Co., 20 Ryan Ranch Road, Monterey, CA 93940.

Administering the Kuder Occupational Interest Survey. The KOIS takes approximately thirty minutes to administer and is designed for individuals from grade nine through adulthood.

Scoring the Kuder Occupational Interest Survey. The KOIS is based on ten interest scales: outdoor, mechanical, computation, scientific, persuasive, artistic, literary, musical, social service, and clerical. It must be machine scored. Profiles from the KOIS organize the results in three major sections:

1. *Interest scales.* The KOIS begins with a narrative of the ten interest scales ranked as high, average, or low by percentiles compared with female and male norming groups.

2. *Occupational groups.* The narrative then provides a list of occupational groups in descending order of similarity, beginning with the most similar, next most similar, and so on, as measured by the interest patterns of the test taker as compared with those in the occupational groups.

3. *College majors scales.* These are presented in descending order of similarity, beginning with the most similar, next most similar, and so on. The separation of college majors from occupations adds flexibility in the usage of this assessment tool at different developmental stages.

Interpreting the Kuder Occupational Interest Survey. Different versions of the computerized profiles from the KOIS are compiled for the counselor and for the test taker. The counselor profile summarizes the data, including comments regarding the validity of this specific profile. For example, the report might comment, "The survey-taker's interest patterns are very unusual. The profile may not be accurate."

The test taker's report includes an interpretive narrative that guides the client through the data. Comments abound, such as, "As you look over your report, remember that your results are estimates based on your current interests." The narrative report provides sufficient information for a thorough interpretation.

STRONG INTEREST INVENTORY

The Strong Interest Inventory (SII) is an assessment that links personality characteristics, primarily through the measurement of interests, with corresponding job titles. The SII compares the interests of the individual being tested with a variety of vocational-group interest patterns already established through many decades of research. A 325 item assessment, the SII measures interests in a wide range of occupations, activities, hobbies, leisure activities, school subjects, and types of people. This assessment may be obtained through Consulting Psychologists Press, 3803 E. Bayshore Drive, Palo Alto, CA 94303.

Administering the Strong Interest Inventory. This assessment typically takes about thirty minutes to administer. The reading level requires a sixth-grade comprehension, and the SII is therefore recommended for individuals age thirteen and older. The reliability and validity of the SII has been well documented.[9]

Scoring the Strong Interest Inventory . Profiles from the SII are divided into four categories:

1. *Holland's types.*[10] Holland's six occupational personality styles—realistic, investigative, artistic, social, enterprising, and conventional—are each reported by a standard score (mean = 50, standard deviation = 10) with a score of very low, low, average, high, or very high.

2. *Basic interest scales.* Each occupational personality style is divided into basic interest scales. For example, the realistic theme focuses on agriculture, nature, adventure, military activities, and mechanical activities. A standard score and norms are given for each basic interest scale.

3. *Specific occupational titles.* Also grouped according to Holland's six types, the test reports results on over two hundred specific occupations. Results indicate whether the subject's interests are very dissimilar, dissimilar, moderately dissimilar, midrange, moderately similar, similar, or very similar to the hobbies, activities, school subjects, and personality preferences of workers in each specific occupation.

4. *Administrative scales.* Ten administrative scales include an Infrequent Response Index (revealing a rare or uncommon pattern of responses, which may signal confusion, intentional foul play, or very unique interests), the Academic Comfort Scale (measuring overall interest in academic pursuits such as reading, research, and writing), and the Introversion-Extroversion Scale (measuring a basic preference for working with people or things).

Interpreting the Strong Interest Inventory. Begin with a review of the general occupational theme scores. They provide a general overview of interest patterns. Then proceed to the increasingly specific basic interest scores, and finally to measures of interest for specific occupations. (See appendix C for a summary evaluation form that can be used as an interpretive tool.)

Interpretation of the SII results is tricky when the profile is unusually flat or unusually elevated.[11] A flat profile, with scores that hover around the average range, may indicate a narrow but enthusiastic interest, little knowledge about the world of work, a mild depression, indecisiveness, or determination not to work. When the profile is elevated, with scores that cluster at the high levels of interest, this may reveal a reluctance to respond negatively or a great diversity of personal interests that causes difficulty in narrowing choices.

SELF-DIRECTED SEARCH

The Self-Directed Search (SDS) is a straightforward, systematic career exploration exercise based on Holland's theory of career development.[12] The assessment involves five levels of career exploration:

1. occupational daydreams
2. preferences for activities
3. competencies
4. preferences for kinds of occupations
5. abilities in various occupational areas

This test may be obtained by contacting Psychological Assessment Resources, Inc., P.O. Box 998, Odessa, FL 33556. 1–800–331–8378.

Administering the Self-Directed Search. A popular interest assessment, the SDS can be self-administered in approximately forty minutes and is designed for self-interpretation, providing results that can be easily integrated into the counseling session. In essence, the SDS guides individuals in:

- developing a list of occupational aspirations

- establishing likes and dislikes for certain activities that can be performed well or competently
- compiling a list of occupations that are appealing
- evaluating themselves on twelve different traits based on previous experience

Scoring the Self-Directed Search. After tabulating his or her scores, the test taker records the three highest scores in descending order. The three highest scores are analyzed by adding scores of responses to (1) most liked activities, (2) activities done most competently, (3) interest in occupations, and (4) self-estimates of traits. These scores reveal a summary code of three letters representing a combination of the occupational personality styles in Holland's typology—realistic, investigative, artistic, social, enterprising, and conventional.

Interpreting the Self-Directed Search. The SDS is used in conjunction with *The Occupations Finder,* a directory with over one thousand occupations coded with Holland's types to match the results from the SDS and organized to provide information about each specific occupation.[13] Holland uses a three-letter code (e.g., ASE is Artistic-Social-Enterprising) listed in descending order of primacy for the occupational environment. An individual could match his or her SDS scores to the same code in the directory to reference careers that provide a fitting environment.

ASSESSING APTITUDES AND ABILITIES

While achievement tests measure the knowledge and skill an individual has already acquired, ability tests seek to measure maximum performance and reveal the level of present ability an individual has. Aptitude measures the capacity or maximum potential that may develop within an individual in the future.[14] *Achievement* is about past performance. *Ability* is about current skills. *Aptitude* is about future potential. However, the line between the three is not always clear. "An important component of the career assessment process is to help clients accept themselves: their strengths as well as what does not come naturally to them," said Barry Lustig, director of the Professional Development Institute, New York. That is exactly what abilities tests attempt to do.

More than any other type of test, the aptitude and abilities tests selected by a counselor usually depend upon the counseling context. Counselors employed by the federal government generally use the United States Employment Service General Aptitude Test Battery (GATB), while those working with the military tend to use the Armed Services Vocational Aptitude Battery (ASVAB). The three most common aptitude/abilities assessments are the Differential Aptitude Tests (DAT), the GATB, and the ASVAB. All three assessments give occupational profiles that match high scores on a variety of aptitudes, providing guidelines for entry into specific occupations.

DIFFERENTIAL APTITUDE TESTS

The DAT was developed by G. Bennett, H. Seashore, and A. Westman. It is focused primarily on abilities and aptitudes related to scholastic achievement. This test measures aptitudes for eight areas: verbal reasoning, numerical ability, abstract reasoning, clerical speed and accuracy, mechanical reasoning, space relations, spelling, and language usage. Widely researched, norms are available from a random sample of over sixty thousand students. This instrument can be obtained by contacting The Psychological Corporation, 555 Academic Court, San Antonio, TX 78204.

Administering the Differential Aptitude Tests. This test is appropriate for individuals grade eight through adulthood. There are four forms available, including a computerized version and a short version for hiring and selection. The other two forms are full-length versions and contain separate norms for men and women.

Scoring the Differential Aptitude Tests. The DAT can be computer scored or hand plotted. Each type of aptitude is graphed on percentiles.

Interpreting the Differential Aptitude Tests. The first step in interpreting the DAT is to identify which, if any, of the percentiles overlap by more then half. These aptitudes are not significantly different. Next, identify those aptitudes that do not overlap by half or at all. No overlap indicates a significant difference. Another important element of interpretation is the combined verbal reasoning and numerical ability scores, which are often used as predictors of ability for English and math courses, respectively. Consult the interpreter's guide for predictive norms based on percentile scores.

GENERAL APTITUDE TEST BATTERY

The GATB was originally developed by the U. S. Employment Service as a tool for occupational direction. Nine aptitudes are measured by the test:

intelligence (G)

numerical aptitude (N)

spatial aptitude (S)

form perception (P)

clerical perception (Q)

motor coordination (K)

finger dexterity (F)

manual dexterity (M)

The GATB may be obtained by contacting the U. S. Government Printing Office, Washington, DC 20402.

Administering the General Aptitude Test Battery. The GATB can be administered by non-United States Employment Service counselors who complete a short training course. The test is timed and requires two and one-half hours for administration.

Scoring the General Aptitude Test Battery. The GATB is one of the most thoroughly researched test batteries. Results are standard scores (mean = 100; standard deviation = 20). Cutoff scores for entry into various occupations are derived from the results of multiple score patterns, which are identified as Occupational Ability Patterns. These Occupational Ability Patterns are used to guide individuals in career exploration through the *Dictionary of Occupational Titles.*

Interpreting the General Aptitude Test Battery. Interpretation of the GATB begins as the counselor consults the profile report for the raw scores translated into standard scores, which yields twelve aptitude scores. The counselor may find it most helpful to focus first on the three highest scores, defining these aptitudes and explaining which occupations involve these aptitudes. This explanation may be followed by a look at the combination of the three highest scores (the Occupational Ability Pattern) of the individual. This pattern can be used as a reference point to consult the Dictionary of Occupational Titles for possible jobs or general fields.

One of the major concerns for interpretation of the GATB is that it has not kept pace with the rapid changes in the world of work prompted by technology. In addition, the test has been criticized for not accurately reflecting norms across racial and ethnic groups.

ARMED SERVICES VOCATIONAL APTITUDE BATTERY

Designed by the Armed Services primarily for high school seniors, the ASVAB is administered to over a million students each year.[15] The ASVAB measures nine aptitudes: coding speed, word knowledge, arithmetic reasoning, tool knowledge, space relations, mechanical comprehension, shop information, automotive information, and electronics information. For more information about the ASVAB, contact the U. S. Department of Defense, Washington, DC 20301.

Administering the Armed Services Vocational Aptitude Battery. Because the ASVAB is used by the Armed Services as a recruitment devise, it is accessible and free.

Scoring the Armed Services Vocational Aptitude Battery. The nine tests included in the ASVAB combine to create three academic scales (academic ability, verbal, and mathematical) and four occupational scales (mechanical and crafts, business and clerical, electronics and electrical, and health, social, and technical). Scores are expressed in percentiles based on national norms.

Interpreting the Armed Services Vocational Aptitude Battery. The *U.S. Army Career and Education Guide* relates the scores to military and civilian occupations. An interpretive workbook is available at no cost to the test taker.

GIVING FEEDBACK TO THE CLIENT

There are three important principles in the interpretation of assessment score profiles:[16]

- *Differences between scores should be interpreted with caution.* It is important to resist the temptation to attribute meaning to small score differences that actually may be attributed to chance. Resist the temptation to narrow the focus to only highest scores, such as an interest score that is high in mathematics, rather than looking at the broader range of high scores.

- *Profiles should be interpreted with concern for the influence of norms.* Whenever possible, score profiles used for predicting career fit and success should be compared with those of competitors rather than the general population (i.e., interest scores on the SII are normed against scores of individuals actually in the careers listed).[17]

- *Scores should be expressed in ranges rather than points.* Ranges are more helpful and more reliable than a single point score for career exploration.

The effective use of tests in career guidance depends on the extent to which counselees understand and accept the results of test performance. Use the following assessment to test your own feedback and reporting skills as a vocational counselor. This checklist is part of Garfield and Prediger's discussion of the testing competencies and responsibilities of vocational counselors.[18] Rate your own skills on the following scale:

1 = I do this routinely as a regular practice.

2 = I have done on occasion.

3 = I do not do but ought to consider doing.

4 = Not applicable to the instrument(s) I am using.

1. Study suggestions for interpretation provided by the test manual or score/report form and determine which of them are supported by the data provided for the test.

2. Review with the counselee the purpose and nature of the test including:

- Why the test was given; what the test can and cannot do.
- Who will receive the test results.
- What the test results cover, and how they will be used.

3. Interpret test results in the context of the testing experience, the client's background, and other assessments of the same characteristics:

- Encourage a discussion of how the client felt about the testing experience in general, his or her performance in particular, and any difficulties or problems encountered (nervousness, fatigue, distractions, etc.
- Examine the possibility that the client's background (race, gender, disability, age) may have influenced test results.
- Seek additional information to explain any inconsistencies that become evident.

4. Apply good counseling techniques to test interpretation:

- Emphasize strengths while objectively discussing weaknesses.
- Allow sufficient time for the client to assimilate information and respond.
- Listen attentively to the counselee's responses (attending to the client first and the test results second).
- Check the client's understanding of the test results from time to time, discerning misconceptions and correcting them.

5. Help the client begin or continue the career-planning process by setting action goals and follow-through counseling sessions.

Assessment is a vital part of effective vocational counseling. Each test provides one piece of valuable information to further self-understanding in the client. However, neither the client nor the counselor can abdicate responsibility for career decisions to assessment results. There is no substitute for the richness of the counseling relationship, which enables one to interpret past achievements, life experiences, and test results uniquely and with artistry. Test scores are not the final word; they are not God-given. The one human factor they cannot measure is motivation. A *C* student with sky-high motivation may make a better professional than an *A* student who has no inner fire.

NOTES

1. W. Sheldon, E. Hartl, and E. McDermott, *Varieties of Delinquent Youth: An Introduction to Constitutional Psychiatry* (New York: Harper, 1949).

2. J. Mitchell, Jr., ed.,*Tests in Print III* (Lincoln, Neb.: University of Nebraska Press, 1983).

3. E. Stephens, *Career Counseling and Placement in Higher Education: A Student Personnel Function* (Bethlehem, Penn.: The College Placement Council, 1970).

4. Ibid.

5. H. Gough, *California Psychological Inventory Administrator's Guide* (Palo Alto, Calif.: Consulting Psychologist Press, 1987).

6. H. Murray, *Explorations in Personality* (New York: Oxford University Press, 1938).

7. V. Zunker, *Using Assessment Results for Career Development*, 4th ed. (Pacific Grove, Calif.: Brooks/Cole, 1994), 84.

8. S. Krebs Hirsh and J. Kummerow, *An Introduction to Type in Organizations* (Palo Alto, Calif.: Consulting Psychologists Press, 1987).

9. A. Anastasi, *Psychological Testing,* 6th ed.(New York: Macmillan, 1988).

10. J. Holland, *Making Vocational Choices: A Theory of Careers*, 2d ed. (Englewood Cliffs, N.J.: Prentice Hall, 1985).

11. J. Hansen, *User's Guide for the SVIB-SII* (Palo Alto, Calif.: Consulting Psychologists Press, 1985).

12. J. Holland, *The Self-Directed Search: Professional Manual* (Odessa, Fla.: Psychological Assessment Resources, 1987).

13. J. Holland, *The Occupations Finder* (Odessa, Fla.: Psychological Assessment Resources, 1987).

14. R. Goldenson, *Longman Dictionary of Psychology and Psychiatry* (New York: Longman, 1984).

15. V. Zunker, *Using Assessment Results for Career Development*, 4th ed. (Pacific Grove, Calif.: Brooks/Cole, 1994).

16. Ibid.

17. L. Cronbach, *Essentials of Psychological Testing*, 4th ed. (New York: Harper and Row, 1984).

18. N. Garfield and D. Rediger, "Testing Competencies and Responsibilities: A Checklist for Vocational Counselors," in *A Counselor's Guide to Vocational Guidance Instruments*, ed. J. Kapes and M. Mastie (Washington, D.C.: National Vocational Guidance Association, 1982).

Chapter Thirteen

Equipping for the Job Search

A POPULAR CARTOON AMONG CAREER counselors depicts a man kneeling beside his bed in prayer saying, "Dear Lord, connect me with a firm of aggressive professionals with proven track records that will let me pursue rapid career growth with a team of professionals involved in state-of-the-art projects in a solid-growth company."

It is not unusual for job seekers to have lofty requests. Sometimes they expect their job to materialize from thin air. In this chapter we focus on equipping the client to assume personal responsibility for finding a job. Career counselors and employment agencies can help, but ultimately the job seeker must put the words in the résumé, complete the application form, do company research, and face the employer.

As someone has said, people can be divided into three groups: those who make things happen, those who watch things happen, and those who wonder what happened. The following information is designed to help clients make things happen. It is divided into strategies for the job search, résumé writing, cover letter writing, and interviews.

JOB SEARCH STRATEGIES

Regardless of the method used, finding a job is a job. It takes time, effort, planning, and preparation on the part of the job seeker. Ways for finding a job can be traditional or nontraditional. A traditional approach to job-hunting emphasizes using all the methods available to communicate with as many employers as one can. For that reason, it is sometimes referred to as the *numbers game*. The nontraditional approach involves identifying and targeting employers through personal research in the hidden job market—jobs that are not officially advertised. Sometimes a combination of the two approaches works best. In order to land a job more quickly, the job seeker must get organized, research companies, learn to network, search the hidden job market, and be persistent.

GETTING ORGANIZED

The job seeker needs a job-search headquarters to keep things organized. Any place will do, but it should be similar to a study area. A good headquarters includes a desk or table where supplies, notes, and incoming mail can be kept. This area serves as an office for finding a job and makes record-keeping easier. Any expense associated with the job search is deductible on federal income-taxes (e. g., travel expenses or fees paid to a career counselor are deductible.)

RESEARCHING COMPANIES

Clients must assume the job of getting a job. This generally begins with researching places where they might work. Every large library has an extensive collection of resources on potential work settings. With the assistance of a librarian, your client should set aside at least two full days strictly for library work. This research will provide a good feel for the target market. The more research clients do, the better cover letters they will write and the more effective will be their interviews. To research a profession, they can use the *Dictionary of Occupational*

Titles, the *Occupational Outlook Handbook,* the *Encyclopedia of Careers and Vocational Guidance,* and trade publications and magazine articles about various professions. The *Encyclopedia of Business Information Sources* lists industry fields such as oil, or finance, or real estate. Under each are listed the most important periodicals, books, and associations devoted to that field, so they can quickly research any field in depth. In addition to libraries, quasi-governmental groups such as regional economic development groups and chambers of commerce have information on local companies. If your clients are doing an out-of-town search, a chamber of commerce is often a good place to start. Of course, the job seekers should take notes on all their research. We recommend a three-by-five card for each organization of interest or notes in a three-ring notebook. (The notebook can also hold machine copies of material.)

Learning to Network

"It's not what you know but who you know," says common wisdom for the job seeker. When asked to identify the first source of information about a newly acquired job, people in three different studies ranked personal contacts highest (66–54 percent).[1] Encourage your clients to use their social contacts for work information. At the very least, job seekers should tell everyone they know about their quest for work. More fish will be caught in a big pond with a broad net than in a small pond with a pole and worm.

Job seekers should never stop after one lead, because a job lead does not necessarily bring a job offer. Clients need to know about as many vacancies as possible, compiling a list of several jobs from which they can make a selection. Interestingly, more job leads are likely to come from acquaintances than from close friends or relatives. This is what researcher Mark Granovetter calls "the strength of weak ties."[2]

Searching the Hidden Job Market

The help-wanted ads in a newspaper and the listings in public and private employment agencies are not the only sources of vacancies. There are more job openings in the hidden job market than are visible to the general public. Only 15–20 percent of all job openings on any given day are published and circulated. Between 80 to 85 percent of all employment comes though the hidden market.[3]

The hidden portion of the job market exists from the time an idea to create a job enters the mind of a person with hiring authority to the time the job is revealed to the public though announcements. The intervening time gives the aggressive job seeker an opportunity to penetrate the hidden market though his or her own network of personal contacts. Many employers prefer to hire though an inside system of their own personal contacts rather than by any other method, feeling that it does not cost them as much and that the information they obtain is more reliable.

BEING PERSISTENT

Persistence in the job search is of great importance to the job-hunter. No job-search system will work without persistence. Disappointments are inevitable, but discouragements are not. In the government's monthly unemployment figures, there is a special category for "discouraged workers"—those who have stopped looking for jobs. Rejection is built into the job-search process. Yet even when clients know the rejection has nothing to do with them personally, their ego gets bashed every time they are turned down.

However, there is an alternative to discouragement and shame. One writer describes it as a *No, No, No, No, No, No, No, No, Yes!* process. Every *No* gets the job seeker that much closer to the *Yes*. It is like selling a house—it only takes one buyer regardless of how many lookers show up.

To persist, candidates must be realistic about the time necessary for job-hunting. Most job hunters spend less than five hours a week on their job search. If they were to make job-hunting their full-time job, thirty-five hours a week, they would speed up the process by a factor of seven and increase their chances accordingly.

RÉSUMÉ WRITING

The importance of résumé writing cannot be stressed too strongly. The résumé (or in some cases the curriculum vitae or personal data sheet) is the first criterion of the selection process. It is the key to opening up opportunities. The résumé gets a job seeker through the door for an interview.

An employer seldom sees a job seeker without a résumé. Richard Bolles, author of *What Color is Your Parachute?*, says that the résumé may serve to jog the employer's memory. Bolles advises mailing a résumé after the interview and tailoring it to the skills needed for the job. It can be sent with a thank-you note attached to a cover letter.[4]

Résumés answer one primary question for the employer: "Why should this person be considered for this job?" They are essential for individuals seeking professional, technical, administrative, or managerial jobs and are often needed for clerical and sales positions.

Preparing an effective résumé is an exercise in introspection. Job seekers need to answer questions about themselves:

Who am I?

What do I do well?

What do I want?

Preparing a résumé is also creative. An approach that works best usually takes several drafts and some experimenting with different formats. Of course, it goes without saying that the basics such as neatness and correct spelling are essential. Study after study shows that employers strongly prefer résumés that are neat, grammatically correct, and free of spelling errors.[5]

The physical appearance of the résumé is also critical. Use high-quality paper. The traditional plain white bond or off-white textured bond is recommended. The material should be balanced on the page so the total effect is attractive and pleasing to the eye. Standard margins are one inch on each side.

Many employers will not take time to read a long résumé. One page is usually sufficient; however, résumés of two pages may be appropriate for people with several years of work experience with many achievements and responsibilities to cover.

Résumé is derived from a French word meaning "summary." It summarizes the job objective, education, work experience, and so on in order to sell the candidate's qualifications to the employer. Résumés can be thought of as a verbal picture of the candidate.

Employers and personnel workers do not have the time or patience to plow through stacks of letters crammed with inappropriate material. A well-designed résumé is concise, to the point, and in sequential order. The résumé should include:

- *Identifying Information.* This includes the job seeker's name, address, and telephone numbers. Both a permanent and a temporary address may be included.

- *Job Objective.* The job objective identifies the responsibilities, challenges, and work activities that the job seeker wishes to assume. Job titles or descriptive phrases should be used to specify the particular job or kind of job being sought (entry-level as well as long-range goals may be indicated).The *Dictionary of Occupational Titles* may be helpful in locating appropriate job titles as well as in putting into words the range of duties sought.

- *Educational Background.* This includes a list of schools attended, dates, degrees, diplomas, and certificates, with emphasis on the highest level achieved and special training pertinent to the candidate's job objective.

- *Experience or Work History.* This is a summary of the job seeker's work experience. Describe the nature of the work, job title, name of employer, and inclusive dates of employment. Work experience relevant to the job objective should be emphasized. For students with little or no relevant experience, it is important to list all summer, part-time, and significant volunteer positions held.

- *Military Record.* This is a brief statement of service obligations, if any, or service experience, if a tour of duty is completed. If the candidate's work history and educational background were mostly military, this information should be included under the previous headings.

- *References.* State simply that references will be supplied on request. However, if the job seeker is registered with a placement office and has a complete credential job-placement file, reference should be made to the availability of the confidential data from that office, noting its full address and telephone number. A job application may ask for two or three people who can be contacted as references. So before beginning your job campaign, identify your references, ask permission to use their names, and obtain their complete addresses and telephone numbers.

- *Personal Data.* Included in this final section is early background (if it is significant), hobbies, and other activities. Personal characteristics such as age, sex, marital status, or physical disabilities may be omitted. The employer can ask for this information after the job seeker is hired.

There are several types of résumés. The most common are chronological, functional, analytical, and imaginative.

1. *Chronological.* This begins with the candidate's most recent educational and work activity. Other experiences are then listed in order of occurrence. Starting and ending dates are used to show how long the person was involved in each activity. This format is most common, especially for job seekers with limited experience. It is easy to follow because of its logical sequence and allows the reader to trace the job seeker's educational and work history rapidly.

2. *Functional.* This approach highlights the function of the positions a candidate has held. The goal of this type of résumé is to place the most significant work experience immediately before the employer. Job titles and specific duties are highlighted to support qualifications for the job. This approach is especially useful for persons with considerable experience, because it allows them to highlight part-time, temporary, and volunteer work in their career field more effectively than the chronological résumé.

3. *Analytical.* This approach emphasizes particular vocational skills or specialized knowledge by grouping

background experiences according to their common features. It does not highlight a chronological sequence or specific job titles.

4. *Imaginative*. The imaginative or creative format is probably the most difficult to prepare and the most risky. The general goal of this approach is to stand out from other applicants in some unique way because of the appearance of the résumé. This format requires a considerable amount of planning, creative writing talent, and a willingness to violate established norms. These résumés may include unique graphic displays, headlines, color, and direct quotations from former employers or teachers. Employers in artistic fields, such as advertising or theater, are most apt to appreciate this type of résumé.

The sample résumés in appendix D highlight the career path of Sandra Parker. As you read each résumé, notice how Parker uses the four different types of résumés to accomplish different job objectives.

A survey of employers in large American corporations reported their views concerning what should or should not be included in a résumé. In terms of correctness of content, poor grammar was ranked as the greatest deficit. Spelling errors ran a close second, followed by poor organization of the résumé itself. Of these employers, 66 percent felt that a one-page résumé was usually sufficient, and 83 percent thought the résumé should never exceed two pages. Beyond the initial contact with the employer, résumés were seen as having two important functions: (1) to serve as an outline around which the interview can be structured; (2) to serve as a concrete reminder to the employer of the job applicant after the interview is over.[6]

THE COVER LETTER

Every résumé needs to be accompanied by a cover letter (also called a letter of application). The cover letter is the first thing employers see when a job seeker initiates contact. Cover letters can be sent to discover job openings, initiate contacts, respond to an advertisement, or follow up on a referral.

The purposes of a cover letter are to introduce the candidate to a prospective employer and to bring attention to the enclosed résumé. The goal of the letter and the résumé is to create a desire in the employer to send the job seeker a job application. Ultimately, the letter, résumé, and application will lead to an interview and a job offer.

Addressing a cover letter to a specific person by name is far more effective than using "Dear Madam," "Dear Sir," or an official title. If the applicant does not know a specific name, telephoning the organization and requesting the name and title of the appropriate person is strongly encouraged. Generally, a secretary or receptionist will provide this information. Using a general salutation makes the letter too impersonal.

Almost all personnel managers in one survey agreed that one page is a sufficient length for a cover letter.[7] Three or four short paragraphs are all that is needed. The first paragraph can state why the candidate is writing and why he or she wants the job. The second paragraph can state the person's qualifications. The third paragraph can bring attention to the enclosed résumé and request an interview. This is only a suggested format; the cover letter should reflect the applicant's personal style.

Some job seekers omit the personalized cover letter when they mail hundreds of résumés in a direct-mail campaign. Research indicates, however, that sending a résumé together with a cover letter is more effective than presenting a résumé alone. (See appendix E for an example of a typical cover letter.)

Interviewing Skills

The hard work of scanning the newspaper want ads, researching companies, and preparing a résumé and a cover letter eventually comes down to going face-to-face with an interviewer. Anxiety inevitably mounts as the interview time approaches. The job seeker feels his or her whole life is going to be decided in the short span of thirty minutes. Everything seems to depend on the interview. However, there is much a vocational counselor can do to ease this agony.

If an applicant is tormenting himself or herself with worry, research has shown it is helpful to imagine the worst.[8] The client should paint the worst possible picture of failure. He or she can envision going into the interviewer's dark office, seeing the interviewer as a crotchety person who wants to reject him or her on the spot, and then being rejected. This is called the worst-case scenario. However, when the client has accepted the worst-case scenario, get back to reality. The world does not end if the client is not offered a position. There are other jobs to seek. The more the client interviews, the easier it becomes. This is the message of the poem by Jacob A. Riis:

> When nothing else seems to help, I go and watch the
> stone cutter hammering away at his rock,
> perhaps a hundred times without a crack
> shown in it. Yet on the hundred-and-first blow
> the rock will split in two, and I know that it was
> not only that blow which split it, but all that had
> gone before.

Effective job interviewing is a skill that can be learned. So a vocational counselor can help applicants improve their interviewing skills by practicing for the interview. For example, clients can imagine they are the interviewer. What kinds of questions would they ask of an applicant for a position in their organization? Frank S. Endicott, former director of placement at Northwestern University, found that interviewers in ninety-two companies asked fifty common questions.[9]

1. What are your long-range and short-range goals and objectives; when and why did you establish these goals; and how are you preparing yourself to achieve them?
2. What specific goals, other than those related to your occupation, have you established for yourself for the next ten years?
3. What do you see yourself doing five years from now?
4. What do you really want to do in life?
5. What are your long-range career objectives?

6. How do you plan to achieve your career goals?

7. What are the most important rewards you expect in your business career?

8. What do you expect to be earning in five years?

9. Why did you choose the career for which you are preparing?

10. Which is more important to you, the money or the type of job?

11. What do you consider to be your greatest strengths and weaknesses?

12. How would you describe yourself?

13. How do you think a friend or professor who knows you well would describe you?

14. What motivates you to put forth your greatest effort?

15. How has your college experience prepared you for a business career?

16. Why should I hire you?

17. What qualifications do you have that make you think you will be successful in business?

18. How do you determine or evaluate success?

19. What do you think it takes to be successful in a company like ours?

20. In what ways do you think you can make a contribution to our company?

21. What qualities should a successful manager possess?

22. Describe the relationship that should exist between a supervisor and those reporting to him or her.

23. What two or three accomplishments have given you the most satisfaction? Why?

24. Describe your most rewarding college experience.

25. If you were hiring a graduate for this position, what qualities would you look for?

26. Why did you select your college or university?

27. What led you to choose your field of major study?
28. What college subjects did you like best? Why?
29. What college subjects did you like least? Why?
30. If you could do so, how would you plan your academic study differently? Why?
31. What changes would you make in your college or university? Why?
32. Do you have plans for continued study? An advanced degree?
33. Do you think that your grades are a good indication of your academic achievement?
34. What have you learned from participation in extracurricular activities?
35. In what kind of work environment are you most comfortable?
36. How do you work under pressure?
37. In what part-time or summer jobs have you been most interested? Why?
38. How would you describe the ideal job for you following graduation?
39. Why did you decide to seek a position with this company?
40. What do you know about our company?
41. What two or three things are most important to you in your job?
42. Are you seeking employment in a company of a certain size? Why?
43. What criteria are you using to evaluate the company for which you hope to work?
44. Do you have a geographical preference? Why?
45. Will you relocate? Does relocation bother you?
46. Are you willing to travel?
47. Are you willing to spend at least six months as a trainee?
48. Why do you think you might like to live in the community in which our company is located?

49. What major problem have you encountered, and how did you deal with it?

50. What have you learned from your mistakes?

If Endicott's list is a bit overwhelming, consider a list of the ten toughest business questions that executives ask of applicants for leadership positions. The list was developed by Joan Detz, a writer and lecturer on communication topics for *New Woman* magazine:[10]

1. *The hypothetical question*: "Suppose you were given an assignment during your first week on the job and couldn't meet the deadline. What would you do?"

Ms. Detz suggests that the job seeker try to avoid doomsday situations like this because they lead to an endless cycle of "what if" follow-up questions. Do not focus on what you would do if you failed; focus on what you will do to make sure that your efforts are a success.

2. *The yes-or-no question*: "Will you be able to do this job on your own, right away?"

Ms. Detz advises that applicants not be hasty with a *yes* answer but respond, "From the information I now have, it looks like things should go smoothly. However, I may need to consult with you if the situation changes or if I need more resources to manage it successfully."

3. *The what-do-you-think-the-other-guy-thinks question*: "How do you think your supervisor will view your leaving your present position?"

Avoid being a mind reader. Instead, you might respond, "My supervisor has agreed to write a reference letter for me, so she apparently understands my need for a change and my decision to advance in my career. If you have any questions about my performance, you might ask her directly."

4. *The ranking question*: "What do you think are the two or three most important concerns of people who are entering the type of position you are applying for?"

This question presupposes that the candidate has a great deal of familiarity with the position and with the other applicants. The applicant should not answer for others but should speak for himself or herself, pointing out that opinions will no doubt vary from applicant to applicant.

    5. *The nonquestion question*: "I've enjoyed reading your credentials, but I don't think your background matches with our needs."

This form of resistance to a person's application is a challenge that should not go unanswered. Ms. Detz advises that the job seeker turn it into a question such as, "You wonder how I can best serve you in the job. Let me tell you what makes me the best candidate . . ."

    6. *The off-the-record question*: "Between you and me, is your company really the best place for me to be looking for someone to fill this position?"

Although questions such as this may seem to provide the applicant with an opportunity to openly express frustrations with a current position (if any), it can come back to haunt the applicant in two ways. First, secrets shared in confidence have a way of getting out. Second, it puts the applicant in an awkward position of gossiping about someone else and may create some doubt about the applicant's sense of loyalty. Therefore, the applicant should not tell the interviewer anything "in confidence" that he or she would not share in public. Instead, focus on how personal background experiences will be of benefit to the employer.

    7. *The A-or-B orientation question*: "What is more important to you, salary or job?"

Most people want a job that pays adequate salary and provides an opportunity for long-term professional growth. An applicant need not exclude one to get the other. Feel free to say, "Both are important to me as opportunities to . . ."

    8. *The why question*: "Most people are alike. Why should I hire you for the position?"

When an applicant hears the word *why*, Ms. Detz advises the individual to put himself or herself in the interviewer's shoes. Think about what the employer needs and what he or she can do to fill those needs. For example, "Judging from the job description and our conversation, I gather that you are looking for someone who is a self-starter, can set goals, and isn't afraid of a challenge. I'm that kind of person. Let me tell you a bit more about how I've demonstrated those qualities in my studies and outside employment."

    9. *The false-premise question*: "I notice you have had a series of short-term positions. I wonder why. Can't you keep a job for a long period?"

If this question is not immediately challenged or corrected, it will continue to haunt the applicant during the interview. A firm response is best. Something like, "In my desire to make my résumé brief and easy for you to read, I did not describe my reasons for leaving the positions I have listed. I'm sorry that it has left you with an inaccurate impression of my background, and I want to thank you for bringing it up so I can provide you with more complete information. Let me explain more fully why I left each position and what I gained from working in each place."

    10. *The open question*: "So tell me all about your last job."

Open-ended questions provide a golden opportunity to show why the applicant is an attractive candidate for the position. Applicants can anticipate the opportunity and be ready in advance with a short summary statement of how they utilized their interests, values, and skills. Applicants may continue by telling how their last job prepared them for the job they are presently seeking. They may start their summary statement with, "My last job required that I be able to. . . . I was successful at it because I was skillful at. . . . It also gave me an opportunity to do the following things that are important to me in a job. These are the qualities I will bring to your position."

In addition to knowing what kind of questions to expect, the applicant can benefit from several simple tips:

Wear clothing that will represent him or her well.

Know exactly where to go.

Arrive on time.

Posture should be relaxed and alert.

Maintain eye contact.

Be equipped with a pen, an extra résumé, and a small notebook.

Know the name and title of the interviewer.

Give the impression of optimism and energy.

Be sincere, brief, and truthful.

Prepare a few good questions to ask the interviewer about the position and the organization (see figure 13.1).

Questions for Job Hunters to Ask Interviewers

1. What kinds of people do you usually hire?
2. What is the growth potential for the company? What new products or services are being planned?
3. Is there a job description of the available position? If so, may I see it? What typical assignments or responsibilities are in this job?
4. Is the job a new position? If not, who was the person on this job before he or she left, and what is that person doing now?
5. What qualities are you looking for in a person you expect to hire for this position?
6. What is management's policy or practice regarding promoting people from within the organization?
7. How will (the economy, a recent governmental action, a strike, the weather, a materials shortage, and so on) affect the operation of the organization (or department)?
8. What efforts are being made to improve (a situation you know about in production, construction, inventory, supply, accounting, management, technical details, and so on)?
9. How much responsibility would I have in (planning, budgeting, decision making, and so on)?
10. Will I be required to travel? How much time would I spend away from the home location?
11. How would you describe working conditions here? (Specific items could be hours, overtime, noise factor, work setting, company policies, etc.)
12. When should I expect you to contact me?

Fig. 13.1

Job search strategies, sources of job leads, writing résumés and cover letters, and interviewing for jobs. What remains? After a successful job search, some people fail to write a thank-you to their potential employer. Clients should be encouraged to send an appreciation note no later than two or three days after the interview. Thoughtfulness marks them as a courteous person and serves to activate the memory of the person who interviewed them.

At best, job seeking is hard work and must be approached as such. Sloppy homework, a disorganized approach, and laziness lengthens the process and contributes to its drudgery. None of the suggestions in this chapter are magic buttons. But taken together, they will ease the way to increase the probability of long-term career success.

NOTES

1. S. Silliker, "The Role of Social Contacts in the Successful Job Search," *Journal of Employment Counseling* 30 (1993): 25–35.

2. M. S. Granovetter, *Getting a Job: A Study of Contacts and Careers* (Cambridge, Mass.: Harvard University Press, 1974).

3. T. Jackson, *Guerrilla Tactics in the New Job Market*, 2d ed. (New York: Bantam Books, 1991).

4. R. N. Bolles, *What Color Is Your Parachute? A Practical Manual for Job-Hunters and Career Changers* (Berkeley, Calif.: Ten Speed Press, 1986).

5. H. H. Meyers, "Writing Résumés Right," *Journal of College Placement* 44 (1984): 19–21.

6. E. J. Rogers "Elements of Effective Job-Hunting," *Journal of College Placement* 40 (1979): 55–58.

7. Meyers, "Résumés," 19–21.

8. P. Hellman, *Ready, Aim, You're Hired! How to Job Interview Successfully Anytime, Anywhere, and With Anyone* (New York: AMACOM, 1986).

9. V. R. Lindquist, *The Northwestern Lindquist-Endicott Report* (Evanston, Ill.: Northwestern University Placement Center, n. d.).

10. Joan Detz, "Ten Toughest Business Questions," *New Woman*, January 1989, 132.

Chapter Fourteen

Developing a Career Resource Center

Gone are the days when a vocational counselor's resources consisted of a few volumes and a drab file of career-related materials. Today a centrally located facility for organizing and displaying up-to-date materials is possible and necessary. An abundance of career-related materials have appeared on the market in the last few years. They are attractive and designed to be openly displayed. Career resource materials have been elevated to a position of central importance and are a critical part of effective vocational counseling.

In this chapter we discuss the basics of a career resource center and identify some of the most important materials needed for starting one.

WHAT IS A CAREER RESOURCE CENTER?

Career Resource Centers (CRC) are also referred to as Career Information Centers and Career Development Resource

Centers. Each serves the same purpose of centrally locating the most timely, accurate, and usable career information available.[1] The purpose of a CRC is to help individuals in the career planning and job-search process. In many respects, the CRC has become the focal point of career-planning and placement programs. The center is used by persons in every phase of career development. Some people are seeking information to narrow down choices while others are looking for broader information. The CRC is designed to meet the unique needs of people in various phases of career decision making.

A CRC does not require a lot of space or money. It can be limited to a corner in a church library or in the waiting area of a counseling office. Locating it directly in the counseling office, however, is not a good idea since clients will need to spend time browsing.

A CRC is often supported by an advisory committee, who serve as its advocates and promoters. The membership of this committee may consist of teachers, counselors, pastors, community members, representatives of local businesses, and so on. In academic settings, alumni are a valuable resource. This committee helps the CRC in a number of ways. The following recommendations are for functions of a CRC advisory committee in a school setting:

1. Develop long- and short-term objectives for the career resource center.

2. Establish relationships with local businesses, industrial complexes, manufacturing firms, and labor unions.

3. Review, evaluate, and recommend occupational materials and equipment for purchase.

4. Develop an adequate budget to maintain the center.

5. Initiate and encourage follow-up studies of graduates.

6. Assist in promoting career-education programs within the district.

7. Encourage teachers and counselors to become familiar with industries and businesses in the community via tours. Write entry-level job descriptions for the elementary reading level.

8. Develop a research design for the evaluation of a center.

9. Assist in identifying sources of funding for centers.

The advisory committee can be a significant part of a CRC. As the CRC becomes operational, the committee will also become actively engaged in evaluating programs and revising objectives for future development. A governing board of this type will be able to promote greater acceptance and wider use of a CRC. Such a board can be particularly important for developing supportive relationships with the local business community.

STARTING A CAREER RESOURCE CENTER

The purpose of a Career Resource Center is to make job- and career-related materials available to job seekers and people making career decisions. However, the visual impact of the center is important. Avoid an odds and ends look. If jobs, work, and careers are as vital to life as we know they are, the center where these materials are gathered must be worthy of its purpose.

To be effective, resources in a CRC should be as direct, personal, and interactive as possible.[2] Simple tools such as computer files of contacts in various occupations (e.g., a list of church members by occupation with work telephone numbers) and attractive bulletin boards displaying current job openings (full-time, part-time, or internship opportunities) are very effective.

In addition to these contacts and a current list of job openings, a CRC should have numerous printed resources covering a wide variety of information to assist people in their career journeys. Most career experts agree that an effective CRC would include resources in the following categories:[3]

1. occupational information

2. armed service information

3. information about colleges and universities

4. information on technical and professional schools

5. financial aid information

6. local job and internship information

7. job-search resources

8. résumé preparation resources

9. information on job interviews

10. career planning information.

The balance of this chapter provides a representative list of resources for counselors to consider when purchasing items for each of these areas.

OCCUPATIONAL INFORMATION

This component is the foundation of a career resource center. The two major needs are (1) descriptions of occupations and (2) projections or outlook information about the future demand for workers in these occupations.

One primary resource each career center must have is *The Occupational Outlook Handbook* (see following list). Revised every two years, this handbook lists hundreds of occupations and is a valuable source of career information including: what workers do on the job, working conditions, training and education needed, earnings, and expected job prospects (based on technological advances, changes in business practices, foreign competition, and shifts in the national economy). The list below provides examples of occupation-oriented resources:

Dictionary of Occupational Titles, Superintendent of Documents, U.S. Government Printing Office, Washington, DC 20402.

Encyclopedia of Careers and Vocational Guidance, Doubleday and Company, Inc., 501 Franklin Avenue, Garden City, NY 11530.

Modern Vocational Trends Reference Handbook, Monarch Press, Division of Simon and Schuster, Inc., 12th Floor, 1320 Avenue of the Americas, New York, NY 10020.

Occupational Briefs, Chronicle Guidance Publications, Inc., Moravia, NY 13118.

Occupational Outlook Handbook, Superintendent of Documents, U. S. Government Printing Office, Washington, DC 20402.

ARMED SERVICE INFORMATION

All branches of the military provide information covering programs. Military related resources include job descriptions for positions found in the military and the addresses of local recruiting offices. The U. S. military provides the following career development publications:

Air Force Information, Headquarters, U. S. Air Force Recruiting Service, Attn.: Director of Advertising and Publicity, Wright Patterson Air Force Base, OH 454333.

Military Career Guide, U. S. Military Entrance Processing Command, 2500 Green Bay Road, North Chicago, IL 60064,

Navy Career Guide, Chief of Naval Personnel, Department of the Navy, Washington, DC 20370.

The U.S. Army Career and Education Guide, Army Careers, U.S. Army Recruiting Command, Hampton, VA 23369.

INFORMATION ABOUT COLLEGES AND UNIVERSITIES

This section of the CRC provides information about two- and four-year baccalaureate and graduate programs. Relevant information includes: geographical location, tuition fees, available financial aid, descriptions of institutions, accreditation information, academic calendars, statistics on the nature of the student body, entrance requirements, application procedures, etc. A collection of the catalogs published by the colleges and universities in the surrounding region is expected. In addition, there are several publications that provide general information about institutions of higher education in the United States.

American Junior Colleges, American Council on Education, 1 Dupont Circle, Washington, DC 20036.

American Universities and Colleges, American Council on Education, 1 Dupont Circle, Washington, DC 20036.

The College Blue Book, Macmillan Information Corporation, 866 Third Avenue, New York, NY 10022.

Peterson's Guides to Graduate and Professional Programs—1994 (available in engineering and applied sciences; business education, health, and law; physical sciences and mathematics; biological and agricultural sciences; humanities and social sciences), Peterson's Guides, Princeton, NJ 08540.

INFORMATION ON TECHNICAL AND PROFESSIONAL SCHOOLS

Vocational, trade, and technical school information should include a listing of private and public schools that offer specific entry-level trade and technical training. A listing of local, regional, and statewide programs will be most helpful.

American Trade School Directory, Croner Publications, Queens Village, NY (need zip).

Lovejoy's Career and Vocational School Guide—A Handbook of Job-Training Opportunities, Simon and Schuster, Inc., 1230 Avenue of the Americas, New York, NY 10020.

FINANCIAL AID INFORMATION

Information about loans, grants, and scholarships from federal, state, private, and local sources will also be helpful. Specific information on the local and state resources is also important. The following publications offer information on financial aid:

Financial Aids for Higher Education, William C. Brown Co., Publisher, 2460 Kerper Blvd., Dubuque, IA 52001.

How to Get Money for : Education, Fellowships and Scholarships, Chilton Book Co., School Library Services, 201 King of Prussia Rd., Radnor, PA 19089.

Scholarships, Fellowships and Loans, Bellman Publishing Co., P.O. Box 164, Arlington, MA 02174.

The Student Guide for Federal Financial Aid Programs, Department of Education, Federal State Aid Information Center, P.O. Box 84, Washington, DC 20044.

LOCAL JOB AND INTERNSHIP INFORMATION

There is a keenly felt need for firsthand experience and on-the-job training. A good CRC will have information about local opportunities and special training programs. Publications that provide this information on programs nationally include:

Alternative to College, Macmillan Information, 866 Third Avenue, New York, NY 10022.

Directory of Internships, Work Experience Programs and On-the-Job Training Opportunities, Ready References Press, Specialized Indexes, Inc., 100 East Thousand Oaks Blvd., Suite 224, Thousand Oaks, CA 91360.

First Supplement to the Directory: On-the-Job Training and Where to Get It, Simon and Schuster, 1230 Avenue of the Americas, New York, NY 10020.

JOB-SEARCH RESOURCES

Providing linkages with job openings is the primary purpose of this section of the resource center. Job-search resources must be relevant to the job market in your community and the surrounding area. It is crucial to gather information about job openings, recruiting, and hiring practices from the major health-care suppliers, retailers, restaurants, hotels, banks, manufacturers, and local and state government agencies. Just contact these employers and ask to be included on the mailing list for open positions as they occur. Also, create a filing system that includes a contact name for the organization and any specific information you may learn.

In addition to actual job openings, the following publications offer assistance with job-search skills:

Graduating into the Nineties: Getting the Most Out of Your First Job after College. Carol Carter and Gary June. The Noonday Press. New York. 1993.

An effective guide to maximize the experiences of the early working years, this book contains interviews with recent graduates and seasoned professionals who also deal with the realities of today's economic climate. The guide also offers suggestions for developing relationships with coworkers and supervisors, handling success and failure, and making decisions about career change. The appendices are an excellent resource for information on how to write well, speak in public, handle business travel, and establish connections with professional associations.

Guerrilla Tactics in the New Job Market. Tom Jackson. Bantam Books. New York. 1991.

This book is for everyone who is looking for their first job, planning a rise through the ranks, or reentering the work force. It provides practical strategies, case studies, and insights including seventy-seven tactics and twenty-five proven fast-track tactics designed to help chart a course to success.

The Hunt. Tom Washington. Mount Vernon Press. Bellevue, Wash. 1992.

This is a comprehensive book on finding a job. It is filled with hundreds of practical ideas, strategies, and tips and contains effective résumé writing techniques. The book also explores the psychology of interviewing.

Marketing Yourself. Catalyst Staff. Bantam Books. New York. 1980.

Catalyst, a national organization of resources for women, provides job information and career counseling for women who are looking for work, changing jobs, or reentering the job market. This step-by-step guide tells how to land a job by presenting yourself effectively on paper and in person.

Network Your Way to Job and Career Success. Ronald L. Krannich and Caryl Rae Krannich. Impact Publications. Manassas Park, Va. 1989.

These authors have more than thirty career books to their credit. In this volume, they provide practical guidance on how to organize effective job networks, prospect for job leads, write networking letters, conduct informational interviews, follow up referrals, and maintain and expand networks that lead to job interviews and offers.

Through the Brick Wall: How to Job-Hunt in a Tight Market. Kate Wendleton. Villard Books. New York. 1992.

This savvy and effective job-search guide teaches how to conduct a job campaign in the toughest of times. Wendleton guides the job seeker in a process of selecting a job target, achieving interviews in the job-target area, and negotiating job offers. Her inspirational style of writing adds to the appeal of this timely book.

Résumé Preparation Resources

There are numbers of self-help materials that assist individuals in writing resumes. In addition, you may wish to compile a loose-leaf notebook of sample résumés that is available for review and comparison. The following is a representative list of the materials available.

The Damn Good Résumé Guide. Yana Parker. Ten Speed Press. Berkeley, Calif. 1989.

This is a self-marketing tool designed with one goal—securing a job interview. It has five essential parts: a clearly stated job objective, the highlights of qualification, a presentation of directly relevant skills and experience, a chronological work history, and a place for listing education and training.

The Perfect Resume. Tom Jackson. Doubleday. New York. 1990.

This résumé book includes over fifty samples of job-winning résumés, easy-to-use résumé drafting forms, special résumés for recent graduates and for women reentering the job market, job-finding tips, salary negotiating strategies, and tips on how to write the perfect cover letter.

Résumé Writing: A Comprehensive How-to-Do-It Guide. Burdette Bostwisk. Wiley. New York. 1990.

This widely recognized comprehensive guide to résumé writing addresses key questions about how to go about the ten most successful résumé styles and how they can be used in a variety of occupations. A variety of cover letters is also included, along with ways to maximize computers and other technology in the job search.

INFORMATION ON JOB INTERVIEWS

The reward of an active job campaign is landing an interview. However, negotiating the interview is often the most threatening aspect of the job search. There are several outstanding publications on the topic of interviewing.

How You Really Get Hired: The Inside Story from a College Recruiter. J. L. LaFevre. Arco. New York. 1989.

This book provides practical tips offered by a seasoned recruiter. It is particularly designed for a recent college graduate. The job-search wisdom includes such directives as, "always wait ten days before responding to a job opening," and "ignore job specifications."

Power Interviews: Job-Winning Tactics from Fortune 500 Recruiters. N. Yeager and L. Hough. Wiley. New York. 1990.

Yeager and Hough provide a comprehensive overview of state-of-the-art interviewing techniques for the 1990s. This book offers insights into the psychological dimensions of interviewing and up-to-date information on trends in corporate America.

Sweaty Palms: The Neglected Art of Being Interviewed. H. Anthony Medley. Ten Speed Press. Berkeley, Calif. 1992.

This book presents job interviewing techniques tailored to the challenging business world of the 1990s. Topics covered include: preparation, presentation, sexual harassment and discrimination, and negotiation.

CAREER PLANNING INFORMATION

Resources that promote effective career planning are crucial to the ongoing effectiveness of the career counseling relationship with nearly every client. Career planning resources engage the client in philosophical reflection and practical exercises that lead to career decision making and vocational assessment. The following publications represent a sampling of a wide range of materials available on this topic.

Career Crash: The New Crisis—and Who Survives. Barry Glassner. Simon and Schuster. New York. 1994.

This timely book examines a new trend in the working lives of Americans—career crash—a predictable outcome of downsizing and career disenchantment. Glassner's book is vivid, inspiring, and offers solutions that go beyond the how-tos of résumé writing and job hunting.

Career Satisfaction and Success. Bernard Haldane. AMACOM. New York. 1988.

This is a book about career planning, career development, and career advancement within an organization. It is a manual of ideas and procedures of ways to determine your own strengths, to set goals and attain them, to find renewal when slowdowns occur, to manage stress, and to change careers. It is a practical, results-oriented book.

Do What You Are. Paul D. Tieger and Barbara Barron-Tieger. Little, Brown and Company. Boston, Mass. 1992.

This book reveals how the principles of personality type unlock the secret of career satisfaction. It is a lively guide to help you discover the right career. It includes an easy-to-understand introduction to personality type, workbook exercises, in-depth interviews, specific job strategies, and an extensive list of occupations that are popular with people of the same type.

Do What You Love and the Money Will Follow: Discovering Your Right Livelihood. Marsha Sinetar. Dell Publishing. New York. 1987.

Sinetar's book provides a step-by-step guide to finding the work that expresses and fulfills your needs, talents, and passions. Sinetar offers suggestions on how to overcome fears, take smaller risks that collectively accomplish the work of larger risks, and to engage in work that is meaningful, growth producing, and filled with joy.

If You Don't Know Where You're Going, You'll Probably End Up Somewhere Else. David Campbell. Tabor Publishing. Allen, Tex. 1974.

This is a lighthearted book that brings understanding and appreciation of your job assets. The purpose of this book is to help readers make the most of what they have. It is a personal growth book designed to help readers discover what they really want to do with their lives.

The Longevity Factor: The New Reality of Long Careers and How It Can Lead to Richer Lives. Lydia Brontë. HarperCollins. New York. 1993.

A thoroughly engaging and well-researched book about the new reality of a career life that stretches well into the years previously considered for retirement—a second middle age in which individuals can thrive in work creativity and productivity.

The Three Boxes of Life. Richard Nelson Bolles. Ten Speed Press. Berkeley, Calif. 1981.

Bolles demonstrates that our lives are rigidly defined into three periods, which he defines as lifelong learning/education, lifelong working, and lifelong playing/leisure. This book, abundant with charts and drawings, provides a structure to deal with the transition into each of the three periods and provides resources and opportunity for growth.

The 1994 What Color Is Your Parachute? Richard Nelson Bolles. Ten Speed Press. Berkely, Calif. 1994.

This book is a classic. It is a practical manual for job-hunters and career changers. It is updated annually. With more than 350 pages (plus appendices), this reference book is not meant to be read from cover to cover. Footnotes are extensive, and there is a lengthy bibliography.

Wishcraft. Barbara Sher. Ballantine Books. New York. 1979.

This book provides a practical program to put your vague yearnings and dreams to work. It shows how to discover your strengths and skills, turn fears and negative feelings into positive tools, diagram the path to your goals, and map out target dates for meeting them. The book also helps you chart progress and create a support network of contacts and sources.

Working. Studs Terkel. Pantheon Books. New York. 1974.

This book is a wordpicture of the American worker. It shows what it means to work in people's own words. This is not a how-to book; it is a book to be studied and enjoyed.

CHRISTIAN CAREER PLANNING

For those of us who are involved in vocational counseling in a Christian setting, it is important that our CRCs include materials that approach career planning from a Christian perspective. The following list of resources focuses on recent career planning publications by Christian authors attempting to integrate their Christian faith with their work.

Decision Making and the Will of God. Gary Friesen. Multnomah Press. Portland, Ore. 1980.

This book sets forth an excellent foundation for sound, biblically informed decision making. While it explores more than work-related issues, the need for its message is felt by every believer who is in a career search.

The Fabric of This World: Inquiries into Calling, Career Choice, and the Design of Human Work. Lee Hardy. Eerdmans. Grand Rapids, Mich. 1990.

This book offers a cogent analysis of the meaning of vocation including the perspectives of Reformed, Greek, and medieval Christian thinking. The primary focus is on the meaning of vocation with a special emphasis on identifying and matching God-given talents with areas of social need. Hardy discusses the impact of job design and management theory on the human experience of work and closes by providing suggestions for restoring a sense of vocation to work.

Finding a Job You Can Love. Ralph Mattson and Arthur Miller. Thomas Nelson Publishers. Nashville, Tenn. 1982.

The authors of this book are principals in the executive search firm, People Management, Inc. They explain how you can find a match between your God-given design and a job or career that expresses that design.

Life Planning: A Christian Approach to Careers. Kirk Farnsworth and Wendell Lawhead. InterVarsity. Downers Grove, Ill.. 1981.

The goal of this workbook is to help readers develop a lifetime approach to evaluating their jobs and themselves. Through a series of twelve sessions designed for small-group use, the book facilitates the discovery of personal values, abilities, gifts, and interests. It also provides helpful advice on making decisions and investigating career opportunities.

Secular Work Is Full-Time Service. Lany Peabody. Christian Literature Crusade. Fort Washington, Penn. 1974.

This little paperback affirms the dignity of everyday workers and their work. It can be used as a tool for small-group discussion.

Why Work?: Careers and Employment in Biblical Perspective. John A. Bernbaum and Simon M. Steer. Baker Book House. Grand Rapids, Mich., 1986.

Written in conjunction with InterVarsity's Marketplace '86 conference, this book is a good preparation for anyone considering career selection. It includes appendices that list Christian professional and academic associations, vocational guidance resources, and other resources on the subject of work.

Your Career in Changing Times. Lee Ellis and Larry Burkett. Moody Press. Chicago, Ill. 1993.

Ellis and Burkett guide the reader in an exploration of merging the personal career journey into the larger picture of God's will through the use of individual gifts. These two experts address a wide range of topics including: recognizing God's call through your gifts, understanding your pattern of strengths for work, choosing an occupation, conducting a job search and landing a job, dealing with job stress, living within a budget, helping children make career decisions, dealing with company downsizing and career turbulence, starting a business, and retirement planning.

NOTES

1. C. Dittenhafer and J. Lewis, *Guidelines for Establishing Career Resource Centers* (Harrisburg, Pa.: Pennsylvania Department of Education, 1973).
2. C. McDaniels and N. Gysberbs, *Counseling for Career Development: Theories, Resources and Practice* (San Francisco: Jossey-Bass, 1992).
3. V. Zunker, *Career Counseling: Applied Concepts of Life Planning,* 4th ed. (Pacific Grove, Calif.: Brooks/Cole Publishing, 1994).

Chapter Fifteen

Keys to a Successful Career

IN HIS POEM, "TWO TRAMPS IN MUD TIME," Robert Frost invites us deep into the forest on a crisp spring morning as he splits oak wood on a chopping block. He is engrossed in his labor. He is enjoying the physical and emotional release provided by "the weight of an ax-head poised aloft." He enjoys "the grip on earth of outspread feet." As he is working, two lumberjacks appear. He reluctantly yields his enjoyable task to them out of compassion for their financial need. But as he watches the men with his ability to see the transcendent in the mundane, Frost concludes:

> My object in living is to unite
> my avocation and my vocation.
> As my two eyes make one in sight,
> only where love and need are one,
> and the work is play for mortal stakes,
> is the deed ever really done
> for Heaven and the future's sakes.[1]

Fulfillment in work develops when our vocation becomes our avocation. Without this integration, pleasure and pride become drudgery and duty; feelings of alienation and exhaustion move in. If these feelings persist, the worker falls victim to burnout. In this final chapter, we examine job burnout and explore the keys for its prevention.

JOB BURNOUT

Although burnout has undoubtedly existed throughout human history, psychologists have only recently studied burnout seriously. Herbert Freudenberger compares a burned-out person to a burned-out building: "What had once been a throbbing, vital structure is now deserted. Where there had been activity, there are now crumbling reminders of energy and life. The outer shell may almost seem intact. Only if you venture inside will you be struck by the full force of the desolation . . . consumed as if by fire, leaving a great emptiness inside, although their outer shells may be more or less unchanged."[2]

Jobs contain built-in dissatisfactions that can lead to burnout. Jerry Edelwich catalogs frustrations that can eventually accrue to burnout:[3]

- *Not enough money.* As a result, people feel their choices are limited and their life is constricted.

- *Too many hours.* Working hours are considered excessive; others may work fewer hours, which is seen as unfair; there is little chance to get away from the job; inadequate vacation time is offered.

- *Career dead end.* People feel blocked or caught in a rut; little or no opportunity exists for advancement to a higher position.

- *Too much paperwork.* Filling out forms and writing numerous reports rather than doing the job described at the time of hiring makes people think they are serving only the organization's needs, not those of people.

- *Not sufficiently trained for the job.* Paraprofessionals, for example, may have to do the work a professional should do. Sometimes, however, the opposite is heard: "I am overtrained for this work."

- *Not appreciated by supervisor.* People feel they are not given responsibility commensurate with their skills and abilities, not consulted about decisions, overlooked by supervisors, and evaluated unfairly or according to irrelevant criteria.

- *No support for important decisions.* A worker is held responsible for a superior's failure to support or implement recommendations.

- *Powerlessness.* A worker experiences little or no chance to make an impact on other people or to influence decisions; recommendations made are ignored or gather dust.

- *Bad office politics.* Internal power politics get nasty; polarization occurs among superiors and subordinates; too much petty infighting, jealousy, and undermining of ambitions and reputations occur.

This list could go on and on. However, Christina Maslach has pinpointed the most salient cause of burnout on the job. She calls it a reaction to stress of any kind.[4] Consider the following scene:

It is 6:00 A.M., the start of another working day. Bleary-eyed from too little sleep, Diane stumbles into the kitchen for a cup of coffee. The telephone rings. It is her husband, out of town on business. He is calling to confirm that she will pick him up at the airport later that day.

As she is packing sack lunches for Josh, her eleven-year-old, and Sarah, her eight-year-old, Diane realizes she has just forty-five minutes to prepare two dozen snacks for Sarah's third-grade class before the carpool arrives. Diane organizes an assembly line of celery sticks and peanut butter and rushes to wake Josh. As usual, he whines about getting out of bed, and his younger sister complains about the clothes her mother has laid out for her.

Finally, Diane gets the kids off to school and gears up for her own day at the office. Before leaving, she frantically tries to straighten up the house—this evening it is

*her turn to host a women's precept Bible study. She leaves
a few dishes in the sink and jumps into her car to join the
rest of the work force in rush-hour traffic. Ten minutes
into her commute, she realizes the report she worked on
last night is still on her nightstand. She has no option but
to drive back and retrieve it.*

*Late for work, Diane opens her office door and finds the
boss pacing inside. Her report was due an hour ago, she is
told; the client is furious. Diane's heart begins to race, her
palms begin to sweat, and she would like nothing more
than to run away.*

*Diane swallows her primal urge and attempts to ex-
plain her tardiness. Her boss grabs the report from her
outstretched hand. "This better not happen again," he
warns. Diane slumps into her chair and fumbles through
the bottom drawer of her desk for a bottle of aspirin. Her
stomach is churning, her back muscles knotting, her blood
pressure climbing.*

It is this kind of stress that Dr. Maslach singles out as the
major cause of burnout in the workplace. Work stress is usually a response to constant emotional strain from interaction
with people. Burnout runs in a cycle of emotional exhaustion,
depersonalization, and a reduced feeling of personal accomplishment. Cynicism replaces idealism. People experiencing
burnout detach themselves emotionally from the needs of
other people. Burned-out people exhibit less caring. Their
attitude toward others is negative. Finally, they redirect their
negativism inward, and burnout turns to a sense of inadequacy on the job. As self-esteem and a belief in personal
competence crumble, the burnout victim often seeks out a vocational counselor.

AVOIDING BURNOUT

What can a vocational counselor do to help people counteract burnout? Here are some of the most common strategies to
reduce the likelihood of burnout. They can apply to the counselor as well as to the client.

1. *Adjust expectations and set realistic goals.* This does not mean giving up your ideals and becoming apathetic. It does mean setting achievable goals based on an honest appraisal of your abilities and values.

2. *Do your job differently; vary your work routines.* Determine which parts of the job can be changed and which cannot. Analyze the consequences of a change in work procedures. Talking to coworkers or your supervisor or taking a workshop or seminar may give you some new ideas about doing your job. Taking action may not be easy, but constant frustration is worse.

3. *Get away from the job for a while.* Getting away can involve a time period ranging from a fifteen-minute coffee break or a one-hour lunch period to a day, a week, or a month. Use a sick day or a vacation period if necessary. Avoid working through lunch hours or coming back to the office in the evening to catch up on work.

4. *Get enough rest and relaxation.* Get sufficient sleep. Use relaxation techniques such as muscle relaxation and deep-breathing exercises. Change your pace and wind down after work. Listen to music. Meditate. Engage in vigorous physical activity. Become absorbed in a hobby. Do something to leave the strains of the job behind.

5. *Seek satisfactions outside of work.* Open up your life beyond the boundaries of your work environment. Family and friends can offer encouragement when work problems thicken. Outside activities and relationships provide outlets for creativity and challenge.

6. *Seek counseling or other professional help.* There is no reason to feel isolated or alone. Take advantage of any counseling services offered by your work, organization, or community.

7. *Leave the job or change occupations.* Such decisions are very personal and individual and should be made only after you have tried all other possible strategies and determined that the difficulties on the job have simply become overwhelming. Make a searching self-analysis, assessing

your goals, values, abilities, temperament, and attitudes. Recycling the career decision-making process and sharpening your job-hunting skills will be necessary.

8. *Keep the Sabbath holy.* From the beginning God blessed and hallowed a Sabbath day. God the Creator himself, after six days of activity, sanctified a seventh day of rest. The Sabbath is a divine institution for rest, relaxation, and worship. "There remains, then, a Sabbath-rest for the people of God; for anyone who enters God's rest also rests from his own work, just as God did from his" (Heb. 4:9–10).

Without a strategic plan to avoid frustration, fatigue, and disillusionment, every worker is walking dangerously close to burnout. However, workers who are not sabotaged by fatigue and frustration are not trouble free. Good jobs are steeped in annoyances, pressures, and problems. The truth is, human labor is no more God's curse than life itself. Though the Fall tainted work, we cannot forget that God introduced the concept of human labor *before* the Fall. When Adam and Eve were still innocent of sin, God gave them a job to do. He called Adam to name the animals and then asked Adam and Eve to subdue the animals, manage the Garden of Eden, and prepare food from the plants and trees. Why would a loving God put his children to work as soon as he created them? Because he knew human labor was a blessing. He knew that even with all its foibles, work would provide one of the greatest sources of human satisfaction.

THE QUIET JOY OF WORK

More time and energy are spent in work than any other waking activity. Sixty-eight percent of us spend more than nine hours each day on the job, including getting to and from work. More than one in five of all employed adults bring work home at least twice a week.

Work is consuming. We complain about work. We try to avoid work. We call in sick to get out of work. But more than anything else, we know we need purposeful work—not for the money alone, but for a sense of personal worth.

Work provides more than financial rewards. It provides spiritual, psychological, and emotional support as well. Sigmund Freud said that to live well we must learn to love well *and* to work well. Kahlil Gibran said, "Work is love made visible."

For most of us, work, whether paid or unpaid, gives us our identity. Work brings personal fulfillment. We love to hate work while we hate to admit we love it. Cartoonists and storytellers have assumed that most people who toil for their daily bread fantasize about winning the lottery, telling the boss what he can do with his old job, kicking the Xerox machine, packing up their Rolodex, and hitting the road. But this is a false picture. In a national survey, more than three-fourths of the respondents said they would choose to remain in their same jobs even though they had, by good fortune, received enough money to live comfortably for the rest of their lives.

Perhaps you are thinking people *need* to say that to feel good about their jobs. Maybe you are wondering what they would really do if it actually happened. The Institute for Socio-Economic Studies wondered the same thing. They looked up more than one thousand people who had won a million dollars or more in a lottery. Only 16 percent actually retired from work altogether. And four out of ten kept working at the same job they had, even though they had no need for the income.

What then draws us to work? An important part of the answer is found in relationships. Marsha Sinetar, author of *Do What You Love and the Money Will Follow,* writes, "Through work and relationships the individual finds a place in the world, belongs to it, and takes responsibility for himself and for others. Work becomes his way of giving of himself. His work or vocation provides him with a way of dedicating himself to live. Through it, he cultivates his talents, stands in for others, exhibits his involvement and connection to the world."[5]

THE WORK WE LOVE

When asked, "What upsets you most about where you work?" employees' number-one complaint was with fellow workers. Penn State psychologist David Day has found that job satisfaction depends more on work relationships than salary. How we fit in with coworkers is often more important than how much we make. Relationships make the difference between the job we love and the job we loath.

What are the ingredients of happiness at work? Hundreds of writers have listed thousands of conditions. However, their wisdom may be boiled down to its essence as two basic needs emerge: (1) The need we have for a good relationship with other people, and (2) the need other people have for a good relationship with us. When these two needs are recognized, internalized, and implemented, every job offers fulfillment.

THE NEED FOR OTHERS

Every effective piece of work is a collaboration. Those who are fulfilled in their work recognize the needs and contributions of others. Luciano de Cresenzo put it this way: "We are, each of us, angels with only one wing. And we can only fly embracing each other."

I (Les) remember my first day of work as a professor. My dean called me into his office and gave me an armful of heavy books. Many were classic works on the philosophy and practice of teaching. We went over some paperwork, and before he sent me on my way, he told me something I didn't expect to hear. "Les, I don't have to tell you how to teach. You wouldn't be here if you couldn't. But I want to give you some advice that helped me when I was in your position. Be kind to the janitor."

In my consuming schedule of teaching, speaking, counseling, and writing, I often think of his counsel. In the factories of Flint, Michigan, where our family once lived, it was said more crudely, "Never cuss a kid." It helps us all when we value the work of the people who help us do our work more effectively.

Kenneth Blanchard and Spencer Johnson wrote a short fable about industrial relations called *The One Minute Manager* that quickly climbed the bestseller lists. Three-quarters of the way through the text, the One-Minute Manger says to his disciple: "Just remember young man, people are not pigeons . . . remember that and respect that. It is a key to good management."[6]

Our need of others is not limited to the people we work *for* or even the people we work *with*. It reaches out to the people we are working to serve—our customers, clients, students, etc.

Years ago, a wealthy man was looking for a hotel room in New York City. A major convention filled the city and, therefore, no rooms were available. The man had made his way from one great hotel to the next only to be turned away. He finally made his way to a small hotel where he pleaded with the young desk clerk for a room. But again, he heard the same story. "I'm sorry sir. I've already turned away dozens of people who have had the same request."

The weary financier leaned on the counter and said to the young man, "Is there not any place where my wife and I can rest?" The clerk said, "Sir, the only room I could give you is my own. I have a bunk in a storeroom. It's clean and warm, but you'd have to share a washroom used by the employees. I'm working most of the night, and I'd be happy to let you stay in my room for no charge." The travelers took his irregular offer.

The next morning, refreshed and rested, the man saw the clerk at the desk. "Son, did you notice who I was as I signed the register last night?" The clerk glanced at the register, "No, I'm sorry."

"My name is John Jacob Astor." Astor made the clerk manager of a hotel yet to be built—the Waldorf-Astoria. The young clerk who had empathy for a couple without a room managed the Waldorf for years.

Once a person genuinely recognizes their need for others—employer, colleague, or customer—they accept the fact that they cannot work alone. With this discovery, they are halfway to finding fulfillment in the workplace.

OTHERS' NEED OF US

There is an ancient tale about a young girl walking through a meadow when she sees a butterfly impaled on a thorn. Artfully, she releases the butterfly, which starts to fly away. Then it comes back, changed into a beautiful fairy. "For your kindness," the fairy tells the little girl, "I will grant your fondest wish." The little girl thinks for a moment and replies, "I want to be happy." The fairy leans toward her, whispers in her ear, and then suddenly vanishes.

As the girl grew, no one in the land was more happy than she. Whenever anyone asked her for the secret of her happiness, she would only smile and say, "I listened to a good fairy."

As she grew old, the neighbors were afraid the fabulous secret might die with her. "Tell us, please," they begged. "Tell us what the fairy said." The lovely old lady simply smiled and said, "She told me that everyone, no matter how secure they seem, has need of me!"

A secret to finding fulfillment at work is to make oneself indispensable to the people one works with. Dr. Hans Selye, the acknowledged father of stress, studied the effects of stress in the workplace and observed that stress is reduced when people make an effort to win the gratitude of their fellow workers. Selye rephrased the biblical quote, "Love thy neighbor as thyself," into his own personal code: "Earn thy neighbor's love." Rather than trying to accumulate more money or power, he suggested we acquire goodwill by helping those we work with. "Hoard goodwill," Dr. Selye advised, "and your house will be a storehouse of happiness."[7]

Making oneself indispensable means making others look good. The famous orchestra conductor Leonard Bernstein was once asked to name the most difficult instrument to play. He responded with quick wit: "Second fiddle." People who are willing to work enthusiastically without recognition are important to harmony in the workplace.

Indispensable workers are not looking for benefits others bring. They are looking for ways to benefit others. This was the attitude St. Francis expressed in his famous prayer:

> Lord, make me an instrument of Thy peace.
> Where there is hatred let me sew love;
> Where there is injury, pardon;
> Where there is doubt, faith;
> Where there is despair, hope;
> Where there is darkness, light;
> Where there is sadness, joy.
>
> O Divine Master, grant that I may not so much seek
> To be consoled as to console;
> To be understood as to understand;

To be loved as to love;
For it is in giving that we receive;
It is in pardoning that we are pardoned;
It is in dying that we are born to eternal life.

The writer of Ecclesiastes understood the fulfillment of work that is based on relationships when he wrote, "Then I realized that it is good and proper for a man to eat and drink, and to find satisfaction in his toilsome labor under the sun during the few days of life God has given him—for this is his lot" (Eccl. 5:18).

NOTES

1. Robert Frost, "Two Tramps in Mud Time," in *The Poetry of Robert Frost,* ed. E. Lathem (New York: Holt, Rinehart and Winston, 1969).

2. H. J. Freudenberger *Burn-out: The High Cost of High Achievment* (Garden City, NJ: Doubleday (1980).

3. J. Edelwich with A. Brodsky *Burn-out: Stages of Disillusionment in the Helping Professions.* (New York: Human Sciences Press, 1980).

4. C. Maslach *Burnout—The Cost of Caring.* (Englewood Cliffs, NJ: Prentice-Hall, 1982).

5. M. Sinetar, *Do What You Love and the Money Will Follow: Discovering Your Righty Livelihood* (New York: Dell Publishing, 1987).

6. K. Blanchard and S. Johnson, *The One-Minute Manager* (New York: Morrow, 1982).

7. H. Selye, *Stress Without Distress* (New York: A Signet Book, New AmericanLibrary, 1974), 122.

Appendix A

Career Maturity Profile

(Please see next page)

CAREER MATURITY PROFILE

Competence Test

	Raw Score	Percentile Rank	Percentile Scale Rate of Career Maturity	Right Response Record + item answered correctly − item answered incorrectly 0 item omitted
Part 1 Knowing Yourself (Self-Appraisal)			1 2 5 10 20 30 40 50 60 70 80 90 95 98 99	2 4 6 8 10 12 14 16 18 20
Part 2 Knowing About Jobs (Occupational Information)			1 2 5 10 20 30 40 50 60 70 80 90 95 98 99	2 4 6 8 10 12 14 16 18 20
Part 3 Choosing a Job (Goal Selection)			1 2 5 10 20 30 40 50 60 70 80 90 95 98 99	2 4 6 8 10 12 14 16 18 20
Part 4 Looking Ahead (Planning)			1 2 5 10 20 30 40 50 60 70 80 90 95 98 99	2 4 6 8 10 12 14 16 18 20
Part 5 What Should They Do? (Problem Solving)			1 2 5 10 20 30 40 50 60 70 80 90 95 98 99	2 4 6 8 10 12 14 16 18 20
Attitude Scale			1 2 5 10 20 30 40 50 60 70 80 90 95 98 99	2 4 6 8 10 12 14 16 18 20 22 24 26 28 30 32 34 36 38 40 42 44 46 48 50

Source: John O. Crites, "Career Maturity Inventory Profile"
(Monterey, Calif.: CTB/McGraw-Hill, 1973). Used by permission.

Appendix B

Social Network Questionnaire

SOCIAL ANCHORAGE	YES	NO	UNCERTAIN
Would you say that you are rooted and have a feeling of familiarity with your neighborhood?	❑	❑	❑
How many years have you lived in your neighborhood?	❑	❑	❑
If you were able to move now, would you do so?	❑	❑	❑
Do you belong to a group of friends that does things together (i.e., play cards, listen to music, go on picnics or church outings, etc.)?	❑	❑	❑
In your daily life, do you have use for the knowledge and skills you have acquired during your life?	❑	❑	❑
Do you feel that you are of great importance to other people and that you have a useful function in society?	❑	❑	❑
Are you a member of any organizations or clubs?	❑	❑	❑
Are you a member of a church?	❑	❑	❑
Are you in any position of responsibility in an organization, club, or your church?	❑	❑	❑

CONTACT FREQUENCY

How often do you meet any of these persons at your or at their homes?

	Often	Seldom	Never
children	❏	❏	❏
relatives	❏	❏	❏
close friends	❏	❏	❏
friends	❏	❏	❏
neighbors	❏	❏	❏
coworkers	❏	❏	❏
church members	❏	❏	❏

SOCIAL PARTICIPATION

	None	1–5 times	6–10 times	more than 10 times
How often in the last year have you taken part in study circles and other courses?	❏	❏	❏	❏
How often in the last year did you take part in meetings of different organizations, clubs, etc.?	❏	❏	❏	❏

How often in the last year have you done any of the following:

	None	1–5 times	6–10 times	more than 10 times
written an article	❏	❏	❏	❏
taken active part in the discussion at a meeting	❏	❏	❏	❏
taken part in a political meeting	❏	❏	❏	❏
tried to influence a decision regarding a political question	❏	❏	❏	❏
appealed against a decision	❏	❏	❏	❏
contacted a consumers' association	❏	❏	❏	❏
gone to a salesman or shop in order to complain	❏	❏	❏	❏
taken part in a political or union rally	❏	❏	❏	❏

	None	1–5 times	6–10 times	more than 10 times
How often in the last year have you been to parties at your friends', relatives', or neighbors' homes?	❏	❏	❏	❏
How often in the last year have you been to church?	❏	❏	❏	❏

ADEQUACY OF SOCIAL PARTICIPATION

Is there anyone in your neighborhood from whom you can borrow things and exchange services? _____

Is there anyone in your neighborhood from whom you can get help if you fall ill? _____

If you need help with something for twenty-four hours, do you have anyone (other than a spouse) you can ask? _____

Do you know anyone who can help you to write an official letter or appeal against a decision made by some authority? _____

AVAILABILITY OF EMOTIONAL SUPPORT	YES	NO	UNCERTAIN
Do you have any friends or relatives whom you like very much and who like you very much?	❏	❏	❏
Do you have any really close friends with whom you feel intimate and with whom you can discuss anything?	❏	❏	❏
If you have continued to work, is it because you want to feel that you are a valuable and important person?	❏	❏	❏
When you have personal problems of any kind, do you have any close friends, relatives, a pastor, or a church Sunday school class to whom you can turn to discuss your problems?	❏	❏	❏

ADEQUACY OF EMOTIONAL SUPPORT

How often do you feel lonely? _____

Do you have the feeling that people appreciate what you do? _____

Do you have enough good friends to be with? _____

Do you think that you see your children too often or too rarely? ____

Source: Adapted from A. Flak et al., "Job Strain and Mortality in Elderly Men: Social Network, Support, and Influences as Buffers," *American Journal of Public Health* 82 (1992): 1136–39. Used by permission.

Appendix C

Strong Interest Inventory Summary Evaluation Form

1. Responses—if less than 310, results are questionable.
2. Infrequent responses (negative number)—check the manual for implications.
3. Academic Comfort Scale: B.A. mean = 50
                                            M.A. mean = 55
                                            Ph.D. mean = 60
4. Introversion-Extroversion Scale: 40 or under = extroverted
                                                       60 or over = introverted
5. LP, IP, DP (boundary 5–60)
   Record section that is outside of limits and refer to page 90 of manual.

   _____   _____   _____

6. Summary code for three highest General Occupational Themes and two examples of variation of theme.

   _____   _____   _____

   _____   _____   _____

   _____   _____   _____

7. Record Basic Interest Scales shown as high and very high.

   _____

8. Record Occupational Scales with scores of 45–55.

   _____

9. Record Occupational Scales with scores of 55 or higher.

   _____

Appendix D

Sample Résumés

Chronological Format

Sandra Parker
201 Galer Street
Portland, Oregon 98109
(206) 890-9751 (home) • (206) 422-6091 (work)

Career Objective

Chief Student Affairs Officer

Education

University of Washington; Ph.D. in Higher Education, College Student Personnel; 1980.

University of Oregon; M.S. in Higher Education, College Student Personnel; 1971.

University of Oregon; B.S. in Physical Education; 1969.

Work Experience

19__–Present   Dean of Student Life, Pacific Lutheran University. Provided leadership for eleven offices that serve different student populations.

19__–19__   Director of Residence Services, University of Oregon. Provided leadership for all university-owned and operated residence halls.

19__–19__   Director of Residence Halls, George Fox College. Administrative responsibility for all university-owned and operated residence halls.

19__–19__   Assistant Director of Residence Halls, George Fox College. Responsible for student life programming, security, and discipline.

19__–19__   Administrative Assistant to the President, George Fox College. Provided administrative support in the Office of the President.

19__–19__   Residence Counselor, University of Oregon. Administrative responsibility for a twelve-story residence hall.

19__–19__   Assistant Area Head, Southern Illinois University. Duties included student life programming and discipline.

Professional Associations

American College Personnel Association

National Association of Student Personnel Administrators

Awards

19__   Outstanding Leadership Award, University of Oregon

19__   Meritorious Service Award to Students, University of Oregon

19__   NCAA athletic scholarship, Southern Illinois University

References

References are available upon request.

Functional Format

Sandra Parker
201 Galer Street
Portland, Oregon 98109
(206) 890-9751 (home) • (206) 422-6091 (work)

CAREER OBJECTIVE
Chief Student Affairs Officer

WORK EXPERIENCE

Dean of Student Life:
Budget, staff, and plan all Student Life Office functions. Provide
leadership for the Offices of International Student and Scholar
Services, Disability Services, Student Organizations and Activities,
Commuter Student Affairs, Judicial Affairs, Women's Services,
and Forensics and Debate. Other responsibilities include student
leadership training and development, Student Life research,
Student Affairs orientation, and other campuswide events. Represent
the Vice President for Student Affairs on various university
committees, meetings, events, and act as the senior Student
Affairs officer in his absence. Teach "Introduction to College
Student Personnel Work" as an Adjunct Professor in the College
of Education. Pacific Lutheran University 19__ –present

Director of Residence Services:
Planned and directed all functions of university-owned and
operated residence halls, food service, student development
programming, maintenance, and business administration.
University of Oregon 19__ –19__

EDUCATION

Ph.D.   University of Washington, 1980
          Major: Higher Education, College Student Personnel
          Minors: Labor Industrial Relations and Management
          Science

M.S.   University of Oregon, 1971
          Major: Higher Education, College Student Personnel
          Minor: Psychology

B.S.   University of Oregon, June, 1969
          Major: Physical Education
          Minor: Psychology

PROFESSIONAL ASSOCIATIONS

American College Personnel Association
National Association of Student Personnel Administrators

AWARDS

Outstanding Leadership Award, University of Oregon, 19__
Meritorious Service Award to Students, University of Oregon, 19__
NCAA athletic scholarship, Southern Illinois University, 1964-1968.

REFERENCES

References are available upon request.

Analytical Format

Sandra Parker
201 Galer Street
Portland, Oregon 98109
(206) 890-9751 (home) • (206) 422-6091 (work)

CAREER OBJECTIVE

Chief Student Affairs Officer

QUALIFICATIONS

MANAGEMENT AND SUPERVISION: As Dean of Student Life at Pacific Lutheran University, eleven separate offices that provide programs and services for different student populations were developed into an organization joined by a common philosophy of student development. Implementation of management by objectives as the planning, management, and evaluation system is central to the operation of this office.

Reorganized the residence hall program at the University of Iowa. Key to the reorganization was the establishment of three assistant directors who assumed comprehensive administrative responsibilities for functionally related areas. Essential to the reorganization was the development of a common operating philosophy as well as the establishment of planning and management systems.

As Assistant Director of Residence Halls at George Fox College, problems of staff morale, decreasing occupancy, and quality of life were resolved. Strategic planning measures were implemented over a three-year period, which reversed the problems previously identified.

FINANCIAL PLANNING AND DEVELOPMENT: Integrated financial and program planning through a common management system. Responsible for the distribution of $1 million for support programs and services provided by eight different offices. Also served as the primary administrator of four successful grant proposals that were designed to enhance the quality of student life.

PROGRAMMING: Implemented a peer support program designed to assist high-risk students who are admitted to the university. The goal of this program was to reverse the 50 percent attrition rate.

Provided leadership in the development of a major student/ faculty/staff program called Project Unity. This program was dramatically effective in terms of reducing conflict in the residence halls. Project Unity was guided by the philosophy of bringing conflicting parties together to work toward common goals.

INSTRUCTION: Adjunct Assistant Professor, College of Education. Taught the introductory courses for master's students in the Student Personnel program. Cotaught the capstone course in the Student Personnel program. The purpose of the course was to assist graduates with the transition from student to professional employee.

EMPLOYERS

Pacific Lutheran University, 1980–present
Univesity of Oregon, 1975–1980
George Fox College, 1970–1975

EDUCATION

1980   Ph.D. in Higher Education, College Student Personnel, University of Washingon
1971   M.S. in Higher Education, College Student Personnel, University of Oregon
1969   B.S. in Physical Education, University of Oregon

REFERENCES

References are available upon request.

Imaginative Format

Sandra Parker
201 Galer Street
Portland, Oregon 98109
(206) 890-9751 (home) • (206) 422-6091 (work)

PHILOSOPHY

Despite our limited behavioral knowledge, the college must recognize that even its instructional goals cannot be effectively achieved unless it assumes some responsibility for facilitating the development of the total human personality.

A student is not a passive digester of knowledge elegantly arranged by superior curriculum design. A student listens, reads, thinks, studies, worries, hopes, loves, and hates.

A student engages in all these activities not as an isolated individual, but as a member of overlapping communities, which greatly influence the student's reaction to the classroom experience.

To teach the subject matter and ignore the realities of the student's life and the social systems of the college is hopelessly naive. (Committee on Higher Education, 1968.)

BACKGROUND

University of Washingon, Ph.D. in Higher Education, College Student Personnel, 1980.

University of Oregon, M.S. in Higher Education, College Student Personnel, 1971.

University of Orgon, B.S. in Physical Education, 1969.

Worked in a variety of Student Affairs positions at University of Oregon while completing the master's degree. These positions included Assistant Area Head in Residence Services, Resident Counselor, and Administrative Assistant to the President. After completing the master's, accepted the Assistant Director of Residence Hall position at George Fox College. Immediately enrolled in the evening doctoral program in College Student Personnel at University of Washington. Completed coursework in five years and was subsequently promoted to Director of Residence Halls. In 1975, left George Fox to assume the Director of

Residence Halls position at the University of Oregon. Completed graduation requirement while serving in this capacity.

In 1980, accepted the Dean of Student Life position at Pacific Lutheran Univeristy and am currently serving in this capacity.

THIS IS WHAT I CAN OFFER YOUR UNIVERSITY

- A philosophy of Student Affairs work that is integral to the mission of your university.
- Over 16 years of professional experience in Student Affairs positions of increasing responsibility.
- Expert managerial and supervisory skills.
- Proven competence in financial planning and development with multimillion-dollar budgets.
- Creative programming based on assessed student needs and interests.
- Effective teaching skills that are grounded in developmental pedagogy.
- A love for working with students and a belief that education can make all the difference in the world.

REFERENCES

References are available upon request.

Appendix E

Sample Cover Letter

Sandra Parker
201 Galer Street
Portland, Oregon 98109

September 15, 19 _

Ms. Jane Thompson
Personnel Director
Seattle Pacific University
Seattle, Washington 98119

Dear Ms. Thompson:

I am seeking a chief student affairs position with a Christian university. My education and experience in administrative education could be valuable to your organization. I have earned a Ph.D. in higher education at the University of Washington. Practical, on-the-job experience includes working as dean of student life at Pacific Lutheran University.

As dean of student life, I am responsible for the budget, staff, and planing of all Student Life Office functions. I provide leadership for many services and campus groups. I am also responsible for student leadership training and development and many campuswide events. I am articulate, a good correspondent, and able to motivate people. I am eager to put my ideas and experience to work for you.

The enclosed résumé summarizes my education and work experience. Please contact me by telephone or mail; I would be pleased to meet with you at your convenience.

Sincerely,

Sandra Parker, Ph.D.

Enclosure: Résumé

Appendix F

Career Management Organizations

Career Impact Ministries
711 Stadium Drive East, Suite 200
Arlington, Texas 76011
817-265-3441

Career Impact Ministries exists to challenge people with a biblical view of work and to provide resources and services to help them live out that view. A few resources worth mentioning include: "On Your Way to Work," a growing series of cassette albums on specific workplace topics; "Standing Out in Your Workplace," a series of case history discussion notebooks for executives; and "Christianity at Work," a monthly newsletter addressing the faith and work of the urban center.

Intercristo
P.O. Box 33487
Seattle, Washington 98133
800-251-7740

Intercristo positions itself as "the Christian career specialists," and the claim is not without merit. Its most impressive resource is "The Career Kit," an extremely useful and affordable notebook and set of tapes that attempt to help one find a rewarding career. The assessment tool in the package is itself worth the price of the notebook. Intercristo also holds seminars across the country on the same topic, along with an individualized career consulting service called CareerWorks.

Intercristo's Christian Placement Network (CPN) is a comprehensive listing of work opportunities in Christian nonprofit ministries worldwide. Intercristo's sister ministry, Tentmakers International, helps Christians integrate their faith and lifework by using secular employment to be a witness for Christ overseas. If your issue is job selection, do not overlook Intercristo. If you are in college, graduate school, or an entry-level position, contacting them is a must.

People Management, Inc.
10 Station Street
Simsbury, Connecticut 06070
203-651-3581

If you are an executive and facing a career change, People Management may be of help. They offer a highly specialized inventory of motivated abilities that is foundational to a variety of consulting services. Two of the principals, Ralph Mattson and Arthur Miller, have authored the excellent book, *Finding a Job You Can Love*.

Probe Ministries
1900 Firman Drive, Suite 100
Richardson, Texas 75081
214-480-0240

Probe Ministries is another organization to consider contacting if you have questions pertaining to apologetics. In many ways a Christian think tank, Probe excels in addressing the many philosophical and sociological tensions Christians confront in our culture. Probe also publishes *Spiritual Fitness in Business,* a helpful newsletter specifically for business and professional people.

Search Ministries, Inc.
P.O. Box 521
Lutherville, Maryland 21093

Search Ministries specializes in equipping Christians to present the gospel to their non-Christian associates in clear, relevant terms. They also have done extensive research in apologetics and have excelled at helping laypeople address the common questions unbelievers ask about Christianity. They have staff across the country and are especially interested in assisting churches in the area of evangelism.

Bibliography

Adams, J. F. *Understanding Adolescence.* Boston: Allyn and Bacon, 1968.

Adams, J., J. Hayes, and B. Hopson, eds. *Transition: Understanding and Managing Personal Change.* Montclaire, N.J.: Allenheld and Osumun, 1977.

Adelson, J. *Handbook of Adolescent Psychology.* New York: Wiley, 1980.

Alder, J. *The Retirement Book: A Complete Early-Planning Guide to Finances, New Activities, and Where to Live.* New York: Morrow, 1975.

Anastasi, A. *Psychological Testing.* 6th ed. New York: Macmillan, 1988.

Angel, J. *Modern Vocational Trends Reference Handbook.* New York: Simon and Schuster, 1970.

Arbeiter, S., C. Aslanian, F. Schmerbeck, and H. Brickell. *40 Million Americans in Career Transition: The Need for Information.* New York: College Entrance Examination Board, 1978.

Armstrong, J. "Decision Behavior and Outcomes of Mid-life Career Changes." *Vocational Guidance Quarterly,* 29 (1981): 205–11.

Atchley, R. *The Sociology of Retirement.* New York: Schenman, 1976.

Axelson, J. *Counseling and Development in a Multicultural Society.* 2d. ed. Pacific Grove, Calif.: Brooks/Cole, 1993.

Ayres, M. "Counseling Hispanic Americans." *Occupational Outlook Quarterly* 23 (1979): 3–8.

Bardwick, J. "The Season's of a Woman's Life." In *Women's Lives: New Theory, Research, and Policy.* Edited by D. McGuigan. Ann Arbor, Mich.: University of Michigan, Center for Continuing Education of Women, 1980.

Barna, G. *The Frog in the Kettle: What Christians Need to Know about Life in the Year 2000.* Ventura, Calif.: Regal Books, 1990.

Bartlett, J., and E. Beck. *Familiar Quotations.* 5th ed. Boston: Little, Brown and Co., 1982.

Baruch, G., L. Biener, and R. Barnett. "Women and Gender in Research on Work and Family Stress." *American Psychologist* 42 (1987): 130–36.

Bateson, M. *Composing A Life: Life as a Work in Progress—The Improvisions of Five Extraordinary Women.* New York: Plume, Penguine Books, 1989.

Baum, L. "Corporate Women: They're About to Break Through to the Top." *Business Week* 22 June 1987, 72–78.

Bernbaum, J., and S. Steer. *Why Work? Careers and Employment in Biblical Prespective.* Grand Rapids: Baker, 1986.

Bernstein, M., and J. Berstein. *Social Security: The System That Works.* New York: Basic Books, 1988.

Beuchner, F. *Wishful Thinking: A Theological ABC.* New York: Harper and Row, 1973.

Blai, B. "Programs for Older Persons: A Compendium." *Journal of Employment Counseling* 19 (1982): 98–105.

Blanchard, K. and S. Johnson. *The One-Minute Manager.* New York: Morrow, 1982.

Block, J. "Psychological Development of Female Children and Adolescents." In *Women: A Developmental Perspective.* Edited by P. Berman and E. Rainey. Washington, D.C.:

Department of Health and Human Services, Public Health Service, National Institute for Health, Pueblo, Colo., 1982.

Block, P. *The Empowered Manager: Positive Political Skills at Work.* San Francisco: Jossey-Bass, 1987.

Bolles, R. *The Three Boxes of Life: And How to Get Out of Them.* Berkeley: Ten Speed Press, 1981.

———. *What Color is Your Parachute? A Practical Manual for Job-hunters and Career Changers.* Berkeley: Ten Speed Press, 1986.

———. *How to Find Your Mission in Life.* Berkeley: Ten Speed Press, 1994.

Bowen, M. *Family Therapy in Clinical Practice.* New York: Jason Aronson, 1978.

Bradely, R. W. "Using Sibling Dyads to Understand Career Development." *The Personnel and Guidance Journal,* 62 (1984): 397–400.

Bradley, R. W., and G. A. Mims. "Using Family Systems and Birth Order Dynamics as the Basis for a College Career Decision-Making Course." *Journal of Counseling and Development* 70 (1992): 445–48.

Bratcher, W. E. "The Influence of the Family on Career Development." *The Personnel and Guidance Journal* (1982): 87–91.

British Psychological Society Bulletin 32 (1979): 309, 312–14.

Brontë, L. *The Longevity Factor: The New Reality of Long Careers and How It Can Lead to Richer Lives.* New York: HarperCollins, 1993.

Brown, D., L. Brooks, A. Roe, P. Lunneborg, S. Weinrach, E. Bordin, H. Hotchkiss, E. Ginzberg, D. Super, L. Mitchell, J. Krumboltz, D. Tiedeman, and A. Miller-Tiedeman. *Career Choice and Development.* San Francisco: Jossey-Bass, 1984.

Burdett, J. "Easing the Way Out: Consultants and Counselors Help Terminated Executives Strategically and Psychologically." *Personnel Administrator,* 33 (1988): 157–66.

Campbell, D. *If You Don't Know Where You're Going, You'll Probably End Up Somewhere Else.* Allen, Tex: Tabor Publishing, 1974.

Carnegie Forum on Education and the Economy. *A Nation Prepared: Teachers for the 21st Century.* Washington, D.C.: 1985.

Carlos, M., and L. Sellers. "Kinship Structure and Moderniza-
    tion in Latin America." *Latin America Research Review* 7
    (1972): 95–124.
Carlson, D. *The Will of the Shepherd*. Eugene, Oreg.: Harvest
    House, 1989.
Carney, C., and C. Wells. *Discover the Career Within You*. 3d. ed.
    Pacific Grove, Calif.: Brooks/Cole, 1991.
Carter, B., and M. McGoldrick. *The Changing Family Life Cycle:
    A Framework for Family Therapy*. 2d ed. Needham Heights,
    Mass.: Allyn and Bacon, 1989.
Carter, C., and June, G. *Graduating into the Nineties: Getting the
    Most Out of Your First Job after College*. New York: The
    Noonday Press, 1993.
Catalyst Staff. *Marketing Yourself*. New York: Bantam Books, 1980.
Catholic Social Teaching on the U.S. Economy, First Draft of
    the U.S. Bishops' Pastoral Letter. *Origins* 40, no. 22/23 (15
    November 1984): para. 158.
Cedoline, J. *Job Burnout in Public Education: Symptoms, Causes,
    and Survival Skills*. New York: Teachers College Press, 1982.
Chance, P. "Biology, Destiny, and All That." *Across the Board*.
    July/August (1988): 19–23.
Chickering, A. "The Young Adult: An Overview." In *Education
    and Identity*. San Fransisco: Jossey-Bass, 1984.
Clinton, J. R. *The Making of a Leader: Recognizing the Lessons and
    Stages of Leadership Development*. Colorado Springs: NavPress,
    1988.
Clopton, W. "Personality and Career Change." *Industrial Ger-
    ontology* 17 (1973): 9–17.
Close, K. *Getting Ready to Retire*. New York: Public Affairs Pam-
    phlets, 1972.
Cloud, H., and J. Townsend. *Boundaries: When to Say Yes, When to
    Say No to Take Control of Your Life*. Grand Rapids: Zondervan,
    1992.
Collins, G. R, and T. E. Clinton. *Baby Boomer Blues: Understanding
    and Counseling Baby Boomers and Their Families*. Dallas: Word,
    1992.
Cook, D. "Impact of Disability on the Individual." In *Rehabili-
    tation Counseling*. Edited by R. Parker, and C. Hansen.
    Boston: Allyn and Bacon, 1981.

Cook, E. P. "The Gendered Context of Life: Implications for Women's and Men's Career-Life Plans." *The Career Development Quarterly* 41 (1993): 227–37.

Corcoran, K., and J. Fischer. *Measures for Clinical Practice: A Sourcebook.* New York: Free Press, 1987.

Corey, G. *Theory and Practice of Group Counseling.* 3d ed. Pacific Grove, Calif.: Brooks/Cole, 1990.

Corlett, D. Shelby. *Retirement Is What You Make It.* Anderson, Ind.: Warner Press, 1973.

Crawford, J. "Retirement and Disengagement." *Human Relations* 24 (1971): 255–78.

Cronbach, L. *Essentials of Psychological Testing.* 4th ed. New York: Harper and Row, 1984.

Cuming, E., and W. Henry. *Growing Old.* New York: Basic Books, Inc., 1961.

Detz, Joan. "Ten Toughest Business Questions." *New Woman,* January 1989, 132.

Dittenhafer, C., and J. Lewis. *Guidelines for Establishing Career Resource Centers.* Harrisburg, Pa.: Pennsylvania Department of Education, 1973.

Dumas, L. "You're Fired." *Health* 20 (July 1988): 38–40, 74.

Dunbar, C., V. Edwards, E. Gede, et al. "Successful Coping Styles in Professional Women." *Canadian Journal of Psychiatry* 24 (1979): 43–46.

Eaton, T., and M. Peterson, *Psychiatry.* 2d ed. Norwalk, Conn.: Medical Examination Publishers, 1969.

Edelwich, J., with A. Brodsky. *Burn-Out: Stages of Disillusionment in the Helping Professions.* New York: Human Sciences Press, 1980.

Ellis, L., and L. Burkett. *Your Career in Changing Times.* Chicago: Moody, 1993.

Erickson, E. *Identity: Youth and Crisis.* New York: Norton, 1980.

Falicov, C. J. "Mexican Families." In *Ethnicity and Family Therapy.* Edited by M. McGoldrick, J. Pearce, and J. Giordano. New York: The Guilford Press, 1982.

Fine, M., and A. Asch. "Disability Beyond Stigma: Social Interactions, Discrimination, and Activism." *Journal of Social Issues* 44 (1988): 3–21.

Flak, A., B. Hanson, S. Isacsson, and P. Ostergren. "Job Strain and Mortality in Elderly Men: Social Network, Support, and Influences as Buffers." *American Journal of Public Health* 82 (1992): 1136–39.

Farnsworth, K., and W. Lawhead. *Life Planning: A Christian Approach to Careers.* Downers Grove, Ill.: InterVarsity, 1979.

Freudenberger, H. "Staff Burnout." *Journal of Social Issues* 30 (1974): 1159–64.

Freudenberger, H., and G. Richelson. *Burnout: The High Cost of High Achievement.* Garden City, N.Y.: Anchor Press, 1980.

Friedman, E. H. *Generation to Generation: Family Process in Church and Synagogue.* New York: Guilford Press, 1985.

Friesen, G., and J. R. Maxson. *Decision Making and the Will of God: A Biblical Alternative to the Traditional View.* Portland, Oreg: Multnomah, 1980.

Frost, Robert. "Two Tramps in Mud Time." In *The Poetry of Robert Frost.* Edited by E. Lathem. New York: Holt, Rinehart and Winston, 1969.

Fuqua, D., D. Blum, and B. Hartman. "Empirical Support for the Different Diagnosis of Career Indecision." *Career Development Quarterly* 36 (1988): 364–73.

Gallup, George, Jr., and David Poling. *The Search for America's Faith.* Nashville: Abingdon, 1980.

Garfield, N., and D. Redige. "Testing Competencies and Responsibilities: A Checklist for Vocational Counselors." In *A Counselor's Guide to Vocational Guidance Instruments.* Edited by J. Kapes and M. Mastie. Washington, D.C., National Vocational Guidance Association, 1982.

Gilligan, C. *In a Different Voice.* Cambridge, Mass.: Harvard University Press, 1982.

Ginzberg, E. "Toward a Theory of Occupational Choice: A Restatement." *Vocational Guidance Quarterly* 20 (1972): 169–76.

Glassner, B. *Career Crash: America's New Crisis and Who Survives.* New York: Simon and Schuster, 1994.

Goldenson, R. *Longman Dictionary of Psychology and Psychiatry.* New York: Longman, 1984.

Gordon, L. V. *The Measurement of Interpersonal Values.* Chicago: Science Research Associates, 1975.

Gordon, T. *Teacher Effectiveness Training: Supplement to the Instructor's Outline.* Pasadena, Calif.: Effectiveness Training Associates, 1972.

Gough, H. *California Psychological Inventory Administrator's Guide.* Palo Alto, Calif.: Consulting Psychologist Press, 1987.

Grace, H. "Industrial Gerontology: Behavioral Science Perspectives on Work and Aging." *Industrial Gerontology: Curriculum Materials.* New York: National Council on the Aging, 1968.

Granovetter, M. *Getting a Job: A Study of Contacts and Careers.* Cambridge, Mass.: Harvard University Press, 1974.

Grossman, J., and N. Chester, eds.. *The Experience and Meaning of Work in Women's Lives.* Hillsdale: N.J.: Erlbaum, 1990.

Guinn, S. "Outplacement: Separating the Myths from the Realities: What Professional Outplacement Should Include." *Organizational Development Journal* 6 (1988): 58–61.

Hansen, J. *User's Guide for the SVIB-SII.* Palo Alto, Calif.: Consulting Psychologists Press, 1985.

Hardy, L. *The Fabric of This World: Inquiries into Calling, Career Choice, and the Design of Human Work.* Grand Rapids: Eerdmans, 1990.

Hellman, P. *Ready, Aim, You're Hired! How to Job Interview Successfully Anytime, Anywhere, and with Anyone.* New York: AMACOM, 1986.

Henderson, G. "American Indians: Introduction." In *Understanding and Counseling Ethnic Minorities.* Edited by G. Henderson. Springfield, Ill.: Charles C. Thomas, 1979.

Hernandez, J., L. Estrada, and D. Alvirez. "Census Data and the Problem of Conceptually Defining the Mexican American Population." *Social Science Quarterly* 56, no. 4 (1973): 671–87.

Herr, E. L., and S. Cramer. *Career Guidance and Counseling Through the Life Span: Systematic Approaches.* 3d ed. Boston: Scott, Foresman , 1988.

Hiestand, D. L. *Changing Careers After Thirty-Five.* New York: Columbia University Press, 1971.

Hill, R. *The Strengths of Black Families.* In *Ethnicity and Family Therapy.* Edited by M. McGoldrick, J. Pearch, and J. Giordano. New York: Emerson Hall, 1972.

Hines, P. M., and N. Boyd-Franklin. "Black Families." In *Ethnicity and Family Therapy.* Edited by M. McGoldrick, J. Pearce, and J. Giordano.New York: Guilford Press, 1982.

Hirsh, S. Krebs, and J. Kummerow. *An Introduction to Type in Organizations.* Palo Alto, Calif.: Consulting Psychologists Press, 1987.

Holland, J. L. *Making Vocational Choices: A Theory of Careers.* 2d ed. Englewood Cliffs, N.J.: Prentice Hall, 1985.

———. *Making Vocational Choices: A Theory of Personalities and Work Environments.* 2d ed. Englewood Cliffs, N.J.: Prentice Hall, 1985.

———. *The Occupatons Finder.* Odessa, Fla.: Psychological Assessment Resources, 1987.

———. *The Self-Directed Search Professional Manual.* Odessa, Fla.: Psychological Assessment Resources, 1987.

House, J. *Work Stress and Social Support.* Reading, Mass.: Addison-Wesley, 1981.

Hyatt, C., and L. Gottlieb. *When Smart People Fail.* New York: Simon and Schuster, 1987.

Jackson, T. *The Perfect Resume.* New York: Doubleday, 1990.

———. *Guerrilla Tactics in the New Job Market.* 2d ed. New York: Bantam Books, 1991.

Jahoda, M. "Work, Employment and Unemployment." *American Psychology* 36 (1981): 184–91.

Jennings, E. *The Executive in Crisis.* New York: McGraw-Hill, 1965.

Jones, D., and S. Moore, eds. *Counseling Adults: Life Cycle Perspectives.* Lawrence, Kans.: University of Kansas, 1985.

Jung, C. *Psychological Types.* New York: Harcourt, 1923.

Kaneshige, E. "Cultural Factors in Group Counseling and Interaction." In *Understanding and Counseling Ethnic Minorities.* Edited by G. Henderson. Springfield, Ill.: Thomas, 1979.

Kanfer, R. , and C. Halin. "Individual Differences in Successful Job Searches Following Layoff." *Personnel Psychology* (1985): 835–47.

Kanter, R. Forward to *The Best Companies for Minorities.* Edited by L. Graham. New York: Penguin Books, Inc., 1993.

Kaufman, H. *Obsolescence and Professional Career Development.* New York: American Management Association, 1974.

Keiffer, J. "So Much for the Great American Dream of Retiring Early." *Generations* 6 (1982): 7–9.

Kelvin, P., and J. Jarrett. *Unemployment: Its Social Psychological Effects.* Cambridge: Cambridge University Press, 1985.

Kenniston, K. *Youth and Dissent: The Rise of the New Opposition.* New York: Harcourt Brace Javanovich, 1972.

Kohlberg, L. *The Philosophy of Moral Development.* New York: Harper and Row, 1981.

Kohut, H., and E. Worlf. "The Disorders of the Self and Their Treatment: An Outline." *International Journal of Psychoanalysis,* 59 (1978): 413–25.

Kramer, H., F. Berger, and G. Miller. "Student Concerns and Sources of Assistance." *Journal of College Student Personnel* 15 (1974).

Krannich, R. *Re-careering in Turbulent Times: Skills and Strategies for Success in Today's Job Market.* Manassas Park, Va.: Impact Publications, 1983.

Krannich, R., and Krannich, C. *Network Your Way to Job and Career Success.* Manassas Park, Va.: Impact Publications, 1989.

Kriegel, L. "Claiming the Self: The Cripple as American Male." In *Disabled People as Second Class Citizens.* Edited by M. Eisenberg, D. Kriggins, and R. Duval. New York: Springer, 1982.

Kruger, P. "What Women Think of Women Bosses." *Working Woman,* June (1993): 40–43, 84–85.

Kubler-Ross, E. *On Death and Dying.* New York: Macmillan, 1969.

Kurtz, R. R. "Using a Transactional Analysis Format in Vocational Group Counseling." *Journal of College Student Personnel* (1974): 447–51.

LaFevre, J. *How You Really Get Hired: The Inside Story from a College Recruiter.* New York: Arco, 1989.

Larsen, L. "The Influence of Parents and Peers During Adolescence: The Situation Hypothesis Revisited." *Journal of Marriage and the Family* 34 (February 1972): 67–74.

Lee, V., and R. Ekstrom. "Student Access Guidance Counseling in High School." *American Educational Research Association Journal* 24 (1987): 287–310.

Lerner, H. *The Dance of Intimacy.* New York: Harper and Row, 1989.

Levinson, D. *The Seasons of a Man's Life.* New York: Ballantine Books, 1978.

Lewis, M., and R. Butler. "Life Review Therapy." *Geriatrics* 29 (1974): 165–73.

Lindquist, V. *The Northwestern Lindquist-Endicott Report.* Evanston, Ill.: Northwestern University Placement Center, n.d.

Lipmen-Blumen, J. "Emerging Patterns of Female Leadership in Formal Organizations: Must the Female Leader Go Formal?" In *The Challenge of Change.* Edited by M. Horner, C. Nadelson, M. Notman. New York: Plenum Press, 1983.

Lucas, M., and D. Epperson, "Personality Types in Vocationally Undecided Students." *Journal of College Student Development* 29 (1966): 460–66.

Mallinckrodt, B., and J. Bennett. "Social Support and the Impact of Job Loss in Dislocated Bluecollar Workers." *Journal of Counseling Psychology* 39 (1992): 483–89.

Marlin, E. "If Your Family Tree Could Talk." *Self,* January 1988, 88–91.

Maslach, C. *Burnout—The Cost of Caring.* Englewood Cliffs, N.J.: Prentice Hall, 1982.

Maslow, A. H. *Motivation and Personality.* 2d ed. New York: Harper, 1970.

Maurer, H. *Not Working: An Oral History of the Unemployed.* New York: Holt, Reinhart and Winston, 1979.

McDaniel, J. "Disability and Vocational Development." *Journal of Rehabilitation* 29 (1963): 16–18.

McDaniels, C. *Developing a Professional Vita or Resume.* Garrett Park, Md.: Garrett Park Press, 1990.

McDaniels, C., and N. C. Gysbers. *Counseling for Career Development: Theories, Resources, and Practice.* San Francisco: Jossey-Bass, 1992.

McGoldrick, M., and R. Gerson. "Genograms and the Family Life Cycle." In *The Changing Family Life Cycle: A Framework for Family Therapy.* Edited by B. Carter and M. McGoldrick. 2d. ed. Needham Heights, Mass.: Allyn and Bacon, 1989.

Medley, H. *Sweaty Palms: The Neglected Art of Being Interviewed.* Berkeley, Calif.: Ten Speed Press, 1992.

Meyers, H. H. "Writing Resumes Right." *Journal of College Placement* 44 (1984): 19–21.

Mirabile, R. "Outplacement as Transition Counseling." *Journal of Employment Counseling* 22 (1985): 39–45.

Mitchell, J., Jr., ed. *Tests in Print III*. Lincoln, Neb.: University of Nebraska Press, 1983.

Moracco, J., P. Butche, and M. Collins. "Professional Career Services: An Exploratory Study." *Journal of Employment Counseling* 28 (1991): 21.

Morrison, A., and M. Von Glinow. "Women and Minorities in Management." *American Psychologist* 45 (1990): 200

Morrison, A. et al. *Breaking the Glass Ceiling: Can Women Reach the Top of America's Largest Corporations?* Reading, Mass.: Addison-Wesley, 1992.

Mulholland, M. R. *Shaped by the Word: The Power of Scripture in Spiritual Formation*. Nashville: The Upper Room, 1985.

Murray, H. *Explorations in Personality*. New York: Oxford University Press, 1938.

Myers, G. E. *Principles and Techniques of Vocational Guidance*. New York: McGraw-Hill, 1941.

Nadelson, C. "Professional Issues for Women." *Women's Disorders* 12 (1989): 225–33.

Naisbitt, J., and P. Aburdene. *Megatrends 2000: Ten New Directions for the 1990s*. New York: Morrow, 1990.

Neapolitan, J. "Occupational Change in Mid-Career: An Exploratory Investigation." *Journal of Vocational Behavior* 16 (1980): 212–25.

Neff, W. *Work and Human Behavior*. 2d ed. Chicago: Aldine, 1985.

Occupational Outlook Handbook. Washington D.C.: U. S. Department of Labor, 1990.

O'Neil, J. "Male Sex Role Conflicts, Sexism, and Masculinity: Psychological Implications for Men, Women, and Counseling Psychologists." *Counseling Psychologist* 9 (1981): 61–80.

Okiishi, R. W. "The Genogram as a Tool in Career Counseling." *Journal of Counseling and Development* 66 (1987): 139–43.

Ornstein, S., and L. Isabella. "Age vs. Stage Models of Career Attitudes of Women: A Partial Replication and Extension." *Journal of Vocational Behavior* 36 (1990): 1–19.

Osipow,. S., C. Carney, J. Winer, B. Yanico, and M. Koschier. *The Career Decision Scale*. Rev. Ed. Odessa, Fla.: Psychological Assessment Resources, 1976.

Osipow, S., C. Carney, and A. Barak. "A Scale of Educational-Vocational Undecidedness: A Topological Approach." *Journal of Vocational Behavior* 9 (1976): 233–434.

Parker, M., S. Peltier, and P. Wolleat. "Understanding Dual Career Couples." *Personnel and Guidance Journal* 60 (1981): 14–18.

Parker, Yana. *The Damn Good Resume Guide*. Berkeley: Ten Speed Press, 1989.

Parrillo, V. *Stranger to These Shoes*. 2d. ed. New York: Wiley, 1985.

Parrott, Les. *How to Choose Your Vocation*. Grand Rapids: Zondervan, 1952.

Parrott, Les. III. *Helping the Struggling Adolescent: A Guide to Thirty Common Problems for Parents, Counselors, and Youth Workers*. Grand Rapids: Zondervan, 1993.

Parrott, Leslie. "Career Decision-Making and Family Functioning." Ph.D. dissertation, Seattle University, 1993.

Parsons, F. *Choosing a Vocation*. Boston: Houghton-Mifflin, 1909.

Pascal, A. et al. *An Evaluation of Policy Related Research on Programs for Mid-life Career Redirection: Volume I—Major Findings*. Washington, D.C.: National Science Foundation, 1975.

———. *An Evaluation of Policy Related Research on Programs for Mid-life Career Redirection: Volume II—Major Findings*. Santa Monica, Calif.: Rand, 1975.

Payne, E., S. Robbins, and L. Dougherty. "Goal Directedness and Older-Adult Adjustment." *Journal of Counseling Psychology* 38 (1991): 302–8.

Perkins, K. "Psychological Implications of Women and Retirement." *Social Work* 37 (1992): 526–32.

Peter, L. J. *The Peter Principle*. New York: Morrow, 1969.

Piaget, J., and B. Inhelder. *The Psychology of the Child*. New York: Basic Books, 1969.

Piotrkowski, C., and R. Repetti. "Dual-earner Families." *Marriage and Family Review* 73 (1984): 73–74.

Purcell, M."Really, I'm Fine—Just Ask Me." *Newsweek*, 20 November 1992.

Ragins, B., and E. Sundstrom. "Gender and Power in Organizations: A Longitudinal Perspective." *Psychological Bulletin* 105 (1989): 51–88.

Rains, J. C., and D. C. Day-Lower. *Modern Work and Human Meaning.* Philadelphia: Westminster Press, 1986.

Rantze, K., and R. Feller. "Counseling Career-plateaued Workers During Times of Social Change." *Journal of Employment Counseling* 22 (1985): 23–28.

Rapoport, R., and R. Rapoport. "The Dual Career Family." In *Career Development and the Counseing of Women.* Edited by L. S. Hanson and R. S. Rapoza. Springfield, Ill.: Thomas, 1978.

Rice, F. *The Adolescent.* Boston: Allyn and Bacon, 1990.

Robbins, S. *Organizational Behavior: Concepts, Controversies, and Applications.* 5th ed. Englewood Cliffs, N.J.: Prentice Hall, 1991.

Roberts, P., and P. Newton. "Levinsonian Studies of Women's Career Stages." *Psychology of Aging* 2 (1987): 154–63.

Rogers, C., G. Gendlin, D. Kiesler, and C. Traus. *The Therapeutic Relationship and Its Impact.* Madison: University of Wisconsin Press, 1967.

Rogers, E. J. "Elements of Effective Job-hunting." *Journal of College Placement* 40 (1979): 55–58.

Rolheiser, R. "The Human Person as Understood by John Shea—The Biblical Perspective." Lecture notes, Insitute for Theological Studies, Seattle University, 1 July 1992.

Rubin, Z. ed. *Doing Unto Others.* Englewood Cliffs, N.J.: Prentice-Hall, 1974.

Sanguiliano, I. *In Her Time.* New York: Morrow, 1978.

Sassen, G. "Success Anxiety in Women: A Constructivist Interpretation of its Sources and its Significance." *Harvard Educational Review* 50 (1980): 13–25.

Schaie, K. *Handbook of the Psychology of Aging.* San Diego: Academic Press, 1990.

Schine, E. "From Hughes to Hell—and Back." *Business Week* 18 October 1993, 76–78.

Scholssberg, N. *Counseling Adults in Transition.* New York: Springer, 1984.

Schultz, D., and S. Schultz. *Psychology and Work Today: An Introduction to Industrial and Organizational Psychology.* 6th ed. New York: Macmillan, 1994.

Sekaran, U. *Dual Career Families: Contemporary Organizational and Counseling Issues.* San Francisco: Jossey-Bass, 1986.

Seldes, George. *The Great Thoughts*. New York: Ballantine Books, 1985.

Seligman, M. *Learned Optimism*. New York: Alfred A. Knopf, 1991.

Sell, C. M. *Transitions Through Adult Life*. Grand Rapids, Mich.: Zondervan, 1985.

Selye, H. *Stress Without Distress*. New York: A Signet Book, New American Library, 1974.

Sharf, R. S. *Applying Career Development Theory to Counseling*. Pacific Grove, Calif.: Books/Cole, 1992.

Shea, J. *Stories of God*. Chicago: University of Chicago, 1978.

————. *Stories of Faith*. Chicago: University of Chicago, 1980.

Sheehy, G. *Passages: Predictable Crises of Adult Life*. New York: Dutton, 1974.

————. *Pathfinders: Overcoming the Crises of Adult Life and Finding Your Own Path to Well-Being*. New York: Morrow, 1981.

Sheldon, W., E. Hartl, and E. McDermott. *Varieties of Delinquent Youth: An Introduction to Constitutional Psychiatry*. New York: Harper, 1949.

Sheppard, H., and S. Rix. *The Graying of Working America: The Coming Crisis in Retirement-Age Policy*. New York: Macmillan, 1977.

Sherman, D., and W. Hendricks. *Your Work Matters to God*. Colorado Springs: NavPress, 1987.

Shon, S., and D. Ja. "Asian Families." In *Ethnicity and Family Therapy*. Edited by M. McGoldrick, J. Pearce, and J. Giordano. New York: Guilford Press, 1982.

Silliker, S. "The Role of Social Contacts in the Successful Job Search." *Journal of Employment Counseling* 30 (1993): 25–35.

Sinetar, M. *Do What You Love and the Money Will Follow: Discovering Your Right Livelihood*. New York: Dell Publishing, 1987.

Sinick, D. *Counseling Older Persons: Careers, Retirement, Dying*. New York: Plenum, Human Sciences Press, 1978.

Skinner, B., and M. Vaughan. *Enjoy Old Age: A Program of Self-Management*. New York: Norton, 1983.

Smedes, L. *A Pretty Good Person*. San Francisco: HarperCollins, 1990.

Smith, E. "Profile of the Black Individual in Vocational Literature." *Journal of Vocational Behavior* 6 (1975): 41–59.

————. "Issues in Racial Minorities' Career Behavior." In *Handbook of Vocational Psychology*. Edited by W. B. Walsh and S. H. Osipow. Hillsdale, N.J.: Erlbaum, 1983.

Solomon, C. M. "Career Under Glass." *Personnel Journal* 69 (1990): 96–105.

Spencer, A. *Seasons*. New York: Paulist Press, 1982.

Starishevsky, R., and N. Matlin. "A Model for the Translation of Self-Concept into Vocational Terms." In *Career Development: Self-Concept Theory*. Edited by D. E. Super, et al. New York: College Entrance Examination Board.

Steinweg, D. "Implications of Current Research for Counseling the Unemployed." *Journal of Employment Counseling* 27 (1990): 37–41.

Stephens, E. *Career Counseling and Placement in Higher Education: A Student Personnel Function*. Bethlehem, Pa.: The College Placement Council, 1970.

Stoltz-Like, M. "The Working Family: Helping Women Balance the Roles of Wife, Mother, and Career Woman." *Career Development Quarterly* 40 (1992): 243–56.

Stone, J., and C. Gregg. "Juvenile Diabetes and Rehabilitation Counseling." *Rehabilitation Counseling Bulletin* 24 (1981): 283–91.

Sullivan, S. "Is There a Time for Everything? Attitudes Related to Women's Sequencing of Career and Family." *Career Development Quarterly* 40 (1992): 235–43.

Super, D. E. "Vocational Development Theory: Persons, Positions, and Processes." In *Perspectives on Vocational Development*. Edited by J. M. Whiteley and A. Resnikoff. Washington D.C.: American Personnel and Guidance Association, 1972.

————. "A Life-Span, Life-Space Approach to Career Development." In *Career Choice and Development: Applying Contemporary Theories to Practice*. Edited by D. Brown, L. Brooks, et al. 2d. ed. San Francisco: Jossey-Bass, 1992.

Tan, A., R. Kendis, J. Fine, and J. Porce. "A Short Measure of the Eriksonian Ego Identity." *Journal of Personality Assessment* 41 (1977).

Taylor, D. *The Myth of Certainty: The Reflective Christian and the Risk of Commitment*. Waco, Tex.: Jarrell, 1986.

Taylor, K. "An Investigation of Vocational Indecision in College Students: Correlates and Moderators." *Journal of
Vocational Behavior* 21 (1982): 318–29.

Taylor, K., and J. Popma, "An Examination of the Relationships
among Career Decision-making Self-efficacy, Career Salience,
Locus of Control and Vocational Indecision." *Journal of Vocational Behavior* 37 (1990): 17–31.

Thomas, A., and N. Stewart. "Counselor Response to Female
Clients with Deviate and Conforming Career Goals." *Journal of Counseling Psychology* 18 (1971): 352–57.

Thomas, L. "Typology of Mid-Life Career Changes." *Journal of
Vocational Behavior* 16 (1980): 173–82.

Tiedeman, D., and R. O'Hara. *Career Development: Choice and
Adjustment.* Princeton, N.J.: College Entrance Examination
Board, 1963.

Trautman, J. *How to Find Your Best Future: A Biblical Approach to
Living Abundantly in a Turbulent World.* Unpublished Manuscript. Seattle, Wash. Intercristo.

———. *Intercristo's Career Concepts: Abridged Thoughts to Encourage and Guide You in the World of Work.* Seattle, Wash.: Intercristo,
1991.

———. "Vocation, Calling, and the Career-Life Journey." Lecture, Seattle Pacific University, 19 January 1994.

Troll, L. *Early and Middle Adulthood.* 2d ed. Pacific Grove, Calif.: Brooks/Cole, 1985.

Troll, L., and C. Nowak. "How Old Are You? The Question of
Age Bias in the Counseling of Adults." *The Counseling Psychologist* 6 (1976):, 41–44.

Turner, R. "The Real Self: From Institute to Impulse." *American
Journal of Sociology* 81 (1976): 989–1016.

U. S. Bureau of the Census. *General Population Characterstics:
United States Summary.* Washington, D.C.: U. S. Government Printing Office, 1980.

U. S. Department of Justice, Civil Rights Division. *Coordination
and Review Section.* 1991.

U. S. Department of Labor. *Counseling and Placement Services for Older Workers.* Washington, D.C.: Superintendent of Documents, U. S. Government Printing Office,
1956.

Vecsey, George. "Norman Vincent Peale, Preacher of Gospel of Optimism Dies at 95." *New York Times*, 26 December 1993.

Vondracek, J., and E. Kirchner. "Vocational Development in Early Childhood: An Examination of Young Children's Expressions of Vocational Aspirations." *Journal of Vocational Behavior* 5 (1974): 251–60.

Voydanoff, P. *Work and Family Life*. Beverly Hills, Calif.: Sage Publications 1987.

Walker, J., D. Kimmel, and K. Price. "Retirement Style and Retirement Satisfaction: Retirees Aren't All Made Alike." *International Journal of Aging and Human Development* 12 (1980): 267–81.

Walters, L., and G. Saddlemire, "Career Planning Needs of College Freshmen and Their Perceptions of Career Planning." *Journal of College Student Personnel* 20 (1979).

Washington, T. *The Hunt*. Bellevue, Wash.: Mount Vernon Press, 1992.

Wegman, R., Chapman, R. and Johnson, M. *Work in the New Economy: Careers and Job Seeking into the 21st Century*. rev. ed. Indianapolis: JIST Works, and Alexandria, Va.: American Association for Counseling and Development, 1989.

Weinstein, M. "A Primer on Unemployment." *Occupational Outlook Quarterly* 23 (1979): 24–27.

Welty, E., and R. Sharp. *The Norton Book of Friendship*. New York: Norton, 1991.

Wendleton, K. *Through the Brick Wall: How to Job-Hunt in a Tight Market*. New York: Villard Books, 1992.

Westcott, N. "Application of the Structured Life-Review Technique in Counseling Elders." *Personnel Guidance Journal* 62 (1983): 180–81.

Willensky, D. "Writing Off the Unemployment Blues." *American Health*, 12 (June 1993): 35.

Worthington, E., J. McLeod, and R. Kessler. "The Importance of Life Events for Explaining Sex Differences in Psychological Distress." In *Gender and Stress*. Edited by R. C. Barnett, L. Biener, and G. K. Baruch. New York: Free Press, 1987.

Yeager, N., and L. Hough. *Power Interviews: Job-Winning Tactics from Fortune 500 Recruiters*. New York: Wiley, 1990.

Yost, E., and M. Corbishley. *Career Counseling: A Psychological Approach.* San Francisco: Jossey-Bass, 1987.

Zaslow, M., and F. Pederson. "Sex Role Conflicts and the Experience of Childbearing." *Professional Psychology* 12 (1981): 47–55.

Zimbardo, P. *Psychology and Life.* Glenview, Ill.: Scott, Foresman, 1979.

Zingaro, J. C. "A Family Systems Approach for the Career Counselor." *The Personnel and Guidance Journal* (1983): 24–27.

Zunker, V. G. *Career Counseling: Applied Concepts of Life Planning.* 3d ed. Pacific Grove, Calif.: Brooks/Cole, 1990.

———. *Career Counseling: Applied Concepts of Life Planning.* 4th ed. Pacific Grove, Calif.: Brooks/Cole, 1994.

———. *Using Assessment Results for Career Development.* 4th ed. Pacific Grove, Calif.: Brooks/Cole, 1994.

Subject Index

About the Authors

Dr. Leslie Parrott is a marriage and family therapist who served as a vocational counselor at Seattle Pacific University for several years. She is also an adjunct professor in the graduate program in family psychology at SPU, where she teaches vocational counseling. Dr. Parrott earned her M.A. in marriage and family therapy from Fuller Theological Seminary and her Ed.D. in educational leadership from Seattle University.

Dr. Les Parrott is Associate Professor of Clinical Psychology at Seattle Pacific University. He holds an M.A. in theology and a Ph.D. in clinical psychology from Fuller Theological Seminary. He is the author of *How to Write Psychology Papers* (HarperCollins), *Helping the Struggling Adolescent* (Zondervan), and *Love's Unseen Enemy: How to Overcome Guilt to Build Healthy Relationships* (Zondervan).

Drs. Les and Leslie Parrott are codirectors of the center for Relationship Development at Seattle Pacific University and are coauthors of *Saving Your Marriage Before It Starts* (Zondervan/HarperCollins) and *Becoming Soul-Mates* (Zondervan).